A Swedish Soldier in the Napoleonic Wars is an important and rare memoir by a low-ranking officer. It contains lively anecdotes and stories of soldiers, commanders, and life on campaign from 1808 to 1814 in Sweden, Denmark, Norway and North Germany. Available for the first time in English, it provides a new perspective of little-known actions, small by the standards of continental Europe, but vital to our understanding of Sweden's part in the war.

In 1807, at the age of 18 and whilst a student at Linköping High School, Carl Magnus Hultin enlisted as a junior officer in the militia, answering the call-to-arms in the nation's efforts to stem the Russian tide before Finland was lost. He then transferred to the regular army as an ensign in the Jönköping Regiment. He took part in the ill-fated Västerbotten expedition against the Russians on Swedish soil in 1809 and witnessed the 1809 coup d'etat to remove the unpopular King Gustav IV Adolf. Following the 'phoney' war with Britain 1811–1812, he served in Mecklenberg, Holstein and Belgium against France and Denmark in the 1813–1814 campaign under Napoleon's former *maréchal*, Bernadotte, who had been elected as Sweden's Crown Prince. Finally, he participated in the 1814 Norwegian campaign that saw the Union of Norway and Sweden, which lasted until 1905. He remained in the army after the war, retiring as a captain in 1842.

Very late in life, he was persuaded to set down his memoirs, which were published in 1872. Two separate editions of the book were reprinted in Sweden in 1954 and 1955 with minimal editing after the expiry of the copyright 70 years after the author's death. The editor's preface to the 1954 edition noted, 'The present volume is … unique to the extent that it may constitute the only document of literary value from our history of war', whilst the 1955 editor noted 'the account … was greatly acclaimed' and that Hultin's friends were 'much entertained by his lively, sometimes rather burlesque tales about military life both on and off campaign.'

This translation, by a descendent of Captain Hultin, includes extensive explanatory notes together with maps and illustrations to support the narrative.

Erik Faithfull has had a life-long interest in military history, most recently that of his Scandinavian ancestry. He is a descendant of both Carl Magnus Hultin and Carl Gustav Armfelt, the subject of his first translated work for Helion, *Carl Gustav Armfelt and the Struggle for Finland during the Great Northern War.*

A Swedish Soldier in the Napoleonic Wars

The Memoirs of Carl Magnus Hultin, 1807-1814

Translated by Erik Faithfull

Helion & Company

Helion & Company Limited
Unit 8 Amherst Business Centre
Budbrooke Road
Warwick
CV34 5WE
England
Tel. 01926 499619
Email: info@helion.co.uk
Website: www.helion.co.uk
Twitter: @helionbooks
Visit our blog at http://blog.helion.co.uk/

Published by Helion & Company 2024
Designed and typeset by Mach 3 Solutions (www.mach3solutions.co.uk)
Cover designed by Paul Hewitt, Battlefield Design (www.battlefield-design.co.uk)

Text and maps © Erik Faithfull 2024
Illustrations © as individually credited
Cover: Carl Magnus Hultin, charcoal drawing by Ingeborg Westfelt-Eggertz (1855–1936).
Illustration from Ellen Key, Minnen av och om Emil Key. The affair at Ratan, 20 August 1809.
Watercolour by C.G. Gillberg (1774–1855). (Library of Congress)

Every reasonable effort has been made to trace copyright holders and to obtain their permission for the use of copyright material. The author and publisher apologise for any errors or omissions in this work, and would be grateful if notified of any corrections that should be incorporated in future reprints or editions of this book.

ISBN 978-1-804514-34-4

British Library Cataloguing-in-Publication Data.
A catalogue record for this book is available from the British Library.

All rights reserved. No part of this publication may be reproduced, stored in a retrieval system, or transmitted, in any form, or by any means, electronic, mechanical, photocopying, recording or otherwise, without the express written consent of Helion & Company Limited.

For details of other military history titles published by Helion & Company Limited, contact the above address, or visit our website: http://www.helion.co.uk

We always welcome receiving book proposals from prospective authors.

Contents

Translator's Foreword		vii
Author's Dedication and Preface (1872)		ix
1	Memories from High School (August 1807–April 1808)	15
2	Preparation for War: The Militia (April–May 1808)	23
3	To Åland and Back (June–September 1808)	28
4	Garrison Duties in Västernorrland (October 1808–February 1809)	37
5	The Revolution (March 1809)	41
6	Transfer to the Regular Army (April–July 1809)	48
7	The Västerbotten Expedition (August–September 1809)	51
8	Interlude (October 1809–December 1810)	56
9	The Phoney War with England (January 1811–December 1812)	59
10	Preparation for War with France (January–July 1813)	70
11	Mecklenburg (August–December 1813)	83
12	Holstein and the Fall of Denmark (December 1813–January 1814)	100
13	Lübeck (January–February 1814)	114
14	To the Rhine and Belgium (February–April 1814)	128
15	Back to the North (May–June 1814)	144
16	Return to Sweden (July 1814)	153
17	The Norwegian Campaign (August 1814)	163
18	After the War in Norway (August–October 1814)	175
19	Home (November–December 1814)	190
20	Epilogue	194
Bibliography		196

Translator's Foreword

This work came about through research into the ancestry of my grandmother, Anne Marie Armfelt. In addition to being a descendant of General Carl Gustav Armfelt (see my previous work for Helion, *Carl Gustav Armfelt and the Struggle for Finland during the Great Northern War*), she was also the great-granddaughter of Carl Magnus Hultin (1789–1883), who had served in the Swedish army during the Napoleonic Wars. Hultin's recollections of that service were published under the title *En Gammal Knekts Minnen* (An Old Soldier's Memoirs) in 1872. Having tracked down a copy, my next translation project was underway.

Two separate editions of Hultin's memoirs were subsequently published in Sweden in 1954 and 1955, after the copyright had expired. Neither was subjected to any significant editing other than subdividing the text into slightly shorter chapters and modernising the spelling; and only one edition was accompanied by a few explanatory endnotes. I have subdivided the text even further in this translation and added a short introductory scene-setting paragraph to each chapter. I have wherever possible identified the people Hultin refers to, typically with a brief supplementary biographical note.[1] In addition, to aid understanding for an English-speaking readership most of whom will not be experts in Sweden's history during the Napoleonic Wars, nor the many classical and contemporary cultural and religious quotations and references Hultin makes use of in his narrative, I have added extensive footnotes. The reader should not, however, feel obliged to read every footnote and, although they have often been very time-consuming to research, they are not the subject of this book, and any errors therein are entirely my own.

Whilst Hultin's memoirs are set out in chronological order as regards the chapters, he often (and necessarily) strays from strict chronology when setting down his recollections of people, places, and incidents. Where he specifies dates and places I have endeavoured to cross check against other sources, not least because Hultin was writing his memoirs some 50 years after the events he describes – up to that time he had been recounting his tales orally and had only been persuaded to write them down as the result of a bet! Of course, one can forgive an unreliable memory after such a period of time but in a few instances I have made amendments to dates in the text which are clearly in error, to avoid unnecessary confusion.

Neither the original nor the 1954/1955 editions were supported by maps or illustrations. This shortcoming has been addressed in this edition for Helion. I have tried to ensure that all the places Hultin describes can be found on the accompanying maps.

---

1 Details of the works consulted can be found in the bibliography.

My thanks to Colin Sutcliffe for a critical review of the manuscript and assistance with some of the supporting research and notes.

Erik Faithfull
Hest Bank, Lancashire, UK

A Note on Units of Measurement

Hultin uses many archaic units of measurement which I have generally converted to contemporary British imperial units. However, to avoid confusion with imperial statute miles, the Swedish mile (*mil*) – which was then about 10.6 kilometres before standardisation to 10 kilometres in 1889 – has been converted to kilometres. Hultin also frequently uses the *aln*, a unit of length equivalent to about 0.59 metres or just under two feet. When used as a measure of distance, 'pace' has been used as a rough equivalent where the context makes it a more appropriate term. Units of weight such as *mark* and *skålpund* are converted to pounds, roughly a half-pound and one pound respectively.

Ranks, Positions and Titles

Ranks, positions, and titles in the text have been translated into English, except where there is no practical equivalent, in which case the Swedish term is retained, with an explanatory note. However, in footnotes, captions and introductory paragraphs, ranks are retained in the relevant native language.

Author's Dedication and Preface (1872)

To Emil Key[1]

The one who persuaded me to write this should be obliged to read it and I therefore dedicate these pages to my friend.

The fortunate old soldier.

These memoirs, which had the honour to appear in the columns of the New Illustrated Magazine,[2] can perhaps now be read by anyone who wished to see them gathered together. So much for the better do I meet this desire, to bring back and relive the memory of those years and to be able to remind any still living companions of the times when Europe's politics were written in red ink.

To write about oneself when you are not a prominent person, when you are over 80 and hardly ever tried to write anything other than reports and memoranda, is indeed thankless; but friends and relatives have countered this view and assured me that the events I could portray would be of interest, as so few of the participants are still living. From the militia, I know of no more than one – and if you, old Gerhard Adolf von Yhlen,[3] happen to read this, you have to concede that people were treated thus at that time and that I have not painted too black a picture.

'We have ranted, raved, quarrelled, drunk, loved, and now have to make way for others who want to do the same.'

Vogel

---

1 Emil Key (1822–1892) was a politician and member of the Riksdag. He was the owner of the Sundholm estate in Småland which included Kallernäs, an old Carolean manor which Hultin leased after retiring from military service in 1842 until his death in 1883.
2 The Ny Illustrerad Tidning was a weekly magazine published from 1865 to 1900. Its content included biographies, short stories, poems, articles on history, science and politics, theatrical and music reviews, etc, with contributions from many of the country's most well-known writers and artists. Hultin's memoirs were serialised in the magazine before publication in book form in 1872.
3 Gerhard Adolf von Yhlen (1790–1872) was a löjtnant in the militia (lantvärnet) in 1809. He died the year Hultin's memoirs were published.

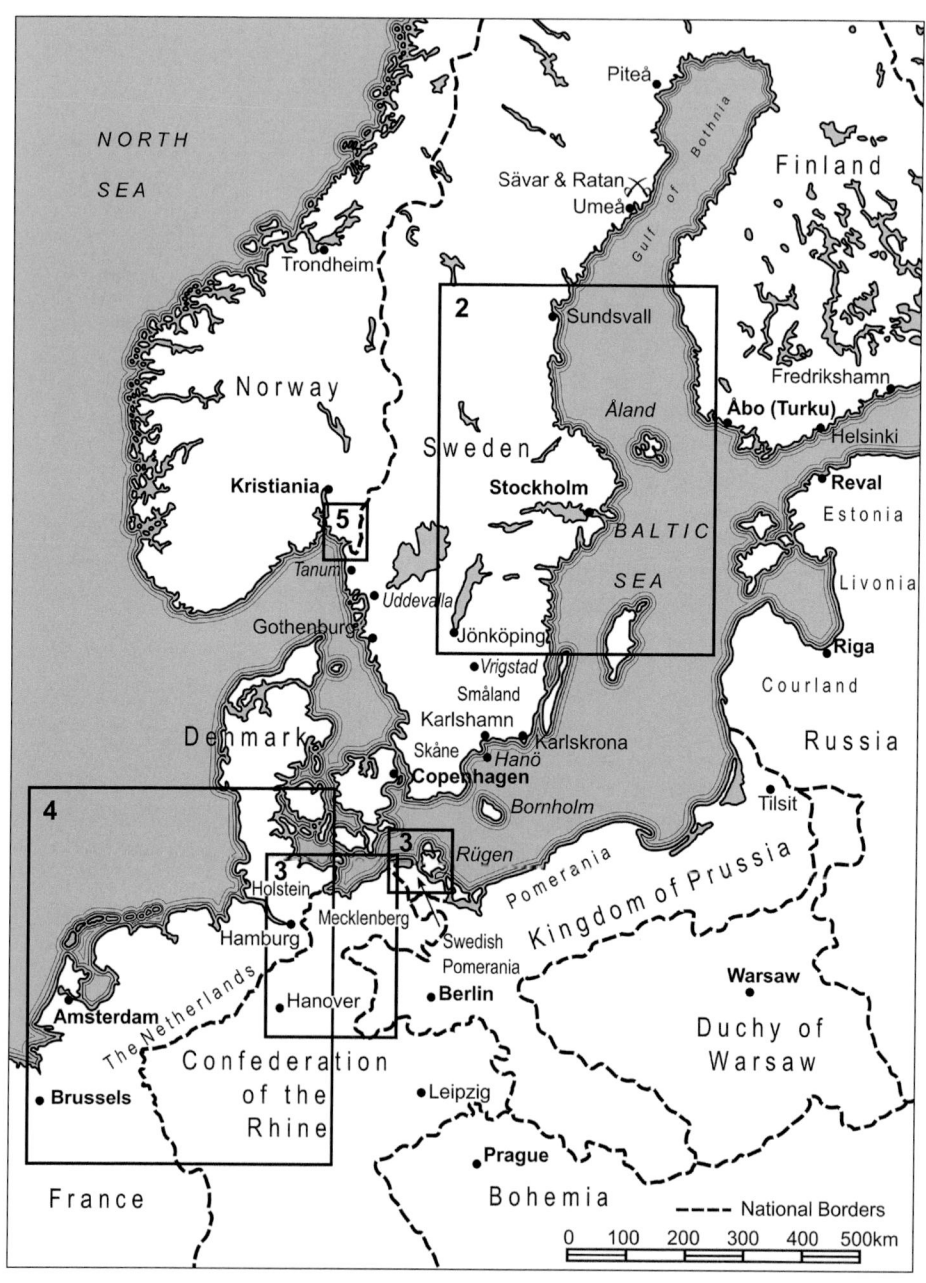

Map 1 Scandinavia and North-West Europe.

Map 2 Eastern Sweden.

Map 3 Holstein, Mecklenburg and Swedish Pomerania.

Map 4 The Road to Brussels.

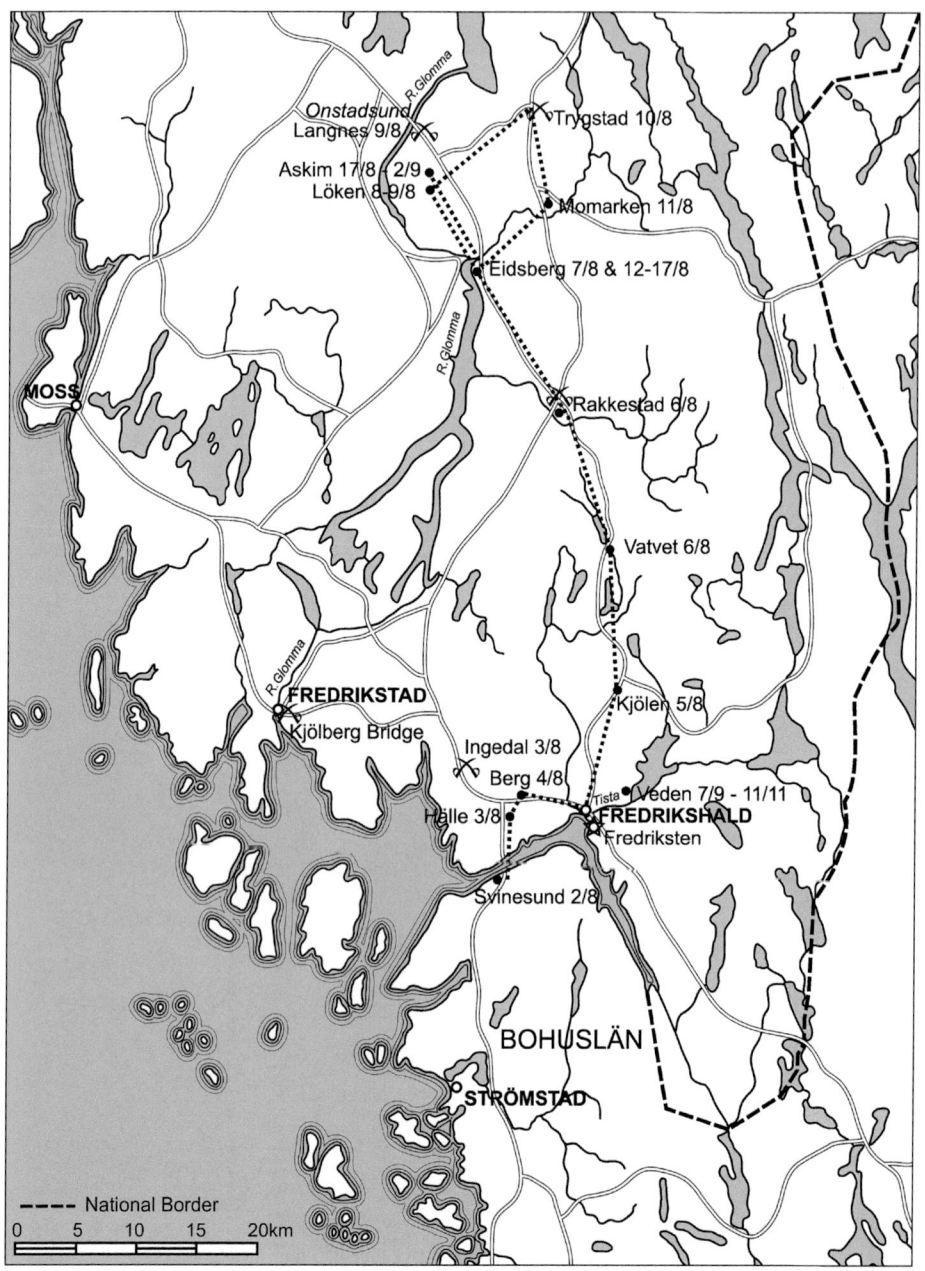

Map 5 The Norwegian Campaign, August 1814 showing principal engagements and approximate movements of Hultin's jäger battalion.

1

Memories from High School (August 1807–April 1808)

The Scandinavian nations, namely Sweden and Denmark-Norway, had tried to maintain neutrality during the Napoleonic Wars.[1] Sweden had entered the Third Coalition against Napoleon in 1805 and had campaigned in North Germany but by January 1807 her sole remaining foothold on the continent was Stralsund in Swedish Pomerania, then under siege by the French Maréchal Mortier. Despite a local armistice agreed in May and the Treaty of Tilsit in July which effectively allied France with Russia and left Sweden with Great Britain as her sole ally, King Gustav IV Adolf took command in Stralsund and resumed hostilities; but the city was forced to capitulate on 24 August, albeit under very favourable terms allowing the defenders to return home with all arms and munitions. At the same time Britain's pre-emptive attack on Copenhagen, capturing the Danish fleet, prompted the Danes to abandon neutrality and side with Napoleon; Sweden was now left in expectation of imminent hostilities with its traditional enemies Denmark-Norway to the west and Russia to the east, as well as France to the south. Hultin was aged 17 at this time and was a student at Linköping High School.

The fatherland's position during Gustav IV Adolf's last year of rule is well known. On his return from Germany, Stockholm was illuminated,[2] and it was said that in a window could be read:

'Wismar is sold and Pomerania is gone,
Our candles burn low but shine on.'[3]

---

1 Since medieval times the kingdoms of Denmark and Norway had been united whilst Finland was under Swedish rule and never formed a separate kingdom.
2 A 'festival of light': all important buildings in the city were illuminated. Private individuals also participated in the celebration with beautifully lit residential buildings.
3 A rhyming couplet in Swedish lamenting the loss of the last of Sweden's possessions on the European mainland. Along with part of the Duchy of Pomerania, the Hanseatic city of Wismar had been a Swedish dominion since the Peace of Westphalia which ended the Thirty Years War. In 1803, Sweden had mortgaged Wismar to Mecklenburg-Schwerin to raise revenue, but it would never return to Swedish ownership. Swedish Pomerania would

This was the overture, the beginning of the tragedy which ended with the loss of Finland in 1808, amid much weeping and gnashing of teeth.[4]

I was then a student in the highest grade at Linköping Gymnasium,[5] reading Latin, Greek, Hebrew, theological dogma and theoretical philosophy. I participated in fights with the city's apprentices, and still hold in fond memory how a carpenter's apprentice once delivered me such a punch on one side of the street that I collapsed into the opposite gutter.

The institution was then, as now, well accredited,[6] and the teachers generally competent, although several eccentrics and pedants were to be found amongst them.

The honourable and faithful Eforus Bishop Lindblom, could represent the prelate both as a man of the cloth and at the banqueting table. He was like a father to the students, much beloved.[7]

The lecturer in history, an elderly man, known as a Jacobin, Red Republican,[8] atheist, etc., held masterful lectures and was very much feared as a guiding spirit in the congregation, for those who displeased him rarely did well. He was always one

Gustaf IV Adolf (1778–1837) in 1806. Miniature by Jacob Axel Gillberg (1769–1845). (Nationalmuseum)

---

    change hands twice more (returned in 1810, lost in 1812, and retaken in 1813), but it was permanently lost to Prussia at the Congress of Vienna in 1815.
4 Matthew 8:12 'But the subjects of the kingdom will be thrown outside, into the darkness, where there will be weeping and gnashing of teeth.'
5 Linköping Gymnasium, today known as the Cathedral School, is Sweden's fourth oldest high school, founded in 1627. The term 'Gymnasium' in Scandinavia and central Europe means a high school preparing students for university rather than its English usage as a room or building for sports and physical activity.
6 For example, Clas Livijn (1781–1844), a writer, military lawyer, civil servant, and prison reformer who had been a student at Linköping a few years before Hultin, considered it superior to Lund University which he also attended. See Johan Mortenson, *Clas Livijn – Ett Nyromantiskt Diktarefragment* (Stockholm, Albert Bonniers, 1913).
7 Jacob Lindblom (1746–1819) had been educated at Linköping school. He became Bishop of Linköping in 1786 and Archbishop of Uppsala in 1805. *Eforus* was a title for a Swedish bishop in his function as chief supervisor for higher education in the diocese.
8 The republican movement in Sweden sprang from the Jacobin movement of the French Revolution but gained little ground until the mid-nineteenth century. 'Red' republicans held the more extremist views.

of the diocese's representatives in the Riksdag and died a Doctor of Theology, albeit with religion being somewhat incidental.[9]

The principal theology lecturer was a venerable, tongue-in-cheek man of honour, though he often credited us with not knowing as much theology as the peasant boys in his prebend pastorate.[10]

The second theology lecturer was a small child-like soul with the stature of a journeyman shoemaker.[11] Everyone was fond of him, but poked fun at him. If he noticed this, he would weep rather than scold. Peace be with you, well-meaning teacher! Although I was a mischievous boy, I knew both then and now to appreciate your pious childish mind. *Sit tibi terra levis!*[12]

The Latin lecturer was probably the most capable teacher, but also the most hated.[13]

The lecturer in Greek, the capable and honest Marcus Wallenberg, was our idol, for when narrow-minded colleagues wanted to punish a boy and struck more severely than he thought appropriate, he would always advise them, 'We should not forget that we were all boys once.' Since then, I have had the honour of meeting him as bishop, and yet he remained the same old Marcus.[14]

One must not imagine that the high-schoolers of the time were all such youngsters as they are today; 24-year-olds were not uncommon. They sported a black robe, came to the academy for one semester, returned home and were ordained into the priesthood.

Everything depended on knowing Latin; sciences were given little attention. However, we sometimes had minds that were good enough to be crowned with laurels and gained European reputation; and those who tutored the boys would before long see them grapple with the Swedish Academy and give our native literature a beneficial boost.[15]

These alumni are now gone but not forgotten, and perhaps it would be of interest to hear how they were in their youth.

Which scientist does not know of Berzelius and imagines the glory of the genius that shone within the youngster's brow? But that was not the case, for his command of Latin was poor and Greek even worse; his intention was only to be able with the grace of God and the mercy of man to work his way up to become a rural chaplain.

---

9   Samuel Gustaf Harlingson (1740–1810) was also a church pastor (*kyrkoherde*) and was highly influential in the Swedish Neo-Romantic movement. That a man described by Hultin as 'atheist' could be a pastor and a Doctor of Theology may seem strange but by the beginning of the nineteenth century Swedish clergymen were required to have a university education thus a questioning attitude more open to liberal and secular ideologies, and often had more secular than religious duties, such as education.
10 Johan Ramstedt (1758–1823). He was pastor in Skeda, just south of Linköping, which was his prebend pastorate – that from which he derived income.
11 Johannes Danielsson Wallman (1753-1823).
12 A funerary inscription dating back to Roman times, literally 'May the earth rest lightly upon you'.
13 Per Arenander (1762–1819).
14 Marcus Wallenberg (1774–1833) had graduated in law from Uppsala in 1797. He became Bishop of Linköping in 1819.
15 The Swedish Academy was founded in 1786 by Gustav III with the aim of promoting and advancing Swedish language and literature.

Subsequently at Uppsala University he heard about a science called chemistry; like St Paul, he was struck by a light from Heaven and within a few years he was Swedish chemistry's leading authority. It is said that during a trip to Linköping he visited his old teacher, the aforementioned Latin lecturer, who received him as his old thick-headed pupil, asking 'and what is Berzelius now?' but when he received the answer, 'I am Professor at the Academy of Sciences' he changed his tune: 'Your most humble servant, Herr Professor, please come and sit down.'[16]

I reach for the sublime when I mention Atterbom. With an angelic appearance, the boy promised what the man delivered. His essays and style were studied and imitated, although few were able to follow his example. His thoughts hovered in the ether oblivious to earthly conditions; perhaps his 'Island of Bliss' was already looming. He was kindness personified and thus sacred to us.[17]

It is but a short step from the sublime to the ridiculous, and thus appears my friend and roommate, the humourist Dahlgren, lean and lanky, drowsy and dreamy.[18] As a comrade he was considered mediocre, both in terms of knowledge and sociability, but flint unexpectedly found steel and gave fire when one May Day some disreputable friends each chipped in one *plåt* – 16 shillings[19] – to be turned into punch. Tasting such profane liquor inside the city's tollgates was hazardous, for if it became known, one got a black mark for the habit and was considered almost infamous, hence Lektorshagen outside the western tollgate was selected as the appointed place. Our friend Dahlgren became somewhat tipsy, stood upon a rock, and extemporised such a comical oration, in the same spirit as took place at The Green Box and on Barbara's Day,[20] that, with admiration and cheers, we got him completely drunk. When, during the height of his fame, I congratulated him on being our greatest humourist, he replied, 'That's why I have to thank you for your appreciation on that May Day at Lektorshagen, because it was there that I found I was good for something!'

---

16 Jöns Jacob Berzelius (1779–1848) is known as 'the father of Swedish chemistry' and one of the founders of modern chemistry. He attended Linköping school before studying medicine at Uppsala University from 1796 to 1801. He was elected to the Royal Swedish Academy of Sciences in 1808.
17 Per Daniel Amadeus Atterbom (1790–1855) was a founder of the Swedish Romantic movement. He was a student at Linköping 1799–1805 before going on to Uppsala University where he became Professor of Philosophy in 1828. Perhaps his most famous poetic work was *Lycksalighetens Ö* (The Island of Bliss) completed in 1827.
18 Carl Fredric Dahlgren (1791–1844) left Linköping school for Uppsala University in 1808 where he was an associate of Atterbom. He was ordained to the priesthood in 1815 and was a representative in the Riksdag. He was a prolific poet and became one of Sweden's best known humorous writers.
19 Originally a *plåt* (plate) was a large copper coin in varying denominations, but at this time the name referred to a 16-shilling banknote (the Swedish word is *skilling*, also commonly spelt *schilling*). 1 riksdaler = 48 *skilling*.
20 The Green Box (*Gröna rutan*) was one of many Bacchanalian Order societies – Bacchus being the Roman god of wine and intoxication. It was formed in Stockholm in 1816 by Dahlgren along with P.A. Sonden, Clas Livijn and others. Barbara's Day, 4 December, was a feast day for a similar Order, *Par Bricole*, founded in 1779.

The psalmist Hedborn, then called Hedenvall, was the oldest in high school, big, strong and a reliable fighter in a scrap, when he could be fiery. As he was very poor, he gave lessons in French for 12 shillings for two hours a week throughout the semester. It should be noted that of living languages only French was read, with the librarian, for one hour a week. Hedborn's poetic ability first became known at the Academy.[21]

P.A. Sonden – Per the sexton – profound, sublime, absent-minded, betrayed already then that in pleasant tones he would sing amen in the Phosphoros mass.[22] He once opened our chamber door and asked, 'Is Dahlgren within?' Dahlgren, who was in his bed in a horizontal position, replied, 'No, he is not,' and with this message our good friend went on his way.

A.J. Cnattingius, thorough, hardworking and orthodox, foreshadowing the theologian and supporter of children he would become.[23]

Hedenborg, who crossed Africa, who explored the pyramids, who wandered through the forests of columns in Nubian temples, who presented valuable antiquities to our museums, already showed an iron constitution that could bear pain. He could starve like a fox and, if needs must, cook pork on the door of a tiled stove. As a very poor soldier's son, he shared mealtimes with his comrades, whose chamber floor was often his bed, with an old coat under his head and a cloak as his quilt.[24]

The happy, jovial Axel von Sydow died as head of the Road and Waterway Corps. Proper good company could scarcely exist unless he was in charge; his mimicry, his mockery, his authority would drive away worry and dissent. He has left a cherished memory.[25]

The versatile Wallman, cynical, self-loving, but honest and good, shared pretzels and sandwiches and was the patron of all the ragamuffins. He himself looked like an alchemist, his room like an artefact display cabinet, where sandwiches, old

---

21 Samuel Johan Hedborn (1783–1849) studied at Uppsala 1806–1809 after departing from Linköping school, becoming good friends with Atterbom and other Swedish Romantics. He was ordained in 1809 and is well known for his two collections of psalms.
22 Per Adolf Sonden (1792–1837), went up to Uppsala in 1809 and contributed to Atterbom's monthly poetry magazine *Phosphoros*, along with Dahlgren and Hedborn. This short-lived publication (1810–1813), the title meaning 'bearer of light' or 'the morning star' gave its name to the Swedish neo-romantic movement *Phosphorism*. Sonden also took part in the Norwegian campaign of 1814 and entered the priesthood in 1817.
23 Anders Jacob Danielsson Cnattingius (1792–1864) was a student at Uppsala from 1810 and was ordained in 1816. Together with Dahlgren he formed *Manhemsförbundet*, an association promoting moral, national, and religious education and he produced many textbooks for the improvement of children's education.
24 Johan Hedenborg (1787–1865) studied medicine at Uppsala from 1810 and subsequently in Stockholm, becoming a Doctor of Medicine in 1822. He also had interests in natural history, archaeology, and languages, and travelled extensively, settling in Rhodes from 1837.
25 Axel Erik von Sydow (1791–1857) studied at Uppsala from 1809 and, with an interlude in 1813 serving as a *löjtnant* in the German and Norwegian campaigns, he graduated in 1818. Thereafter his career was as a civil engineer; he was admitted to the Swedish Academy of Sciences in 1839 and became head of the semi-military Road and Waterway Corps when it was formed in 1851.

stockings and the like would be found jumbled together. Since then, as a teacher, he was very much loved, and deserved it, too.[26]

More could be listed who became prominent in various branches of science, but too many to elaborate.

That both talent and dunderheads were to be found, one can probably understand. So, for example one genius would in an essay invoke Charles XII, but spelled '*hjälte*' (hero) as '*gälte*' and to make it complete, he forgot the umlaut, so that the sentence read: 'Charles XII, the great boar,' which brought such delight, that the writer, who was somewhat corpulent and died as a custom-house clerk in Linköping, throughout his entire life was known as 'the great boar.'

Another had to translate '*glada vänner*' (happy friends) into a script in Latin. Weak in Latin, he had to use Schenberg's Lexicon, wherein he found that the word *glada* (in fact meaning a kite, the bird of prey) was thus translated as *milvus*, hence he wrote '*milvi amici*' and thereby acquired by his comrades the nickname Milvus as long as he lived.[27]

Talents were little valued by our teachers, but they were nevertheless found: the school orchestra was large and not to be despised, though the musical director, who succeeded the skilled Mecklin, was an incompetent old boot.[28] At that time, the violins of Messrs Wennerberg, Ekbäck and Barkenbom could be heard anywhere and concerts were welcomed; on beautiful summer evenings music was performed on the Kittelberg outside the city, when the country's daughters would let themselves be seen.

Our time passed easily but was monotonous; the bright sparks loafed around, the dunces worked until the sweat dripped from their brows. We knew little about the position of the fatherland, for in the few newspapers available (in quarto format) all political talk was forbidden.

Boys like to play at war, and our Viking heritage was most pronounced during regimental officers' meetings, which were held in the town. We borrowed muskets from the corporals and engaged a drunken Jernfelt's corporal named Kallerman,[29] for a couple more drinks to practice us in exercises from the drill book for an hour, not then knowing that many would benefit from this game, which was not approved of by the teachers.

---

26 Johan Haqvin Wallman (1792–1853) was the son of Hultin's theology lecturer, Johan Wallman. He became Associate Professor of Natural History at Linköping a few years later in 1822.
27 Schenberg's Lexicon was a Swedish-Latin dictionary for schools first published in 1739. *Glada* is both the plural form of the adjective *glad* (happy) and a bird of the kite family which has the Latin name *milvus*, hence the student's confusion.
28 Johan Adolf Mecklin (1761–1803) was director of music and cathedral organist in Linköping from 1789. His unnamed replacement about whom Hultin is rather disparaging was presumably Zacharias Köhler (1765–1812) who held the same position from 1804 until his death in 1812.
29 A *Major* Jernfelt of the local provincial regiment, the Östgöta (Östergötland) Infantry, was wounded during that regiment's distinguished service in the Russian War 1788–1790 so it is likely therefore that Kallerman was a *korpral* in the *Major*'s company.

It was well known that the war in Finland was going badly,[30] but that matter concerned the king, not us, and the moans and groans we heard from people was regarded as just routine. However, we were awakened from our complacency by the Royal Ordinance of 26 March 1808, which called to arms all young people from 18 to 25 years, under the name of *lant-värn* (militia).[31] Some cried, some swore, others laughed, and the teachers shook their heads in disapproval.

One beautiful morning, shortly afterwards, the head-master, after finishing prayers at school, read a letter from brigade commander Colonel Skjöldebrand,[32] saying that high school students, who had both the desire and the aptitude, could obtain positions as officers in the militia, if they reported to his headquarters in Skänninge. The Vice-Chancellor discouraged us from such an uncertain venture and held out the prospect that the strict regulations issued might be relaxed. But the enterprise had its supporters; they reasoned that if it became necessary to take up arms, it would be easier serving as an officer than as a soldier, whereupon four students departed for Skänninge that same day and did not return. More followed suit until 10 comrades had signed up; they sometimes paid us a visit, praising their good fortune for abandoning theological dogma and getting 36 shillings a day.

Certainly, I wanted to follow their example but did not dare without my parents' consent, so I wrote to them and asked, and received the answer that I should follow

Count Anders Fredrik Skjöldebrand (1757–1834). Miniature by Giovanni Domenico Bossi (1767–1853), 1811. (Nationalmuseum)

---

30 Russia had commenced their invasion on 21 February 1808 and within a month had taken most of southern Finland including the capital Åbo (Finnish: Turku).

31 The 1872 edition incorrectly gives the month as May rather than March, the error repeated in the later editions. And whilst the King's original order issued on 14 March 1808 (the same day that Denmark's declaration of war was received) did indeed called for *all* healthy unmarried men between the ages of 18 and 25 to be called-up, this was supplemented by an order on 26 March which set a limit on the numbers raised to 30,500. Hultin had turned 18 the previous October and was thus liable for service.

32 Count Anders Fredrik Skjöldebrand (1757–1834) had commenced military service as a *kornett* in the South Scania cavalry in 1774; he acted as adjutant to Duke Charles (later Charles XIII) in the fleet in 1789 during the Russian War and retired as an *överste* (colonel) in the Life Drabants in 1797. He re-entered service in 1808 being appointed *överste* of the newly raised Östgöta militia.

my inclination, with a hint that, if it was necessary to enlist, it would be as well to be first rather than last.

I visited the headmaster and asked for permission to visit my comrades at Skänninge, but he, who sensed the danger, gave me a fatherly and flattering admonition not to throw my good mind in with a bunch of soldiers and said I would be losing much by laying my books to rest, but wished me well.

I was hesitant, but the next day Colonel Skjöldebrand came into town and I asked if there were any officer's positions vacant, to which he kindly replied that he could not decide now, but if I turned up in Skänninge the following week, I would have an answer.

By chance, a few of my old comrades came to visit at this time, took me aside and pressured me to join, and told me that the colonel had been asking searching questions about me. 'Come along! You get a free ride with us, easy treatment, accommodation and pay in Skänninge.'

2

Preparation for War: The Militia (April–May 1808)

From the outset, prospects for developing the militia into an effective fighting force were poor. The call-up took place at the same time as that of the reservists for the provincial regiments which raised around 15,000 men,[1] so the remaining raw material available for the planned 30,500 strong militia was the poorest and least suited; retired officers were re-commissioned as company commanders and above, but competent officers were few and numbers had to be supplemented from university and college students who had very little time to learn how to handle the men to be placed under their command.

No sooner said than done. The journey went well. I attended upon the colonel, who, after some consideration, furnished me the appointment of ensign in the Östgöta (Östergötland) militia, and ordered me to report for duty. I then met his principal staff officer, Elias Norlin,[2] a former captain in the Swedish Guard Regiment, who seemed rather abrupt, and asked me to sit for a while. He wrote, crossed out, pondered, spat, wrote, and crossed out, and finally he got up, counted out some money, wrote some words on a scrap of paper and said, 'Present this to the provost for your billets, and here is a month's pay; but the ensign now has opportunity to help me write for a while.' And right away I was set to work, writing general orders, requisitions, official letters etc. so much to his satisfaction that he designated me to assist in this role in the forthcoming expedition.

The next day I received a rusty old musket, with which I headed for the parade ground where my new comrades had gathered. It was a remarkable company, consisting of a pair of former officers who had probably been invalided out through

---

[1] Sweden's regular army essentially comprised provincial (*indelta*) regiments raised under the so-called allotment system and enlisted (*värvade*) regiments which included the guard regiments, garrison troops, artillery and other specialist units. For the provincial infantry regiments, every parish was divided into districts (*rote*) comprising 2–4 farmsteads, each rote being required to provide and maintain one soldier. Although the regiments were permanent and the men long-serving, they were only mobilised in time of war and otherwise only required to take part in regimental musters typically for three weeks each summer. Each soldier was provided with a croft and land sufficient to support himself and his family when not at war. Reservists (*vargering*) were raised by every two rote having to provide an additional soldier.

[2] Elias Norlin (1779–1865) who later became *överstelöjtnant* in the Västgöta-Dals Regiment.

bad feet, a couple of former non-commissioned officers who had been dismissed the service for drunkenness, the rest comprising high school students, bookkeepers, inspectors, a foundry proprietor, and a tanner's apprentice. Some had fragments of uniform, most were dressed as they pleased. A couple turned out with hunting rifles; the Royal Decree allowed such for both officers and men because there was a great shortage of muskets. Our non-commissioned officers comprised apprentice boys, stewards, servants, and the like. Together we would now have to organise and train a group of farm boys taken directly from the plough!

The higher command were certainly honest and decent people, but belonged in the lower echelons as regards fitness for duty.

The brigade commander, Colonel and later His Excellency Count A. F. Skjöldebrand, was a highly gifted, gracious man, a scientist, a talented writer and a successful poet, in his time a great musician, an artist, a language expert, an excellent horseman, and had a long time previously been a major in the former Östgöta cavalry.[3] He understood order and discipline well enough, but forming a brigade of infantry from scratch was beyond his ability.

His adjutant, the abovementioned Captain Norlin, was an excellent officer and did all that he could. It was entirely to his credit that anything serviceable was accomplished with such unpromising material. But, like many officers of the time, his command of the written language was limited; as evidence it can be cited that in Sundsvall he threatened me with arrest because I would not spell '*packkistor*' (packing chests) with one 'k' as he had written the word in the draft, '*packistor*'.[4]

To provide further understanding about those entrusted with command I want to list the officers of the 1st Battalion to which I belonged.

The battalion commander, old Count C. W. Douglas, had formerly been a captain in the Östgöta cavalry but long since retired from service, was honourable, pleasant, and well liked, and wanted to be better than his abilities allowed.[5]

The first company commander, Norlin, a relative of the adjutant, was an old gout-ridden merchant naval captain, with the honorary rank of ensign at the Admiralty. Wearing naval uniform, he never drew his sword for the company more than once, and then much to the amusement of our young men. At sea, however, we benefitted from the assistance of this old man, which tale will be told in due course.

The second company commander, Stålhammar, had never been anything other than a chamber-page,[6] with more aptitude for companionship and showmanship than for military service.

---

3   The former Östgöta Cavalry Regiment and Östgöta Infantry Regiment were combined to form the Life Grenadier Regiment in 1791 although they remained as semi-independent units, the *rotehåll* division and the *rusthåll* division.
4   A typical compound word derived from *packa* (meaning to pack) and *kista* meaning a storage box and thus properly spelt with double k.
5   Carl Wilhelm Douglas (1754–1822) had been appointed *ryttmästare* (equivalent to a captain) in the Östgöta cavalry in 1780. He was the great-great grandson of Count Robert Douglas, a Scotsman who had entered Swedish service in 1627, fought with distinction during the Thirty Years War and Charles X's Polish War and was ennobled Count Skänninge in 1654.
6   A chamber-page (*kammarpage*) was a youth of the nobility who waited upon princely or other high-ranking persons within their apartments.

The third company commander, von Breda, an artist, elegant and bright, painted portraits better than he handled military service.

The fourth company commander, a former Fågelberg high school student, had enough aptitude and desire, but what could one expect from a youth with only a month of experience?

The remaining commissioned officers were high school students. In the other battalions, the commanders were of similar or perhaps poorer material.

I have since served 34 years and for 14 years had the honour of commanding an *indelta* (provincial) company and know how it should be, but still cannot understand today how it was possible for our militia to hang together as well as it did, although it was subsequently disbanded. Had non-commissioned officers and corporals been drawn from the established regiments, so that at least one was present in each company to guide and correct the well-meaning young officers, perhaps things would have gone better. But as it was, the officers could barely take care of themselves, let alone their men.

Exercises continued and Captain Norlin did his best, so that I, having already been instructed in musket drill by Corporal Kallerman, in eight days learned the great skill of controlling a *stångpluton*,[7] but that was all.

The officers' training having ended, we were sent to our postings: the 1st Battalion to Linköping, the 2nd Battalion to Norrköping, and 3rd Battalion to Vadstena. Although a kind of brigade adjutant, I was, as an ensign, assigned to the 4th Company, where the captain, the lieutenant and I were three high school students, but in reverse order of seniority, because in high school I was the most senior and the captain the least; but we nevertheless got on well enough.

The day after our arrival, the militia mustered in the castle courtyard,[8] and there were witnessed both lamentable and absurd scenes; relatives and friends had followed them, some crying, some drunk, hugging their loved ones, offering them brandy and waffles. After they had been inspected by the Governor, the aging Rear Admiral Strömfelt,[9] they were divided into companies. The boys maintained reasonable self-control. We had feared a riot, but things settled down, and now we were left to fend for ourselves, three boys as officers with 154 farm-hands, without knowing how we should bear our responsibility to the men entrusted to us. The lieutenant, being most resourceful, went off to inquire as to what the other companies were doing, with the result that the men were ordered to assemble at Magasinstorget at 6:00 a.m. the next morning.[10]

I have heard talk of negro companies in the West Indies as being a travesty of soldiery, but it can hardly be truer of or more ridiculous than this parade. Neither officers nor non-commissioned officers had received full uniforms; some wore

---

7   A *stångpluton* (lit. pole-platoon) was part of a *stångbattaljon*, a unit assembled for command exercises, whereby the unit was only represented by platoon flankmen carrying poles providing the correct unit frontage.
8   Linköping Castle, a Renaissance style municipal building which was the Östergötland County governor's residence.
9   Count Fredrik Georg Strömfelt (1738–1814) was 70 years of age at this time. He had served in the navy from 1755 to 1783 and then as governor of Östergötland until 1810.
10 Magasinstorget is a small square in Linköping close to the river.

Linköping in the late eighteenth century, by Elias Martin (1739–1818). The view is of the eastern toll gate along Storgatan towards the Governor's residence and castle grounds in the distance. The river bridge is just beyond the gate, the cathedral is to the right. Linköping was then a small provincial market town, population circa 1,800 in 1750 rising to 3,000 in 1810. (Kungl. Konsthögskolan, Stockholm, via Alvin National Digital Cultural Heritage Platform)

headgear of their own design, some civilian hats or green peaked caps which were then fashionable; one wore a uniform with light blue trousers. None carried sidearms. There now stood 161 men including officers, variously dressed and without weapons since our muskets had not yet arrived and were later only initially provided for half the strength.

The farm boys were generally well-clothed, although between jerkin and trousers one could read their initials L. J. S., P. L. S. etc. sewn with red woollen yarn onto their shirts. But some wretches might have no shirt at all and only fragments of clothing to cover themselves. Two lacked both socks and shoes, which, however, was soon remedied by collecting surplus from the officers, because the boys' footsteps had to be able to make sound when ordered to halt or stand to attention.

However, most attention was paid to headgear, because His Royal Majesty's very specific and defined General Order decreed that a white linen band should be wrapped around the crown of the hat, and on the left side a five-inch-long worsted plume was to be attached, and these items – together with an old cartridge box – were the only equipment the Crown had provided. Imagine such a masquerade, with hats of various models and shapes, some so unsightly that a tuft of red hair protruding on the right side in conjunction with a yellow plume on the left gave the appearance of the horns of the demon Mephistopheles.

That this hat decoration was seen as of the highest symbolic importance to the fatherland is evidenced in the General Order of 15 June which decreed as punishment in the first degree, i.e., for minor misdeeds, eight days detention; but in the second degree, i.e., for more serious errors, the miscreant was to be stripped of his decoration for between two and eight days. They were however exempted, or at least generally spared, from corporal punishment.

The first service activity was to give the boys their soldier names,[11] and from this selection one could conclude that our company commander was well-read, because they included Romulus, Remus, Bucephalus, Achilles, Patroclus and the like; but regarding their board and lodgings, I believe that our captain and lieutenant knew as little as I did.

We eventually received old surplus muskets of many types, most more dangerous to the shooter than to the enemy, and the recruits' training continued such that after three weeks they could handle their weapons well and march passably. Had they been properly armed and had an experienced officer to lead them into battle, I think they would have fought well, for they were hateful of the Russians.

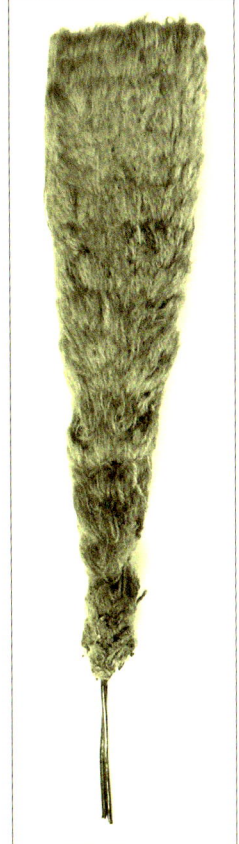

Swedish infantryman's plume from the Napoleonic wars. (Armémuseum)

---

11 Since family surnames were uncommon until the twentieth century, many soldiers in a unit might have exactly the same name. Soldier names were therefore used to ensure each man could be uniquely identified, and the choice of names was generally the responsibility of the company commander.

3

To Åland and Back (June–September 1808)

Russian progress since commencing their invasion of Finland on 21 February was demoralising, but by the end of May 1808 the situation was looking more promising, despite the surrender on 6 May of the massive Sveaborg fortress outside Helsinki with its garrison of some 6,000 men, 700 guns and most of the archipelago fleet. Swedish forces were advancing from the north and the Åland Islands had been recaptured. A predominantly militia force was assembled there in June for a planned attack in the southwest of Finland.

At the end of May, orders came for us to depart for Finland; we were to march across the country – steamboats and trains were then unknown. Everything was to be transported by the peasantry's own horses, and it seemed incomprehensible that this would suffice; troop transport was sought north and south, and I heard some drivers say they had journeyed as far as 80 kilometres.

The day of our departure from Linköping was miserable; we were considered to be lambs to the slaughter. Family and friends gathered to say their final farewells, streets and windows were full of people crying, our solemn former schoolfellows embraced us with tears and the ladies, with and opposite whom we danced, threw flowers and tributes to bid us farewell.

But the journey went without incident and the boys were in good spirits. In Södermanland they laughed when, being accustomed to thick peas, they were treated in that neighbourhood to thin pea gruel.[1]

As we approached Stockholm, we assembled at Liljeholmen, because of course the brigade wished to parade in a march past through the capital, and the men's courage was then put to a hard test, for unexpectedly a salute was given from Kastellholmen and the distant noise made them anxious, causing a rumour to race through the ranks that the Russians were already here.[2] This had the consequence that a parish tailor fled and several people claimed to have contracted cholera.

---

1   Hultin is presumably drawing a comparison between their local and typically thick pea soup and a rather thinner version they were served in Södermanland. Pea soup in many forms has been a staple in Sweden since the Middle Ages and is still traditionally served on Thursdays.
2   Presumably a salute by cannon fire from Kastellet, the small castle on Kastellholmen which is an island in the centre of Stockholm. Liljeholmen is about four kilometres WSW of there. Salutes were generally only fired for incoming and outgoing ships.

With an inebriated non-commissioned officer as a guide, I was sent to the Adjutant General to deliver the brigade's proposal and was introduced to the then serving Adjutant General Melin,[3] who was called 'carrion scum' by Armfelt,[4] and who, with military gauntlets tucked into his belt, looked critically over my attire and barked, 'The brigade may march through the city and here are orders for the brigade commander.' This highly important officer seemed to me to bear a close relation to our beloved native Småland oxen!

We were probably the first militia unit that passed through, for we aroused great compassion, which was expressed in words and gestures, but this did not alleviate our hunger or thirst.

We rested for a couple of hours at Roslagstull,[5] and those who were not afraid to go astray and had money visited inns, taverns, and market stalls. We had now seen Stockholm, although many did not see the city sights but enjoyed its pleasures and amenities and gathered material to tell drunken tales to our fellow countrymen on our homecoming. The wooden drum being sounded (we had no other),[6] we loaded the wagons and were now told that we were going to Grisslehamn and from there to Åland, where we were expected by the king, who did not dare to cross to Finland until he had such brisk lads with him.

At Grisslehamn we boarded Roslag boats, and whilst we had some provisions, of pitiful nature, no one had thought to provide water, so we might have died of thirst had the voyage had not been favoured by reasonably fair wind.

After about nine hours we landed at Marsund and were quartered on the hills, because there were no settlements nearby. The peasants were boastful, saying they did not need us, for they could kill the Russians better than we, to which end they presented us with evidence. The guerrilla action under priest Gummerus had ended just days before our arrival, and that commander had succeeded in isolating and capturing a Russian outpost and clubbing several to death, and the forests and hills were rumoured to be full of both Russian skeletons and weapons.[7] These latter at least we needed, and consequently a rather gullible group set out to unearth these treasures, but found nothing but a dead owl and a manure fork. However, we bought

---

3 From the time of Gustav III, the position in wartime of *generaladjutant för expeditionen*, or simply at this time known as *generaladjutant*, corresponded approximately to the chief of staff of later times. Georg Henrik of Melin (1769–1839) was appointed as the King's *generaladjutant* in October 1808. He later sought to defend Gustav IV Adolf during the coup d'état in 1809.
4 Finnish-born Gustaf Mauritz Armfelt (1757–1814) was commander of the western army on the Norwegian border at this time; a supporter of Gustav IV, he was instrumental in obtaining Finnish autonomy from Russia after the war and consequently seen by many in Sweden as a traitor.
5 A customs toll gate about three kilometres north of Stockholm's Old Town (*Gamla Stan*).
6 In line with the general lack of equipment, the militia were supplied with wooden drums instead of the standard army type which were made of brass.
7 A small Russian force of about 450 men had occupied the islands in the spring of 1808; Johan Henrik Gummerus (1774–1836) together with Governor Eric Arén had mobilised the peasantry in similar numbers to oppose them. By 11 May the entire Russian force had been captured, with only a handful of casualties on either side.

Roslag boats (*Roslagskutor*) were designed to operate in the Roslag archipelago and the Åland islands and ranged from seven to 22 meters in length. They remained in widespread use for transport of goods until the early twentieth century. Ink drawing by Jacob Hägg (1839–1932). (Sjöhistoriska museet)

some old swords from the peasants, which smelled of Russian leather,[8] so that some of the non-commissioned officers were thereby armed.

After a few days, we marched further inland, were given some tattered old tents, pitched camp on a sandy plain near a bay in Jomala parish,[9] and lived quite comfortably, at least when there was something to eat.

My skills in hunting and fishing now benefitted myself and my companions, because the bays teemed with seabirds and a fishing rod brought in as many small fish as we needed, so that we had roast meat – albeit tasting of fish-oil – and fried

---

8   Russian leather was a high-quality leather impregnated with birch oil that rendered it both soft and waterproof as well as providing its distinctive pleasant odour. It was a significant export from Russia in the seventeenth and eighteenth centuries and only began to be replicated elsewhere in Europe in the early nineteenth century. The reference here presumably relates to the scabbards in which the swords would have been kept, typically of leather-covered wood.
9   The original text states 'Jonsala' but this is assumed to be a typographical error, there is no such parish today or shown on the 1789 map; Jomala is one of the principal parishes on Fasta Åland and fits the description. It is about 20 kilometres from Marsund so likely reached within a single day's march.

Fasta Åland, detail from 1789 map by the Swedish Royal Land Survey (Kungliga Lantmäteriet). (Lund University Library collection via Alvin National Digital Cultural Heritage Platform)

ruffe.[10] If one had been able to ferret out a ½ pound of butter from a farm or croft, we would have had a feast, because mouldy rye bread was all that could be obtained from the stores.[11] Our exercises were not arduous and we had no-one sick.

The tranquillity was once disturbed when a dense smoke unexpectedly appeared over the archipelago, which was thought to be due to Russian action and caused an alarm. Ammunition was hurriedly distributed, and we were expecting to face the enemy when the old sailor Captain Norlin came hobbling out of the croft wherein

---

10 The ruffe (*gärs*) is a small freshwater fish, common throughout Finland's inland and offshore waters and typically around four to six inches long.
11 A soft acidic rye bread known as *ankarstock* was used in both the army and navy, supplied by the crown bakeries. A loaf was intended to provide two days ration.

King Gustav IV Adolf inspects troops on parade on Grelsby meadow, Åland, 31 July 1808. The infantry marching past is the Guards Brigade, the cavalry is a detachment of the Lifeguard of Horse. (Finnish Heritage Agency Historical Picture Collection)

he was quartered for his health, and, laughing, asked if we had never seen a sea mist before, whereby we were simultaneously reassured and ashamed.

On a late summer's evening we were told that at nine o'clock the next morning we were to assemble at Grelsby for a parade.[12] There upon a field were formed up about 5,000 men, mostly militia,[13] and our young king rode past the ranks, proud and erect, graciously nodding, after which a small couch was produced and placed in the centre of the field, upon which he sat, with four tall, gaunt Life Drabants[14] posted around him, and the service began.

The heat was exceptional, one of the lifeguards and several other men fainted, but the king sat with his coat done up to his neck, without having mind for anything but the sermon and his psalm book. I had seen the king a couple of times before, but now he was not the same, both drowsiness and distraction overcame him.

After the service, the king handed out the first gold medals for bravery in the field. Baron von Vegesack of the Älvsborg Regiment and an officer of the Jämtland

---

12 Hultin states more precisely that they were notified of the parade on *Midsommarafton* (Midsummer's Eve) which would mean it took place on 24 June, but other sources indicate the Östgöta militia only arrived on Åland on 24 July and the parade took place on 31 July.
13 The army return of 28 July indicates the Åland force then comprised a Guards Brigade under *Major* Fleetwood with one battalion from each of the Finnish, Swedish, and Svea Lifeguard regiments; the Uppland militia (three battalions) under *Generalmajor* Lantingshausen; the Östgöta militia (three battalions) under *Överste* Skjöldebrand; one company of the Åland militia; a detachment of the Lifeguard of Horse; and two 3-pounder batteries of the Svea artillery regiment, totalling just under 4,500 men excluding officers.
14 *Kunglig Majestäts Livdrabantkår* – His Royal Majesty's Life Drabant corps – was at this time primarily a palace guard of 150–200 men in four companies. A second Life Drabant unit was formed for Duke Charles in 1790. Hundreds of officers passed through its ranks. It was disbanded in 1809 when Charles became king.

mounted jäger squadron were the lucky recipients.[15] We were then dismissed to entertain ourselves as best we could.

I cannot fail to mention a circumstance that then personally touched me. Among the spectators on that Grelsby meadow I saw a priest leading a little girl. Fourteen years later, this girl became my wife.[16] It is surely unnecessary and impolitic for a man to praise his wife, but in fairness I confess that she has been my best friend and brought me the greatest of happiness for almost half a century.

On the way back, it was fun to hear the boys' reflections on this solemn day and the eminent people encountered. It was considered a great blunder that I had not known to bow when I saluted the king. They had also seen a moth-eaten and serious-looking man and wondered whether he, like us, was hungry and could not afford such fine clothes as the highest-ranking general. When we found out who they meant by that, it turned out to be the king's personal bodyguard![17]

Safe and sound we returned to our camp and resumed our usual pursuits, that is, exercise for a couple of hours and then fishing, hunting or sleep.

Baron Eberhard von Vegesack (1763–1818). Lithograph by Johan Elias Cardon (1802–1878). (Finnish Heritage Agency Historical Picture Collection)

---

15 The medal *För tapperhet i fält* (For valour in the field) was created by Gustav III in 1789 during the Russian War, in the form of a silver medal for non-commissioned officers and other ranks. In 1808, Gustav IV introduced a gold version for officers; Hultin indicates that these two officers were the first recipients. *Generalmajor* Eberhard von Vegesack (1763–1818) was much decorated for bravery during his long military career. This award related to his command of the seaborne landing at Lemo just south of Åbo (Turku) on 19/20 June with the aim of capturing that city. He led a force of about 2,800 men from the Åland army including one battalion of guards and the Uppland militia brigade and was opposed by a superior Russian force of 3,600. After initial success he was forced to retreat, re-embarking his men, and heading back to Åland. Each side lost about 200 men.
16 Constance Wänman (1803–1883), daughter of the Hammarland parish priest Israel Gustaf Wänman (1762–1821) and Henrietta Sophia Cronhielm (1773–1848). The family relocated to Sweden after the war with Russia.
17 The *kammarhusar* was the king's personal bodyguard and would wear something resembling a hussar uniform regardless of whether or not he had been a hussar.

We would subsequently learn of the degrading of the guard regiments which aroused both surprise and pity and was perhaps a primary contributor to Gustav IV Adolf's overthrow.[18] We would then see the occasional former officer in new uniform with a non-commissioned officer's buttons and yellow plume and learn how they had had to grit their teeth. The injustice was so much greater as it was applied to everyone without exception, even those who were not involved in the infamous retreat. Many ex-officers became employed as adjutants, such as for example our chief staff officer Captain Norlin. More were posted to serve in other regiments. Many men from these regiments had never been to Finland, let alone Helsinge, but they likewise had their buttons torn off and lost their rank, which at that time was doubly harsh, because the youngest ensigns were dispersed to provincial regiments alongside the most senior lieutenants. One could therefore imagine what resentment the degrading would bring to the families of the nobility who had sons and relatives in these regiments. One began to hear whispers that things would not turn out well for the king, but God preserve anyone who dared to speak openly of this. But the nation still remained staunchly royalist, and the distrust of 'gentlemen' had grown further since the last war, the Anjala Conspiracy and Gustav III's murder.[19] A military revolution, which perhaps was being planned and which subsequently succeeded and saved the kingdom, would at that time hardly have been likely to succeed. From older comrades we subsequently heard that a coup was in consideration in 1804 in Stralsund,[20] but that they did not dare due to the Finns who were there present.

Åland is not fertile but is a beautiful land. Getting to know it would require a whole summer, because it comprises over 80 inhabited islands and countless islets and skerries, mostly covered with deciduous forest. Its flora includes several alpine plants, its fauna being the same as the Scandinavian mainland. Its predators include the fox, and, during extreme winters, wolves which cross over the frozen sea, but they are hunted down and killed. The archipelago is full of sea birds, fishing is profitable

---

18 The landing at and retreat from Helsinge 26–28 September 1808 was one of the final actions on Finnish soil during the 1808–1809 war with Russia. It appeared that the three Guards regiments present did not perform well and the evacuation onto naval transports on 28th was certainly chaotic. As a consequence, in an order dated 12 October 1808, Gustav IV Adolf demoted some 120 Guards officers, abolishing their rank and privileges; the Svea Life Guard and the Finnish Guard Regiment were degraded to become ordinary enlisted regiments, known as Fleetwood's and Palén's after their respective commanding officers, and the Swedish Guard Regiment was disbanded and the men divided between those two new units. This action brought widespread resentment, particularly amongst the nobility.

19 Officers opposed to Gustav III's Russian War (1788–1790) opened secret communications with Catherine the Great to try to end the war; this became known as the Anjala conspiracy; 113 officers signed their support. This unpopular war was one of the factors leading to the assassination of the king in March 1792, along with the increasing of his own absolutist powers whilst reducing the privileges of the nobility. He was succeeded by his son, Gustav IV Adolf.

20 When the French invaded Hanover in 1803, Gustav IV Adolf sought to ally with Britain and Russia to launch an attack from Stralsund in Swedish Pomerania, as a prelude to which he sent troops there during 1803–1805, declaring war in October 1805 thus involving the nation in the War of the Third Coalition against Napoleon.

Swedish troops on Åland: Foot Guard; Upplander; Horse Guard; Militiaman. (Illustration by Magnus Adlercreutz from C.O. Nordensvan, *Finska Kriget 1808-09* (Stockholm: Albert Bonniers, 1898))

and seal hunting is a significant activity.

The Ålanders are a strong and hardy people, who speak fairly pure Swedish, aim to live well, principally on fish, but value a piece of seal meat and a quart of brandy. I once had the pleasure of tasting a regional dish comprising boiled dumplings of oatmeal and seal blubber and can attest that it was accompanied with brandy. The peasants were neither simple nor dumb; if beaten, they would strike back.

At the end of August, 500 men together with their officers were ordered to Karlskrona, and we never saw them again.[21] At their eventual home-coming, half were missing, either lying in hospital or in their graves, for at that time our men were cared for worse than I ever cared for my dogs.

Every other day rumours arose that next week the king would accompany us to Finland, and then the devil take the Russians, but the weeks went by and both the king and ourselves stayed put, until mid-September when the order to break camp arrived, in the middle of the night; but instead of heading east, we marched west, back to Marsund, where we were encamped for a week on its familiar hills, until a fleet of Roslag boats arrived, which we quickly boarded; but then lay at anchor for several days through lack of suitable wind.

---

21 Karlskrona was the country's principal naval base on the Baltic. Many of the militia were directed to serve as manpower in the galley fleet. The General Staff history (*Sveriges krig åren 1808 och 1809*) indicates one battalion of the Uppland militia and one of the Östgöta militia were despatched to the fleet on 2 August, rather than the end of August.

So far, everything had been a game, we had no-one sick and out of 1,600 men not one had died, but now our sorrows began: half-naked and starved, wet and frozen stiff, thrown about like herring in the open boats, in rain and foul weather, and although provided with salted meat and peas we had no means to cook a meal on board. As a result of storms and headwinds, we were at sea for 17 days,[22] and twice would have been lost, had not old Norlin, as a practical seaman with knowledge of the archipelago, searched out and anchored between skerries. He also received praise in the newspapers for this action. During these interludes, men gathered brushwood and branches and boiled their peas in crevices in the rocks, and the officers had to buy fish, otherwise we would have starved to death. Fortunately, we had some lads with us from the Östergötland archipelago, who could assist in manoeuvring the ship, for the commander 'Jerk Jersa' and the chief mate, his son, who constituted the official crew, were feckless and poor navigators.

---

22 The General Staff history states that, as a result of news that Norwegian troops had broken into Jämtland and Härjedalen, the king ordered Skjöldebrand to Sundsvall with the four remaining battalions of the Uppland and Östgöta militia; departing on 17 August they arrived in Sundsvall on 25 August 'after a rather adventurous journey under difficult wind conditions.' This indicates a nine-day voyage rather than Hultin's recollection of 17 days, but individual boats may well have taken longer battling the poor conditions. Assuming the boats remained close to the coast, the journey by sea would be at least 350 kilometres.

4

Garrison Duties in Västernorrland (October 1808–February 1809)

The planned invasion of Finland from Åland never took place and the assembled forces returned to Sweden. Hultin's unit was posted to garrison duties around Sundsvall where they remained for the winter. Finland was formally abandoned to Russia by the Convention of Olkijoki signed on 19 November, but this did not end the war and Tsar Alexander now had designs on conquering the Swedish mainland.

After much misery we came to Sundsvall, with over 50 sick delivered to hospital. The town had recently been destroyed by fire,[1] so that the whole force could not be accommodated there. The 1st Battalion was quartered in Njurunda parish, 15 kilometres away; myself together with a non-commissioned officer and 36 men were quartered at Mjösund farm, where both officers and men recovered.

The Njurunda river discharges here into the Baltic and affords excellent fishing. Salmon and whitefish were daily dishes, which were much enjoyed boiled or fried; but when offered *gravlax*[2] or *surströmming*,[3] which were common, our good-natured Östgöta humour surfaced as we laughed, spat, and swore. Game was in abundance and with the hounds, which always accompanied the soldiers, we engaged in hunting; but the peasantry caught most with snares, so that you could often buy a hazel grouse for a few shillings.

The local bread did not suit Östgöta stomachs, and no wonder, when one learnt that the grain (principally barley) is not always ripe, they harvest the ears more or less mature and are not concerned if any straw comes off with it. This is then ground with chaff and all, made into a dough without yeast and rolled out in round cakes of three to four feet in diameter,[4] the thinner the better, which are then baked on a hot plate of iron or stone. In appearance it looks like cardboard and is very dry.

---

1   Fire was a constant hazard in towns whose buildings were predominantly made of wood. In September 1803, following a prolonged drought, a fire started in Sundsvall which, fanned by a strong north-westerly wind, destroyed over 200 buildings and made homeless more than 900 of the population of just over 1,000.
2   Raw salmon traditionally salted and fermented by burying it in the sand.
3   Lightly salted fermented raw Baltic Sea herring, near rotten and famed for its pungent smell.
4   Hultin states the diameter as 1½ to 2 *aln*.

With *surströmming* added between layers, the peasants could easily devour a piece two-foot square! The people were agile, handsome, and probably the most honest in all of Sweden.

We met here with the Uppland militia, who were better off than us, both in terms of their officers and their clothing.

Every fortnight, quarters were exchanged; those who had been in the countryside then undertook garrison duty in the town, where the locals were quite charitable. When the winter cold began, the burghers provided an old overcoat for each guard post, which the man on duty was permitted to wear, and this was essential, for in December the temperature reached -25 to -28°C.[5] We received some clothing from our hometowns through generous collections made on our behalf, so that about 20 sets per company could be distributed to the most needy. But most did not reach us in time; the materials remained in the county administration's safekeeping for our homecoming. What happened to it subsequently is one of 'natures mysteries', but certainly the militia never gained any benefit therefrom. Most did not need them either, because they lay dead and buried in the ground.[6]

For three months, about 2,000 men were idle in this place, instead of going over to Finland and helping our vigorous Finns, who alone fought against the Russian colossus. But the poor mad king was now thoroughly unpopular and ripe for his fall, and probably both we and his own perverse actions must serve as agents of his departure.

Garrison service was not arduous, but we had an outpost on Brämö island about 20 kilometres from Sundsvall, comprising a subaltern and 50 men, which was adventurous, because if a storm occurred, there was great difficulty getting over with provisions. I too had the pleasure of a 14-day posting there and occasionally going hungry.[7] The island was uninhabited. Although there was a collection of small, pleasant wooden houses and an even smaller church, it was now deserted, because Sundsvall's burghers, who in summer used it as a base for fishing, were now back in the town and left us their houses, in which we established ourselves most comfortably.[8] When supplies were interrupted for a few days, we lived on sea birds and bilberries. During easterly storms, the small harbour was so rife with herring gulls (*Larus argentatus*) that we would simply split our musket balls into eight pieces and fire into the middle of the flock to kill several birds with one shot. And I have never

---

5 Historical daily mean temperature records for Stockholm 1756–2005 indicate that the winter of 1808–1809 was particularly cold with several days being the coldest ever recorded. The present mean daily minimum temperature at Sundsvall airport in December is circa −17°C and the record low since 1943 circa −37°C.

6 The majority of losses in the militia (some 6,000) were as a result of sickness, to such an extent that a collective term *lantvärnssjukan* (militia disease) was coined to cover losses from a range of common diseases including dysentery, typhus, and typhoid fever.

7 Hultin uses an idiom '*suga på ramarna*' literally 'suck on paws' meaning to exist frugally, from an old and erroneous notion attributed to Carl Linnaeus in 1748 that a bear, when it is starving, maintains life by sucking on its paws.

8 This description of Brämö is very much still the case today. The island has an area of about 15km^2 and lies two kilometres off the mainland coast. It is now a nature reserve with just two small settlements and no roads.

seen elsewhere as many bilberries as were to be found here; crushed and mixed with flour, they yielded edible pancakes. The boys, mindful of Östergötland's meat stews, derisively referred to bilberries as *Brämö peas*.

What else the posting was intended to achieve, I still cannot understand, for in the event of an enemy attack it was a rat trap. But in summer it would have been good fun to play Robinson Crusoe there.

In November our beloved brigade commander departed, having been ordered to Gävle to take command of the Life Grenadier brigade and with it cross over to Finland, and as his chief of staff was at that time indisposed due to a broken bone, I was assigned to accompany him. The brigade, slightly more than 2,000 men, embarked on old and barely seaworthy merchant ships, and the expedition failed as might have been expected, because after a couple of days it was driven back by storms and headwinds and had to seek shelter in harbours and inlets from Öregrund to Härnösand. One ship foundered at Ängesberg on the approaches to Gävle, where Ensign de Geer drowned together with 120 Life Grenadiers.[9] I escaped all this, because at the departure of the expedition I had been ordered to return to Sundsvall.

Things were bad, the hospitals were full, and those who laid there were mostly awaiting the grave, although medical staff of barbers and apothecaries did everything they could. Now and again we met a former high school companion serving as a battalion physician in the Uppland militia, and when we questioned him in astonishment as to how he had been able to complete the training so quickly, he replied, 'I spent six weeks in Stockholm and Hallman made me a doctor, so if you become ill, come and see me, I have Hoffman's drops and wormwood drops.'[10]

Meanwhile, the 2nd Battalion was moved to Härnösand and thus we got accommodation in the town, whose residents we had to thank for help, both with clothes and food.

Apart from guard duties, our main work was to dig graves for our deceased comrades in the frozen earth at our new cemetery. Our priest, the young honourable Alexander Palmblad, was among the first.[11]

It sounds incredible, but nevertheless true, that in the extreme cold men went on guard with their feet and legs wrapped with spun straw. Our needs and hardships

---

9 The General Staff history indicates that the Life Grenadier Regiment had set out on 18 September 1808, and, although disrupted by storms, by mid-October 700 men had arrived in Finland.
10 Johan Gustaf Hallman (1769–1814) was head of the army physician's corps (*fältläkarekåren*) 1808–1810. To address the poor provisions for medical care following the outbreak of the war, he was commissioned to admit promising young candidates to be taught field medicine in a temporary educational institution. Seventy-six students were selected, although only six continued their medical studies after the war. Hoffman's drops were an intoxicating compound of one part ether to three parts alcohol, named after the German physician and chemist Friedrich Hoffmann (1660–1742). Wormwood drops comprised an extract of wormwood (*artemisia absinthium*) for medicinal purposes particularly for indigestion as well as treatment of more serious diseases.
11 Alexander Herman Palmblad (1780–1808) from Tingstad near Norrköping was ordained in 1806 and died aged 28 as field preacher in the Östgöta militia in Sundsvall on 19 September 1808.

increased greatly because we did not receive any pay for two months. For the men this was not so harsh, for they were accustomed to poor provisions and little money besides, but the officers, and especially the poor non-commissioned officers, who were in need, had to work or beg to raise money. Those who had learned a trade fared best, for they could sometimes find work with the town's craftsmen.

One Count Frölich, probably of the *Adelsfanan*, now had command in the town and over the troops.[12] From where or how he came to this position, I do not know, for I never saw him in uniform, but I would sometimes assist his administration with writing. He often asked me what the men said about the situation, if they were very dissatisfied with the lack of pay. He did not seem to be too concerned when I said yes to this, from which I can now conclude that even he was harbouring thoughts of revolution.

In February, during the sharpest winter cold, a movement order arrived, not for Finland but to our home province, and lucky was the man that could lay abed in hay in the spacious Norrland wagons.[13] However, each night's camp delivered its share of frostbitten, sick, and dead. Our journey went through Sala and Västerås to Norrköping, where we went into quarters.

I cannot be precise regarding numbers, but certainly in the end, of the 1,800 healthy young men who in May the year before had set out ready to fight, not 600 returned fit for service, so that, allowing for the Karlskrona contingent which departed from Åland and of which almost half later returned, we were missing 1,000 men.[14] With proper supervision and suitable equipment, these bitter events should not have cost so many lives. But this is how the country's youth were being treated at that time, and perhaps with some intent, to prepare them for the mad king's fall.

I received 14 days leave to visit my family and found them well, although they burbled on about the great military action that was being advocated. I was duly quizzed and then ridiculed because I had not seen any Russians, other than in Sundsvall where I had seen a transport carrying prisoners of war.

Upon my return to Norrköping, I found that major changes had taken place. Most of the men were re-assigned as grenadiers or reservists and the remainder were demobilised.[15] The officers received one month's pay, travel money to return home and a 'thank you for your good service'. As for me, I was posted to Stockholm with the brigade's campaign records and documents, whence I immediately departed.

---

12 Possibly Count Johan Frölich (1754–1826) who had resigned military service in 1787 and was resident in Sundsvall until his death in 1826. The *Adelsfanan* (lit. Noble Banner) was Sweden's first regular cavalry unit, raised from the nobility. However, by 1743 it had become a unit on paper only and membership incurred no obligations to serve but retained certain privileges.
13 *Norrland* is a common term for the northern half of Sweden.
14 Hultin's text states the initial strength as 1,600 but this does not fit the subsequent numbers quoted; the initial strength of the militia regiments was nominally 1,800 men in three battalions of four companies of 150 men. As noted earlier, 500 had been despatched to Karlskrona in August 1808, so if 200 subsequently returned ('almost half') this would give the stated total loss of around 1,000. But by either reckoning more than half had died and without ever engaging the enemy.
15 Presumably by 'grenadiers' Hultin means the Life Grenadiers, the local regiment based at Linköping.

5

The Revolution (March 1809)

Sweden's revolution of 1809 was a bloodless affair, a coup d'etat to remove the unpopular King Gustav IV Adolf, particularly given his handling of the war against Russia. There was no intent to dispense with the monarchy, but rather to restore the balance of power between king and parliament (the Riksdag) from the absolutism which had been imposed by his predecessor Gustav III, who himself had seized power from the Riksdag in the coup of 1772 and who was assassinated in 1792. Hultin by chance was in Stockholm at the time of Gustav IV's arrest and was witness to the events.

In Stockholm, I was pleased to meet again my former brigade commander, and, after the expedition's actions had been recorded, comments addressed and verification arranged, I had plenty of time to stroll. The city was full of off-duty officers, some Finns, some militia, and the young men amused themselves and would create a scene when opportunity arose. However, I availed myself of Hallman's institute for the training of field physicians and although I did not learn much, I have since benefitted therefrom.

The king spent most of his time at Haga,[1] and when he passed along the streets it was best to fasten every button on one's coat and wear one's hat in the correct manner. He was least welcomed at the Royal Guard parades, which he regularly inspected twice a week, for he would mete out eight to 14 days detention[2] for an unfastened button, a wrinkled corner on the armband,[3] or an incorrectly worn neckcloth. I saw the king personally fasten the top coat button on Colonel Hierta,[4] who had already handed in his resignation from service and was probably on his last guard parade. This royal button-fastening was accompanied by the words, 'We thought Hierta, who is such an experienced officer, would know how to dress.'

One fine day, whispers were heard that the Russians were on Åland and intended to pay a visit to Stockholm. The city's nobility and wealthy merchant families

---

1   Haga Palace, about five kilometres north of the centre of Stockholm, was completed for Gustav IV Adolf in 1805 in Haga Park, which itself had been established by Gustav III between 1780 and 1797.
2   Hultin uses the contemporary Swedish slang term *fria husrum*, literally free housing.
3   *Armklädet*: a white cloth worn in a bow around the left upper arm of all Swedish officers between 1772 and 1809 to signify the approval of the 1772 revolution.
4   Likely to be *Överste* Axel Adam Hierta (1749–1820) who had been in military service since joining the Cadet Corps in Karlskrona in 1760.

started packing. A few days later there was a rumour that the Western Army had revolted and was on its way to Stockholm,[5] but this was not believed, until Sunday, 12 March, when His Majesty came from Haga with all the cavalry he could muster. The gates of the Royal Palace were closed, the guard at all toll gates was strengthened to discourage those who wanted to get away, adjutants and chamberlains galloped about, and the citizens began to look apprehensive. The Guard regiments were absent and only a small military force remained in the city.[6] In the evening I was ordered to be ready the next day to follow the troops who would be marching south and so at 9:00 a.m. I turned up at the Palace.

At dawn on 13 March, I went up to the expedition office to pick up my writing supplies etc. There I met the colonel's valet, an old acquaintance since the campaign, busy with packing. 'The Ensign would not believe the trouble that occurred here last night,' he said. 'Visitors have come and gone, such that the colonel has not slept a wink until now. He has ordered me to load his pistols, and so the Ensign can assist me.' 'What in God's name is going on?' I asked. 'Well, we will probably follow the king to Södertälje today.'[7] And that is all I was told about a revolution in which my commanding officer was one of the principal characters, although this was little evident.[8]

At the Palace, where only the west gate next to the Royal Guard Wing was open, I reported for duty at nine o'clock, and met many acquaintances, for all the officers who did not belong to any of the units stationed in the city had received the same order and were gathered in the Drabants waiting room.[9]

There, the rumour of the Western Army's revolt was confirmed and that we were facing civil war. Important men passed in and out looking more concerned than we, and adjutants fussed about as usual. Much noise was heard from within adjacent rooms, which we thought to be a consequence of packing, but a while afterwards General Adlercreutz,[10] whom I had often seen with my commanding officer, came

---

5   The Western Army – that facing Norway and amounting to some 15,000 men in total – was under the command of Gustav Mauritz Armfelt who was a strong supporter of Gustav IV and opposed to the revolutionaries. But *Överstelöjtnant* Georg Adlersparre, who had been recently relieved of his command on the Norwegian front, issued a revolutionary manifesto in Karlstad on 7 March and then set off for Stockholm with an insurgent force of 3,000 men.
6   The degraded Guard regiments (now Fleetwood's and Palén's) were on Åland.
7   The King was planning to flee with family, court, loyal troops, and the reserves of the national bank to join the army under loyal *General* Toll in Skåne. His route would pass through Södertälje about 40 kilometres southwest of Stockholm.
8   Skjöldebrand had been involved in plotting the overthrow of the king for several months and saw an opportunity when called to Stockholm in February 1809 but his attempts to win over Duke Charles and high officials did not bear fruit, and he had a falling out with those who finally carried out the coup, so remained outside when it took place.
9   The Royal Guard Wing (*Högvaktsflygeln*) is the northernmost of the two curved wings on the west side of Stockholm Palace; the Drabants waiting room (*Stånddrabantsalen*) is a room on the first floor (now known as the Bernadotte floor) facing the west entrance and used by the King's bodyguards, the Drabants.
10 Finnish-born Carl Johan Adlercreutz (1757–1815) was a popular war-hero who had entered military service aged 13 and excelled in both the Russian War 1788–1790 and the Finnish war 1808–1809 during which he was promoted to *Generalmajor*. He also served in the 1813 campaign against Napoleon and against Norway in 1814; he died after a short illness in 1815.

THE REVOLUTION (MARCH 1809) 43

Stockholm Palace in the 1780s viewed from the Skeppsholm bridge, by Elias Martin (1739–1818). The view today is almost identical. (Nationalmuseum)

The west front and curved Royal Guard Wing of Stockholm Palace in the 1800s. Lithograph by Carl Johan Billmark (1804-70). (Lund University Library via Alvin National Digital Cultural Heritage Platform)

General Carl Johan Adlercreutz (1757–1815). Portrait by Carl Wilhelm Nordgren (1804–1857). (Nationalmuseum)

out with the Adjutant General's baton in his hand. He looked upset, stopped in the middle of the hall, and spoke in a loud voice, 'By virtue of the office I hold as Adjutant General, I command you gentlemen to remain calm. His Royal Majesty is unfit to rule.'

One can imagine what astonishment and surprise this brought about. People looked at one other, turning pale with anxiety and then started whispering, 'What in heaven's name is going on? Has he been murdered – or have they arrested him?' A young officer drew his sword and proclaimed, 'You shall not arrest the king as long as I live!' But an older colleague took him by the arm and whispered, 'Beware, at the first sign of resistance, at the slightest action in his defence, he might be killed, assuming he is still alive.'

Later I heard it said that this action was intended to save the kingdom in the greatest emergency. We knew nothing of the king's attempted escape and recapture by von Greiff.[11]

It was past one o'clock and we wanted to leave but the west gate was now also closed. The hungry crowd began to grumble, which resulted in cold food and wine being served on tables and benches, which was eagerly consumed and calmed our royalism. Later, the entrance was opened from time to time, and one was allowed to pass as befitted a junior officer.

I did catch a brief glimpse of the king, reclining on a chair in the White Room, looking more dead than alive.[12] It has been said that he was treated improperly, but I cannot be certain about that.

---

11 Johan Ludvig Bogislaus von Greiff (1757–1828) had served as a cavalryman in the Russian War 1788–1790 but had resigned from military service in 1801 and since 1803 held the position of Court Huntmaster (*hovjägmästare*). When after the coup the king tried to flee through the Palace courtyard, he was seized by von Greiff, who also subsequently escorted the king and his family into confinement at Gripsholm castle.

12 The White Room was the Queen's dining room and adjoined the Queen's Drabants room on the east side of the Palace. Von Greiff's account of his capture of the king records that

Gustav IV's re-capture by Johan Ludvig Bogislaus von Greiff, 13 March 1809. Undated water colour. (Nationalmuseum)

Thus, the autocratic king in his palace, together with his loyal commanders, had now been arrested by five enterprising officers, with no harm caused other than a broken door.[13] Give me such a revolution again!

I do not wish to interrupt my simple story to make reflections, but I cannot imagine without horror what could have happened if the king had appealed to us. We, a group of young boys, who were brought up on the principles of monarchy, who did not reason about the position of the fatherland, about the king's ineptitude, or the calamities of a civil war, but who had such military discipline that we would obey and protect the king – we, and I felt that way myself, would have taken his side. I do not claim that the revolution would thereby have failed, but a scene from Constantinople could have been enacted at Stockholm's Palace.[14]

Say what you will about Gustav Adolf, but as an individual he should have been worthy of respect. Frugal, fair, and a man of his word, he could have been the sovereign that Sweden needed, had his upbringing and religious musings not clouded his judgement. In addition, he was misled, ill-served and, as a result of the rumours concerning his birth, destined to be dethroned.[15]

---

after being taken to the White Room, the king felt ill and vomited, and was then attended by his physician.
13 In fact, von Greiff had the honour of suffering the only wound in the affair when the king struck him with his sword causing a minor cut to his forearm.
14 Likely a reference to the reputation of the Ottoman court for palace intrigue and murder of their Sultans, often involving the army, such as the coup in 1807 by the Janissaries which was followed by another in 1808 when Sultan Selim was murdered.
15 Rumours concerning Gustav Adolf's parentage relate to Count Adolf Fredrik Munck (1749–1831), a Finnish noble who became an intimate friend of Gustav III and Queen Sophie Magdalena, to the extent of being hired in 1775 to assist and instruct them in consummating

Around three o'clock we departed, to be questioned left and right in the streets and squares about what we had and had not seen. We then re-established ourselves as if nothing had happened and a similar situation prevailed in the city. Of course, there were murmurings in various circles, but no action was taken.

'Old Duke' Charles had ruled as regent in the past and would now have his hands full trying to fix up the mess.[16] Willing or not, he had to step up, at least until the commander of the Western Army arrived to take charge.

The Western Army held its triumphant procession. They had consented to march to Stockholm, to receive double pay and have a good time. But they were not minded to go to Åland, where old man von Döbeln alone showed the Russians his sharp teeth.[17]

Proclamations came thick and fast, read and forgotten. In good time, the Estates met, otherwise the Western Army, like Rome's Praetorians, might have imposed a king upon us.[18]

Duke Charles (1748–1818), crowned King Charles XIII on 29 June 1809. Portrait by Carl Fredrik von Breda (1759–1818). (Nationalmuseum)

---

their marriage. At the same time, he was having an affair with the Queen's chamber maid. The future King Gustav IV Adolf was born in 1778 and rumours rapidly emerged as to whether Munck might be the father.

16 '*Gamle Hertig*' or 'Old Duke' was the nickname of Gustav III's brother, Duke Charles, who was soon to be crowned King Charles XIII. He had been *amiral* (admiral) of the fleet during the Russian War 1788–1790 and had already served as regent between 1792 and 1796 following the assassination of Gustav III.

17 Baron Georg Carl von Döbeln (1758–1820) had been assigned to defend the Åland islands in February and put up a stout resistance when the Russians attacked on 14 March, the day after the coup, but, unable to defeat them, he successfully withdrew his troops across the frozen sea to Grisslehamn three days later.

18 A parliament (Riksdag) was convened on 1 May; by 27 June a new constitution had been drawn up and accepted by all the Estates following which Duke Charles was crowned Charles XIII on 29 June. This marked Sweden's permanent transition from an absolute monarchy to a constitutional monarchy.

Now everything fell into good order. The citizens were cultivated with spirits and brotherly toasts, the current four Estates representation was maintained, retaining the nobility and clergy, with their privileges and prerogatives, which could then so easily have been thrown into the fire. The imperfect new constitution was then patched and repaired for 56 years, before a brusque king and a wise council would totally shred it.[19]

---

19 The historic Riksdag representing the four Estates – nobility, clergy, burghers and peasants – was abolished in 1865 during the reign of Charles XV in favour of the modern two-chamber parliament. The architect of this reform was Louis Gerhard de Geer who also became Sweden's first Prime Minister in 1876.

6

Transfer to the Regular Army (April–July 1809)

> *The militia were by now a spent force. They would not be effectively disbanded until the end of the war with Russia in September 1809, but from June 1808 the best men had, in any case, been a primary source of replacements for the regular army and militia unit losses were not made good, so by the summer of 1809 their numbers had more than halved. Some one in five of those conscripted had succumbed to disease. Hultin was minded to continue to serve his country, and so looked to secure a new position.*

It was now time for me to move on, for the militia raised by our former king was to be disbanded, with no prospects in my favour.

The army was overwhelmed with surplus officers. A multitude of Finns, who did not wish to submit to the knout, had left service and payroll there and come over, and these had to be found positions.[1] Nor was it possible to exclude those who sought employment from the militia, so that, especially in the southern regiments, there were excessive numbers.

In the Life Drabant corps, whose reputation and credit were nothing to brag about, I could receive a salary immediately, but Colonel Skjöldebrand, who, although no longer my commanding officer, nevertheless showed me paternal goodness, dissuaded me from there and secured me a posting in the Jönköping Regiment, although the prospects were not too bright, for there were 30 ensigns, thus 22 without pay.

It sounds incredible, but it was not until 1812, three years later, that I would receive a salary, as most of the appointed Finns failed to appear and old officers had resigned because they had grown weary of service. The regiment by then also had a

---

1 The Russians had issued a proclamation inviting serving Finnish soldiers to desert, and offering financial inducements to hand over their weapons, and equipment, including horses. Refusing to 'submit to the knout' – the knout being a form of whip commonly and barbarically used for both corporal and capital punishment in Russia at that time – meant refusing to accept life under Russian rule. However, although on 1 April Tsar Alexander declared Finland part of the Russian empire and demanded that the Finns swear loyalty, the country was to be an autonomous state which would maintain its own religion, laws and privileges and would be governed by native Finns; this new state of affairs was quite readily accepted by many, particularly amongst the higher echelons of society.

new commander, who swept away much chaff and the officer cadre was increased by four captains and four lieutenants. Thus, promotion could be swift. At that time, an ensign's salary amounted to 110 riksdaler.

Nevertheless, I had now obtained a placement, clothed myself in the grey uniform of the provincial army – the militia had swaggered around in blue – and attended upon my new commander, General Baron Bennet, a distinguished but ugly old man with a pigtail and the motto, 'Damn ceremony.'[2]

He gave me instruction in the regulations and articles of war, on which I would report once a week, and he wanted to take care of both my work and my social life, promising that everything should work out fine, and, knowing me to enjoy restaurants as well as less salubrious establishments, he was thus both my commander and my guardian.

He was considered a good commanding officer, with a powerful voice like a trombone, who supported and assisted many impoverished officers and non-commissioned officers; he had nine covers to his account during gatherings at the dinner table, where, in turn, an officer from each company and their orderly (at that time a non-commissioned officer) was invited. To our misfortune, as Vice President of the College of War, the standard bearer for the Royal Order of the Seraphim, and more, he had to remain based in Stockholm.[3] There is a story from the renowned General Bergenstråhle, that when visiting a market in Jönköping dressed in civilian attire, he addressed a soldier and asked about various things, at which the soldier enquired, 'Who would my lord be?' And when he answered, 'I am your colonel, my boy,' the soldier saluted and said, 'God bless the colonel! I have served for 12 years, but never in that time seen any colonel!'[4]

Jacket worn by *Fänrik* Carl Fredrik Lindeberg of the Jönköping Regiment at the Battle of Ratan in 1809, at which he was wounded in the left arm. Hultin would have been similarly attired. (Armémuseum)

---

2   Baron Wilhelm Bennet (1757–1824) began his military service as a volunteer in the Life Guard in 1775 and served as a *kapten* in the Russian War of 1788–1790. He was commanding officer of the Jönköping Regiment from 1797 until his resignation from service as a *generalmajor* in 1810.
3   Fredrik I created three orders of chivalry in 1748: the Royal Order of the Seraphim, the Royal Order of the Sword, and the Royal Order of the Polar Star. A fourth, the Royal Order of Vasa was added by Gustav III in 1772. The Order of the Seraphim was the highest award, and its banner bearer was a key official.
4   Gustaf Bergenstråhle (1771–1829) took part in the Russian War 1788–1790, served as *generaladjutant* to Armfelt during the Norwegian War of 1808 and commanded the 5th

Through the old man's absence, the regiment, and above all the officers, went into decline, being guided by some schemers in whom he had placed his trust. Whilst exercise and discipline were kept sufficiently under control, for with such unusually good and diligent material as this regiment had in its ranks they could hardly fail, the attitude and conduct of the officers was wretched.

As an example of a regimental commander's autocratic authority at that time, I must also tell you something that, when compared with a commanding officer of today, sounds incredible. A Life Drabant was posted as a lieutenant in the regiment. Outsiders in general and Life Drabants in particular were never welcomed. When the officers attended upon the Colonel and the new officer was presented by the Lieutenant Colonel, the old man said, 'Well, my good man, you have come here unheard of by me. What His Royal Majesty cares to do, I cannot undo, but be sure that you will never receive a salary as long as I am in command; only when I am gone might you rectify this matter.'

Jäger of the Jönköping Regiment, illustration from 'Remarks on the organization and present state of the Swedish Army' by Frederic, Baron von Eben, 1808. (Armémuseum)

Brigade during the German and Norwegian campaigns of 1813–1814. He was appointed *överste* of the Jönköping regiment in October 1810 and remained its commander until his promotion to *generalmajor* in 1816.

7

The Västerbotten Expedition (August–September 1809)

Peace negotiations with Russia had commenced in July, by which time Russian forces were occupying the Swedish coast along the Gulf of Bothnia as far south as Umeå in Västerbotten (Westrobothnia). Russia was seeking to consolidate her gains, but although Sweden had accepted that Finland would be lost, ceding large parts of Northern Sweden and the Åland Islands would be too great a loss to bear. The Västerbotten expedition was therefore planned to land an army north of the Russian forces around Umeå, cut them off and force their surrender, liberating the province and strengthening Sweden's hand in the negotiations. Although the expedition was not deemed to be a success, the Russians did retreat and Sweden did largely achieve her aims in the peace treaty which was signed at Fredrikshamn in Finland on 17 September, ending the war with Russia and creating the Grand Duchy of Finland as an autonomous state within the Russian Empire.

I joined the regiment, which was marching to Västerbotten, boarded ship at Gräddö and landed at Ratan. The outcome of this well-conceived but poorly executed expedition is too well known to be described.[1]

It is said that General von Döbeln, when, some time afterwards, he passed by and saw the position at Djäkneboda, proclaimed with his typical delight, 'If I'd had but 500 old women, no Russian would have escaped here.'[2]

The strategic judgment of an inexperienced ensign cannot be great, but it was clear to me that planning and co-ordination were lacking. The battalion commanders who wanted to fight, fought, whilst others looked on. The commander of the regiment's 2nd Battalion, then Major Kuylenstjerna, was among those who, several

---

1 The Swedish force of some 6,800 men under *General* Wachtmeister landed at Ratan on 18 August; marched south towards Umeå and fought and lost a battle with the Russian army of about 6,000 men under General Kamensky at Sävar the following day. The Swedes then retreated back to Ratan where they repulsed the pursuing Russian attack on 20 August, after which Kamensky retreated northwards to Piteå and the Swedes liberated Umeå. During this short campaign the Swedes suffered about 1,000 casualties; the Russians lost around 1,800.
2 Djäkneboda is five kilometres inland from Ratan.

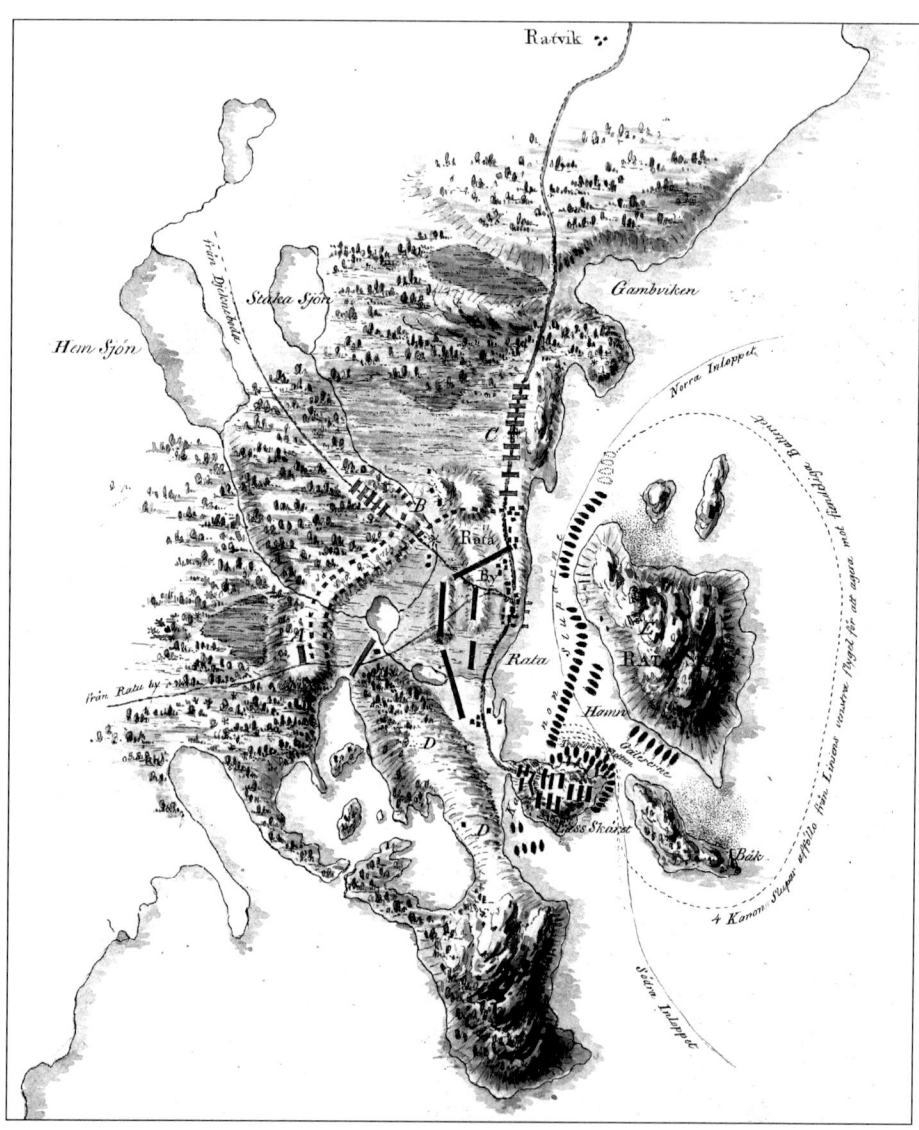

Plan of the Battle of Ratan, 20 August 1809. Watercolour by C.G. Gillberg (1774–1855). (Library of Congress)

times, showed what Swedish troops can accomplish when properly led.³ When he was finally called upon to surrender, being trapped, he gave a typically Swedish answer, 'Be off you scoundrels or you'll feel our bite.' He lost a third of the battalion but broke through.⁴

I want to relate some events which characterise the Swede's abhorrence for captivity and for his enemies.

A reservist was captured during the hand-to-hand fighting between the skirmish lines and taken away, guarded by two Russians. After a couple of hours march, he made signs that he needed to stop for a call of nature, whereupon one Russian went on ahead and the other remained guarding the prisoner. He then discreetly drew his knife, which a Smålander is never without, stabbed the guard in the throat, grabbed his musket and aimed it at the other Russian, who took flight, after which he set off through the woods, chanced upon the Södermanland Regiment and was back with us the next day, with a Russian musket on his shoulder. This man, a blacksmith by trade, later served in the ranks of our lieutenant colonel's company where I was his lieutenant for several years, but I never dared to punish him for fear he might have killed me, as he had a fierce temper.

A soldier who, during the retreat from Sävar, stopped to drink and was surprised by the Russians, ended up with only the barrel of his broken musket in his hands but still refusing to surrender. This calm, handsome fellow would later be a corporal in my company, and I often talked to him about the incident, laughing at his tale of trying to escape when he was surrounded by, he claimed, over 50 enemy soldiers. Of course, they had wanted to take this fine young man alive, to offer him quarter, but he misunderstood their shouts of 'Pardon, comrade' and naturally kicked up the dust in their midst. He also believed that a prisoner would be immediately put in fetters and manacles. But he was nevertheless taken captive and was so well treated that, had he known, that he would probably not have put up such a fight.

A soldier in the Östbo company,⁵ rapidly loading his musket as the Russian skirmish line retreated, had barely got the ball down and taken aim at the nearest Russian, when the latter held his hand aloft showing that it was shot through and bloody. He ceased his aim, saying 'You'll do no more harm today, I'll try for another.' His company commander, who happened to be nearby, ensured that another man did fall to his shot.

Ensign Bengt Ennes,⁶ who was commanding the battalion's skirmish line, noticed that several musket balls had been fired at him, one of which went through his coat

---

3 *Major* Carl Kuylenstierna (1762–1829) exchanged into the Jönköping Regiment in 1783 and took part in the wars in Finland 1788–1790, in Pomerania 1805–1807 and the Västerbotten expedition in 1809 and retired as *överstelöjtnant* in 1810.
4 The Jönköping Regiment fielded three battalions in this battle; the 1st Battalion (Hultin's) appears to have done little or no fighting, the 3rd saw some action opposing a Russian attack. The greatest losses were suffered by the 2nd Battalion when it was ordered to counterattack.
5 A company of the Jönköping regiment named after its recruiting area, Östbo district in central Småland.
6 Most likely Bengt Georg Ennes (1781–1849); his elder brother Barthold Anders Ennes (1764–1841) was a *kapten* in the regiment at this time; their father Bengt Johan Ennes (1728–1811) had also been a *major* in the regiment.

The Battle of Ratan, 20 August 1809. Watercolour by C.G. Gillberg (1774–1855). (Library of Congress)

tails, but as he had much to observe, he did not see where they were coming from, so he told the nearest soldier, 'There is some devil who is constantly shooting at me, can you see where he is?' The soldier, whose name was Skön, from the lieutenant colonel's company, replied, 'He is behind the hay barn there, see now he has just appeared.' 'Then drive that scoundrel off and be quick before he can reload.' Skön ran up to the wall of the barn, then crept up to the gable end, but carelessly held his musket in front of him, so that the Russian must have seen the barrel sticking out, for he took to his heels and fled across a courtyard, but Skön shot him and although the Russian fell head over heels, he was only wounded, for another came up and carried him off on his back. Skön re-loaded and took aim. Ennes shouted that he should let them go, but at that moment the shot was fired, and both men fell.

A reservist in a cannon sloop was hit by a musket ball in the back and was thrown into a boat with other dead.[7] However, he was still conscious, heard and understood everything that was said, but lacked the ability to raise a finger or show the smallest sign of life. Some Russian prisoners were being used to dump, or, to use nautical language, stow, bodies in the boat and one of them took the man's wallet containing 36 shillings. That the Smålander was still aware of events can be inferred by the fact that it pained him much that he could not punch the Russian in the face. After the fighting, the dead were brought ashore to be buried. The man could hear this and was resigned to his fate, but still tried in vain to give a sign of life. Eventually, Major Kuylenstjerna came to the Dal Regiment and asked for him – they were born in the same place and had played together as boys. He observed a movement of his eyelid; the doctors examined him and found he was indeed still alive. He was taken to the

---

7   A cannon sloop was a small shallow draft rowed vessel designed for use in the archipelago, typically at this time mounting two 24-pounder cannon and having 10 pairs of oars requiring two men per oar, sometimes also fitted with two fold-down masts. Reservists or militia would most likely have served as oarsmen.

Model of a cannon sloop made by Fredrik Henrik af Chapman to his 1776 design. (Sjöhistoriska museet)

hospital in Umeå and was unconscious for a month. The ball was cut out from the right side of his chest, and he recovered. He subsequently served for 20 years as a corporal in my company, wore a medal for bravery with the ball next to the medal ribbon. He was frequently examined by doctors who would opine that, according to all the rules of their profession, they would never have ventured to risk such an operation.

The expedition might well have ended differently if Döbeln or Adlercreutz had commanded, but the former was considered Gustavian and the latter would not leave Adlersparre alone to manage Old Duke Charles. The result was that we were beaten, the Russians broke free, and the Kronoberg and Jönköping regiments footed the bill. The latter regiment, which including their reservists went into the campaign 1,400 strong, could afterwards hardly field 800 men under arms. Three officers were killed in the fighting, and many were wounded.[8]

After this well-conducted affair (!) we clambered aboard open cannon sloops, and, through storm and tempest, arrived weather-beaten and decimated back in Stockholm, to meet there our commanding officer, safe and sound, who in bicorne hat and pigtail led us to the Palace to 'pay our respects', where the Old Gentleman with a shining sword in a trembling hand created a few knights among us, after which we departed to march home.[9]

---

8   Mankell notes that the 1st Battalion did not come under fire and although the other two battalions did indeed take the lion's share of the Swedish losses, the total loss to the regiment was 168 men dead and wounded. See Julius Mankell, *Anteckningar rörande svenska regementernas historia* (Örebro: N.M. Lindh, 2nd edition, 1866).
9   The 'Old Gentleman' (*gamle herrn*), meaning the new king, Charles XIII, formerly Duke Charles.

8

Interlude (October 1809–December 1810)

Soon after the end of the war with Russia, a treaty was signed in Jönköping in December 1809 ending the war with Denmark-Norway. The Treaty of Paris in January 1810 ended war with France. The year 1810 was thus relatively peaceful for Sweden, although momentous in other ways. The aging and childless Charles XIII was incapacitated by a heart attack in November 1809, and his nominated successor, Christian August of Denmark, died a few months after arriving in Sweden, in May 1810. Of several alternative candidates who might be acceptable to Napoleon, Maréchal Jean-Baptiste Bernadotte was elected, becoming Crown Prince Karl Johan in November 1810, and effectively taking over from control of government from that time. Bernadotte would become Charles XIV of Sweden on the old king's death in February 1818.

During the year 1810 a battalion of the regiment was transferred to Gotland, but I was permitted to stay at home. We then received a new commander, the eminent General Bergenstråhle. He was perhaps the most capable regimental commander in the army, with two qualities that befit a leader: He was nobody's favourite and never insulted anyone. He was furthermore an exceptional man, calm, serious and quiet. From lieutenant colonel to ensign, all were treated equally, and when something was done wrong, firm correction was delivered without regard to rank, but the incident was then forgotten. He rarely conversed with anyone other than on duty, and his attitude earned him the sobriquet 'His Excellency' both within and outside the regiment.

Our lieutenant colonel, the jovial von Hartmansdorff, once had the opportunity to tell him that such an isolated relationship would not endear him to his officers, but he replied, 'I don't want to be cherished, I want to be feared.'[1]

In the beginning he was indeed truly feared, but soon came to be valued, for he was a confident advocate, who, even in the upper echelons, dared to speak his mind, and his iron will was needed to reorganise a neglected regiment. When the regiment was presented for some big-wig and something went awry, he did not, like other hotheads, swear and scream, but said quite calmly, 'We can do this and shall do it again, as long as battalion and platoon commanders are calm, then I am sure it is possible.'

---

1 *Överstelöjtnant* Christoffer Svante von Hartmansdorff (1771–1818) would go on to become *överste* of the Jönköping Regiment in 1816 on Bergenstråhle's promotion to *generalmajor*.

Crown Prince Karl Johan, formerly *Maréchal* Jean Baptiste Bernadotte (1763–1844), at the entry into Leipzig in 1813 at the head of his staff. Oil on canvas by Fredric Westin (1782-1862). (Skoklosters slott)

When Crown Prince Karl Johan later visited us on campaign, it was difficult to judge whether he or our regimental commander was of greater importance. Of course, he had been appointed to the regiment alongside many foreign officers who were excellent men and necessary to revitalise us, but he made the officer cadre so serviceable that I can confirm that there was barely a single weak link among us on campaign.

9

The Phoney War with England (January 1811–December 1812)

Although the Treaty of Paris required Sweden to join Napoleon's Continental System (the trade embargo against Great Britain), it was not enthusiastically embraced, and significant illicit trade continued. France finally threatened war on Sweden if they did not comply, and so Sweden formally declared war on Britain in November 1810. However, little changed during 1811, and in consequence in January 1812 Napoleon sent Maréchal Davout to occupy Swedish Pomerania, which had only been returned to Sweden two years earlier. This in turn led Crown Prince Karl Johan to declare Swedish neutrality. Soon after Napoleon's invasion of Russia had begun in July 1812, Sweden allied herself with Britain and Russia with the Treaty of Örebro, but would not be engaged in direct action against France until 1813.

In early 1811, I was sent with a detachment to Karlshamn.[1] We were at that time engaged in the peculiar war with England during which not a shot was fired. Napoleon had forced us to join the Continental System and declare war upon England, and we expected an English fleet to bombard our fortresses and blockade our ports. Upon arriving in Karlshamn, I was billeted with 50 men in the citadel, destined to remain in this hovel for 18 months, and to top it all, the commander, Captain Burman, an old man, died just days after my arrival.[2] One can imagine the distress of this young, inexperienced boy, being left alone with a garrison of 50 soldiers, 12 artillerists (fine lads), a naval petty officer and six ratings, fearing a bombardment, for an English squadron was said to be already in the Sound.[3]

---

1 Karlshamn was a strategic port on the southern Baltic coast which had been ceded to Sweden from Denmark following the Treaty of Roskilde in 1658. The citadel (*kastell*) was constructed on an island in the harbour, dating from 1675, and remained part of the country's formal defences until 1865.
2 *Kapten* Johan Burman (1731–1810) had served as commander at Karlshamn citadel since 1782. Records indicate he died on 27 December 1810 (at the age of 79) and was buried on 5 January, so if Hultin was indeed present when he died, he must have arrived in late December 1810 rather than early 1811. However, that would be inconsistent with Hultin's statement that they remained here for 18 months and his later statement that they were stood down in November 1812.
3 The Öresund channel separating Sweden from Denmark.

View over Karlshamn main square towards the citadel (*kastell*) in the harbour, 1904. The new town hall in the foreground was built in 1900 but otherwise the view would have been little different in 1811. (Image from *Hemmets bildmaterial* magazine, Tekniska Museet, Stockholm)

Fortunately, the new commander, Lieutenant Benzelstjerna, soon arrived, also rather old, a man of honour, but who had done little service as an officer since the battle of Svensksund, where he distinguished himself and received the beautiful Svensksund medal. He had been in the merchant navy for 25 years and well understood naval matters and activities in the harbour, but his understanding of the army was even less than mine.[4] Of course, he had no other choice but to accept me as adjutant and garrison lieutenant. We put our heads together and got on so well the whole time that I always thereafter missed him like a father, although he might have been old enough to be my grandfather.

When English warships were observed off the coast, the citadel garrison was reinforced, especially with artillery, so that both commander and lieutenant had something to respond with. A battalion of the Kronoberg Regiment and 300 men of the Jönköping Regiment were posted in the town, whilst in the entrance to the harbour

---

4   Jesper Albrecht Benzelstierna (1763–1833) had first gone to sea as a teenager at the end of the 1770s, becoming skipper of his own boat, then joined the navy as a *fänrik* (ensign) serving in the Russian War 1788–1790 during which he earned medals at Hoglund (1788) and Svenskund (1790), and reached the rank of *löjtnant* before resigning the service in the mid-1790s. He then continued his career in the merchant navy but in December 1808 returned to service where he was transferred to the army and promoted to *kapten*. He took up the post as commandant at Karlshamn in the spring of 1811, moving there with his family from Stockholm. The Battle of Svensksund in July 1790 was the largest naval battle ever to take place in the Baltic and a famous Swedish victory which effectively ended the war against Russia.

Karlshamn citadel, little changed since Hultin's time. (Creative Commons CC BY-SA 4.0)

were placed four blockade brigs, well-armed, and in the harbour itself six cannon sloops, so at least we had some resistance to offer.

Our way of life on this forsaken rock was to be surrounded by friends and comrades and never finding oneself alone. We established our own housekeeping with a weekly rota, received abuse over food, arguing with the gluttons to press them for higher contributions, played cards, board games and most notably the fiddle, so that it became a saying at Karlshamn citadel that hell was to be a cat or a fiddle, because if a cat appeared it would be chased by dogs, and if a fiddle appeared it would be scraped by every man. From time to time, the town's dance and billiard halls were visited, where quarrels and brawls would frequently occur.

One must not imagine the officers of the time to be as educated and courteous as they are today. The constant orders and the experience of war made them bullies, their ignorance and dishonesty instilled in them a dislike for both learning and compassion. In small towns, they typically went to dances with the intention of outraging the ladies and driving away the civilians. This was considered as bravura and could make one renowned.

However, Crusenstolpe, who in such a partisan manner tried to rob Karl Johan of all merit, must admit that he would ensure that our officers were educated men, and this practice has continued, so that the position now, both in culture and knowledge, bears comparison with any other army.[5]

---

5   Magnus Jakob Crusenstolpe (1795–1865) was a Swedish historian who held much influence with Karl Johan (as Charles XIV) early in his career but later fell out to become one of his bitterest opponents.

A small town dance attended by soldiers and civilians. Watercolour by Carl Johan Ljunggren (1790–1852) dated 1818.[6] (Nationalmuseum)

One day, two ships of the line and three frigates bearing English flags anchored at Hanö island, 10 kilometres from the castle.[7] Alarms were sounded, the cannon were loaded, the cannon-ball furnaces lit, and we prepared for what we assumed was about to come.[8] But the squadron remained there for a day, then several days, and ultimately until the autumn. They disregarded us and we became so used to the British that we could consider them to be comrades.

Merchant ships would depart from the harbour to anchor in the midst of the enemy, others arrived from other ports, and when sufficient numbers were gathered, a man-of-war went with them to escort them through the Sound, thereafter to be met by French privateers, who plundered friend and foe alike.

---

6   Carl Johan Ljunggren (1790–1852) had studied at the Royal Academy of Art in Stockholm before joining the army in 1805. He participated in the 1808 campaigns in Norway and in Finland and the 1813 campaign, including the Battle of Leipzig where he was wounded; but he recovered enough to fight in the Norwegian campaign in 1814. He retired from service with the rank of *major* in 1827. He wrote memoirs of his campaigns, published posthumously, and produced many drawings of contemporary military and civilian life.
7   The British fleet of 11 battleships under Vice Admiral James Saumarez had arrived off Gothenburg on 2 May 1811 where it would remain all that summer; part of the fleet had then been dispatched to Hanö, which served as the fleet's base of operations in the Baltic during the 'phoney' war with Sweden 1810–1812. The fleet only saw some minor actions against the Danes in 1811, but disastrously lost three ships on the return voyage to England in December 1811 from which just 30 men were saved.
8   Cannon-ball furnaces were for the production of heated shot intended to set fire to enemy ships.

Such a benign enemy could not instil fear, and we often encountered their civilian-dressed officers armed only with bottles of port wine and rum, since they had little taste for punch.

Enticed by some acquaintances engaged in smuggling, I also once visited Hanö, in civilian attire, and found with astonishment that this islet, usually inhabited by sheep, hares, ospreys and other seabirds, was now full of makeshift houses and wooden huts, packed with colonial goods, and a crowd such as one would find at a market. German seemed to be the *lingua franca*. That smuggling on a large scale was practiced by both Germans and Swedes is certain, for customs officials were insufficient in number and would in any case look the other way. The army had nothing to do with customs enforcement – the garrison officers only had responsibility for ships' passengers and to check that they, especially foreigners, were duly provided with passes.

In the harbour under the citadel's guard there were 21 condemned ships loaded with expensive colonial goods. According to the Continental System's rules, these were to be burnt, but the cargo was considered too valuable, and it was therefore decided to auction the goods. Coffee, sugar, and cotton were sold off in batches weighing 1,000 pounds for a few shillings; logwood[9] and mahogany at almost at the same price as firewood. Many trading houses rapidly became wealthy, their accountants and counterjumpers[10] had money to burn and flaunted it. It was said that the profits, which amounted to millions, were shared amicably between the English and Swedish Crowns, whilst the unfortunate owners of the goods, mostly Germans from the Hanseatic cities, bore the loss. Although soldiers were stationed on every deck of these ships, substantial quantities of goods were also stolen, for their captains and crews did not consider the Crown's claims to the seizures to be legal and wanted their share, which gave rise to theft, dispute, and courts-martial.

As an intermediary I was twice tasked with delivering letters on board the proud HMS Victory on which Nelson fell. This three-decker carried 120 guns and four howitzers.[11] Meeting two drinking companions there, they asked why I came with a white flag when we were such good friends? Admiral Saumarez, to whom I handed the letters, looked like a county official.

Now that we had become so familiar with our enemies, military service passed more quickly, and we enjoyed ourselves, for we were many. We numbered five officers from the regiment, four from the artillery on the blockade brigs and cannon sloops and six from the navy, all young and carefree. In the town, which we often visited, regimental comrades and Kronoberg men, who sometimes joined us, would meet and then our joy would raise the roof. The old commander looked on and laughed. He drank like a brother with us all but was known as 'Uncle.'

---

9   Logwood, *haematoxylum campechianum*, was a valuable natural source of dye.
10 A counterjumper (*bodknodd*) is an archaic slang term for a salesman or shop assistant.
11 In fact, *Victory* originally mounted 100 guns; four were added in 1799. As a result of her age and the damage suffered at Trafalgar, in 1807 she had been downgraded to second-rate, her 28 middle deck 24-pounders being replaced with 18-pounders and two 32-pounders removed. HMS *Victory* was at this time the flagship of Vice Admiral Saumarez, who had been given command of the Baltic fleet in 1808.

Vice Admiral James Saumarez (1757–1836). (Frontispiece from Sir John Ross, *Memoirs and correspondence of Admiral Lord Saumarez* (London: Richard Bentley 1838, vol.2)

Vice Admiral James Saumarez's flagship, HMS *Victory*, in Portsmouth Harbour, circa 1900 but much as she would have looked in 1812. (Library of Congress)

A couple of our comrades had brought dogs, and, when hares were plentiful on the islands in the archipelago, hunting parties were often arranged, hazardous ventures during which fellows sometimes nearly drowned. The harbour, particularly in the autumn, was full of seabirds. On one occasion I decided to take a pot-shot at them with an 18-pounder loaded with triple canister, aimed high and got – nothing.

In the autumn, the English fleet went home,[12] and the garrison both at the castle and in the town was reduced, but I with my 50 men was entrusted to remain on The Rock,[13] to play three-man bridge with the commander and the artillery commander (another old man) during the long winter evenings. Ship movements had ceased, and in the harbour we had no other duty than the guarding of condemned vessels which had not been able to unload their cargo.

However, it happened in late autumn after the English had left the Baltic that the guard at the flagstaff reported one morning that a strange vessel was lying at the harbour entrance. I had never seen its like, nor the flag it carried. The commander came out and declared with just a glance, 'It's a lugger and her flag is French'. A boat was sent across and returned with the information that she was a French privateer with a 60-man crew and was accompanied by her captain who was dressed in French naval officer's uniform. He presented a Letter of Marque,[14] signed by the Emperor Napoleon and valid for one year. The Letter had expired, but there was an endorsement by the French envoy in Hamburg stating that it was valid for another six months. With Letters of Marque, one has to be very careful. The commander was unsure as to whether this endorsement was valid and wished to send the letter to Admiral Puke, who was commander-in-chief in Karlskrona,[15] but the Frenchman firmly declared that he would not willingly hand over the document on which his security depended, and that, if it was necessary for it to be examined in Karlskrona, he himself wanted to present it, which is why it was decided that I should accompany him there.

We received a courier pass and departed. I had the honour of becoming more acquainted with this captain in the French fleet, Herr Michelon de la Luserie, and found that he had experienced much. He had received several wounds, and was both a great joker and a companionable reveller. He was well received by the High Admiral and invited to dinner, and I received orders that he should be treated kindly and that all the amenities that the port afforded should be arranged for him.

---

12 On 9 November 1811 a convoy of 120 merchantmen left Hanö escorted by the British warships. See R. C. Anderson, *Naval Wars in the Baltic, 1522–1850* (London: Francis Edwards Ltd, 1969).

13 Hultin uses the term *syndaklippan*, (lit. sin-rock) which was a vernacular name for a rock-like fortress erected on an island and in particular referring to the 1833–1863 rebuilt Vaxholm fortress situated on an island in the Stockholm archipelago, which also served as a prison. Translation as 'The Rock' i.e., Alcatraz seems apposite.

14 A Letter of Marque was the privateer's licence from his government to attack and seize vessels of nations with which his own country was at war.

15 *Amiral* Johan af Puke (1751–1816) had served in the Russian War 1788–1790 and was commander-in-chief at Karlskrona from 1803. He was appointed *överamiral* in 1809 and commanded the Västerbotten expedition in that year.

On the way home we had the foulest of weather, with rain and snow. At the inn, when he found there was nothing offered that he would care to eat, he shouted and swore profusely, until I procured a batch of eggs for him.[16] Then he cheered up and drew from his travelling-case something which I have not seen before or since, a flask made of India rubber in the form of a ball with a small neck, which he opened, demanded clean glasses and offered me a drink of what he called '*vin da cap*' which could play havoc with a fellow's insides; it tasted like a liqueur and had a sharp bite to it.[17]

Upon our return, we found his lugger moored below the citadel; its supply of gun powder, which was not large, had been deposited in the powder store and the

Amiral Johan af Puke (1751–1816), circa 1797. (Swedish Portraits Archive, portrattarkiv.se)

crew had been forbidden to go ashore. But now they were provided with all kinds of freedom, they carried out repairs, took on water, and the captain visited the city's taverns and *schweizerier*,[18] but for his safety I usually had to accompany him for the town was full of German ship-owners, who would shout 'crucify him!' It was feared that he and the great nation to which he belonged would be offended.

After about a week, orders arrived directly from the adjutant general's office, that an officer should board the French privateer *le Balayeur*, request the crew list,[19] summon the crew, establish whether any served in the French army and to which regiments, and most notably, 'should any of them have been born in Sweden, Pomerania or Rügen, he is to be arrested and taken under guard to Karlskrona.'

---

16 The road between Karlskrona and Karlshamn is about 55 kilometres, so by coach the journey would likely have required only one overnight stop.
17 *Vin da cap*, perhaps from the northern tip of Corsica, and possibly a forerunner of that island's most famous liqueur, Cap Corse Mattei, created in 1872, a bittersweet mix of local Muscat and Cinchona which was in common use as a malaria/fever remedy on board ships by the early nineteenth century.
18 *Schweizerier*, after the Swedish word for Swiss, were cafes selling pies, pastries etc and alcoholic beverages.
19 *Folkpass*: A document required since the mid-eighteenth century being a detailed list of the ship's crew and any passengers, expected to include name, age, place of residence and place of birth, marital status, and employment terms.

I was entrusted to perform this mustering of gallows physiognomies.[20] Most were from the Netherlands, Germany, and Denmark. Only two men had served in the army. Just one young man, named Peter Lock, was born in Stockholm, so he was taken, despite the captain's protests. On the way ashore he thanked us for his liberation, stating that he had intended to escape, but had not managed to find an opportunity. On arrival at the citadel, he was taken to the guard house.

Hardly had I been able to report to the commander, when the guard corporal reported that the new prisoner wanted to speak to me. When I got there, he asked if he was going to be arrested. I informed him that he would be despatched to Karlskrona the following day. Then he began to cry and asked to speak to me in confidence. He told me that he his real name was Losch and he was a sub-lieutenant in the Archipelago Fleet,[21] in which his father was a major. He had been a merchant seaman, suffered shipwreck in the Netherlands, and had taken service on the privateer, which was destined for the Baltic, and reiterated that he thereby hoped that he could escape and come home, but had found no chance to do so.

When the commander learned of the circumstances, he was troubled and said, 'This seems more than likely, because I have seen Herr Losch a couple of times at Skeppsholmen, just not been introduced.' He went down to the guard, recognised the man, and whispered to me, 'He is nevertheless a former comrade; we cannot send him under guard as a prisoner to Karlskrona, so we shall report the situation and employ him in the commanding officer's headquarters.' Accommodation was prepared in the citadel, but we had to provide him with clothing etc. to avoid him becoming a formal addition to the garrison.

The position was reported to Stockholm and Karlskrona and Herr Losch remained at the citadel, whilst the privateer was repaired, provisioned and, after courtesies were exchanged, saluted as she set sail. A few days later, orders arrived by courier from Stockholm stating that 'because the French privateer has held and tried to induce a Swedish officer into his service, he should be detained until further notice.' This order came too late, because by then the privateer was in Denmark. Shortly thereafter, two of our naval brigs – *Svalan* and little *Vänta* – arrived with the news that the French had occupied Pomerania and made the garrison in Stralsund prisoners of war, so that we could now add a theme to the preludes of war that were being played.

At Christmas time, an unusually small sloop had arrived, under Rostock's flag,[22] which had on board three Prussian cavalry officers, unusually decent men who, as far as I could gather, were of Prussian noble lineage, and provided with the requisite passports. They took quarters in the town and remained there for a long time, so we wondered what their intention was.

---

20 A Shakespearean allusion from The Tempest, Act 1 Scene 1, '... his complexion is perfect gallows' meaning someone destined to be hanged.
21 The *arméns flotta* (Army Fleet) or *skärgårdsflottan* (Archipelago Fleet) was established in 1756 for coastal protection to operate close inshore where conventional naval vessels could not venture. It employed shallow draft vessels such as galleys and was largely independent of both army and navy.
22 The Hanseatic port of Rostock in the Duchy of Mecklenburg was at the time under French control.

Soldiers soon get acquainted, and I developed a close relationship with them. Finally, they entrusted me with the information that they were squadron commanders from the Prussian Horse Guards who had deserted their regiment because it was preparing to assist Napoleon in his war against Russia, and they did not wish to fight for their fatherland's oppressors, but instead intended to travel from Gothenburg to Spain to fight against him. I reminded them that they only had passports to Karlshamn, and that strangers were still carefully observed in Sweden, so that without further passports, which the local authorities were not allowed to issue to foreigners without permission from a higher authority, it would be difficult to get to Gothenburg. The lieutenant – von Massow – said that he was personally known to His Excellency von Engeström, who spent much time in Berlin at his father's house, and I advised him to apply directly to him, which had the consequence that both passports and a courteous letter promptly arrived.[23] I mention this, because, strangely enough, during the German campaign I met the captain – von Barner – who had command of a dragoon regiment. Von Massow was by then major in the Second Brandenburg Hussar Regiment, but I did not meet him. The cornet – von Müller – had fallen in Spain.

Winter passed monotonously. Sure enough, I sometimes froze in the Crown's neglected accommodation, but this I have experienced both before and since. Finally, spring came – spring in Blekinge! To anyone who has not seen it, I advise going there, in the hope that our lumberjacks have not caused such devastation there as elsewhere.

When on a calm, beautiful morning, one witnesses the sun's orb rising from the Baltic Sea and gilding countless islets, skerries, hills and valleys covered with all varieties of Scandinavia's deciduous and coniferous trees and overflowing with both common and rare flowers – when one breathes the fine scent of honeysuckle and hawthorn, when one hears cuckoos and thrushes begin the dawn chorus, the occasional nightingale's song like a piccolo, pigeons cooing the bass, the grouse on the hilltop sounding like a snare-drum, seabirds in the reeds like castanets setting the beat, the crow like an arts critic enjoying the concert and shouting bravo, whilst archipelago quarrymen blasting rock salute the seal and eider – one who sees Blekinge thus in the spring and does not feel his heart swell and soul elevate is a philistine with taste for nothing but tobacco and small beer. The materialist, amongst whom I unfortunately must count myself, can also appreciate beauty when he sees the amount of cod, flounder and Baltic herring the local fishermen land. It is strange that the praises of this little province have been so little sung. It probably deserves it as much as 'Värmland, you beautiful, you glorious land.'[24]

The menfolk are lively and not to be toyed with, because they readily reach for their knives. The women are renowned for their beauty, such that the Royal Theatre might get increased funding by recruiting their ballet troupe from amongst them.

---

23 Count Lars von Engeström (1751–1826) was a Swedish diplomat and politician. Through marriage he had inherited an estate in Prussian Poland in 1790 and from 1798 to 1803 had served as envoy to the Prussian court. He was Sweden's Minister for Foreign Affairs 1809–1824.
24 The title of a popular song from a three-act musical play by Anders Fryxell, 1822.

An English squadron arrived and anchored as usual at Hanö, although our cannon were not loaded. Rumours began that the English would become our allies, although the state of war continued.

The harbour became a hive of activity, ships were hired and prepared as troop transports. One could see that another guiding hand beat the pace of the government, because preparations went well with both organization and implementation. It was expected that during the summer an army corps would be transferred to Pomerania, but whether to aid or to defeat Napoleon, we did not know. Certainly, our relationship with him was considered a little tense, but that our French marshal would wage war upon his Emperor and help our hereditary enemy seemed unlikely and was scorned as political rumour.

In the harbour, the transport vessels were eventually ready, but it was becoming quite late in the year. So, we would wait until the following spring, when we hoped to mimic the Dalecarlians who in 1804 crossed to Stralsund.[25] They had had unusually difficult weather on the crossing and had fared badly, but as soon as they got ashore and had been well fed, they asked, 'so, where is Bonaparte now? Surely there is no further sea passage needed to reach him?'

In November 1812, orders came to stand down and return to our homes. I would leave The Rock to which I had been tethered for close to one and three-quarter years, I would leave the honourable old man who was more my comrade than my commander and I would leave many friends. That I could not do this without regret is certain, but I was happy enough that my men would be free to see their families and Småland's pine forests and heathery hills. We marched away and arrived just in time for *Julgröt!*[26]

The soldiers felt good, and many brought home cash, for those who wanted to earn money when off-duty always had rewarding opportunities to do so, but many were as broke as I, who lived in an expensive place the whole time and had just 36 shillings a day to get by.

---

25 As part of his plan for a joint strike against Napoleon with British and Russian allies, Gustav IV Adolf had despatched reinforcements to bolster the garrison of Stralsund in Swedish Pomerania between summer 1803 and autumn 1804. *Dalecarlian* refers to people from the county of Dalarna.

26 *Julgröt* – Christmas porridge – is a traditional Scandinavian Christmas dish of rice, cinnamon, and milk.

10

Preparation for War with France (January–July 1813)

Although Sweden had harboured hope that Karl Johan would help them recover Finland, the Crown Prince had rapidly realised that this would not be possible and had instead, by the Treaty of St Petersburg, 5 April 1812, obtained the support of Tsar Alexander I for the annexation of Norway, seen as a much more practicable and potentially beneficial prospect. However, he also considered it essential to have Britain's support, and made Sweden's commitment of forces for the Allies forthcoming campaign to defeat Napoleon conditional upon that support, which he obtained by the Treaty of Stockholm, 3 March 1813. A Swedish force of some 30,000 men was mobilised for the campaign during April and May and transported across to Rügen in Swedish Pomerania, which the French had evacuated following the loss of the Grand Armée on the retreat from Moscow.

During the winter of 1812/1813, I had intended to walk out amongst the Småland hares, but the regimental commanding officer said, 'Those who take the salary, do the service' and instead required me to walk out with the troops! The officers held instructional meetings, church parades, exams and inspections, whilst the non-commissioned officers and corporals exercised recruits in their recruiting areas (*rote*), until the beginning of April, when marching orders arrived, and the regiment gathered at Vrigstad.[1]

I had not seen the regiment since 1809, when it was starved, broken, and decimated. Now it was complete, newly dressed, exercised and had officers with both skill and drive.

We marched to Karlskrona, embarked on the ship of the line *Gustaf the Great*, and two days later anchored at Cape Perd.[2]

---

1 Hultin states May, but the regimental records and other parts of Hultin's account confirm this must have been the beginning of April. The regimental record indicates departure from Vrigstad on 16 April. (See the Jönköping regimental diary reproduced in Peter Wieselgren *Bihang till Ny Smålands Beskrifning* (Jönköping: Sandwall, 1847).
2 From Vrigstad in Jönköping county to Karlskrona on the south coast is about 165 kilometres, a march likely to take about 10 days. Cape Perd (Nordperd) is the southeast tip of the island of Rügen, a voyage of about 250 kilometres from Karlskrona. The ship was originally a 74-gun ship of the line launched in 1799 named *Gustaf IV Adolf* which served as a flagship in the

Model of the 74-gun Gustaf IV Adolf, later renamed Gustaf the Great, constructed in 1790. (Photo: Anneli Karlsson, Sjöhistoriska museet)

Despite the fine weather, sea sickness was endemic and gave rise to both miserable and laughable crises. We had, amongst our patients, an elderly captain, Ridderstråhle, the most sober man I ever knew, who found it impossible to endure the sea and therefore usually stood at the rails in an unfortunate state. The sailors, who regarded this as a slight against themselves and the beautiful weather, quietly asked us, 'Does that gentleman suffer from the same affliction on land?'

Soldiers always feel bad aboard ship, despite every care of their officers. They are packed below decks, lacking fresh air, fresh water, and comfortable berths. But sailors also have to face the unpleasantness of having to clean up after them.

1808 naval campaign but became a block ship in Karlskrona 1810–1811, after which she was renamed *Gustaf den Store* (Gustaf the Great); she would again become a flagship with Charles XIII on board during the attack on Fredrikstad in 1814.

Swedish Pomerania and the island of Rügen, from a map published in London, 1813. (Public Domain)

We disembarked on Rügen and were provided with quarters, some in Bergen (a small town) and others in villages.[3] We were now in Germany but did not understand the vernacular German which was like Hebrew to us. Although I had read some German and in Karlshamn spoke a little, I could not make myself understood. Thus, unless we could find a gentleman or a scholar, we had to communicate with sign language! The soldiers who spoke the dialect of Småland fared best.

We were now divided into field battalions, and I had the good fortune to be assigned to the 3rd Battalion, which had a lively commander. Many knew and remember the late General Boij, who maintained his vivacity and vigour to the end.[4]

---

3 Bergen was (and remains) the largest settlement on Rügen, its principal town.
4 Johan Fredrik Boij (1786–1861) was then a *major* in the Jönköping Regiment and chief adjutant to Charles XIII. He had a very long and distinguished military career, commencing as a 15-year-old *löjtnant* in 1801 and ending as a *generallöjtnant* in 1858 aged 74. He served

Johan Fredrik Boij (1786–1861) in the hussar uniform of the Lifeguard of Horse. Detail from a painting by Carl Frederik Kiörboe (1799–1876). (Nationalmuseum)

He was at this time a major and wanted everyone to be like him. He was also given the youngest officers and men, whom he drove apace, and few battalions could have been more mobile and better exercised than his. He practiced manoeuvring in line together with all of our cavalry. The Crown Prince looked on, laughed, and would often say the only Swedish words he knew, 'Very good, thank you my children.'

Off duty, he was like a brother, and loved to join us at our bivouacs with a potato stew around the campfire. He devised the most absurd games, and if he was told that someone was strong, he would insist on wrestling with him. Then he would not tolerate any consideration for his rank, which is why it could sometimes happen that a soldier threw our major to the ground, causing his ribs to rattle. For this, the soldier would be rewarded with schnapps, praise, and some beer-money. And when the bullets were flying, he wanted to be there – perhaps more than he needed to. As a lieutenant in the Göta artillery in 1805 he had also merited and received the Order of the Sword.[5]

One might surmise that a commander who so fatigued his men would not be cherished, but I have never seen officers and soldiers lament as much as when he resigned from the battalion to take up the post of chief of staff to General Posse.[6]

---

with distinction throughout Sweden's campaigns during the Napoleonic Wars and was ennobled under the name 'Boy' in 1818.
5   The Order of the Sword (*svärdsorden*) was awarded for bravery in the field.
6   *Generalmajor* Carl Henrik Posse of Säby (1767–1843) had been given command of the 1st Division in the Swedish Corps of Crown Prince Karl Johan's Army of the North for the forthcoming campaign and would be engaged in the major battles of Großbeeren, Dennewitz and Leipzig.

Putbus Palace in 1813 by Michael Gustaf Anckarsvärd (1792–1878) who was then a lieutenant in the Svea Lifeguard. (Uppsala University Library collection via Alvin National Digital Cultural Heritage Platform)

We remained on Rügen – in their letters home the soldiers spelt it *Rygen* – for three weeks. I had the good fortune of being accommodated with the Major for 14 days at Putbus,[7] where one felt like a prince, although most of the time one had to be over-dressed as if on parade and we received dinner – without schnapps – at four in the afternoon.

His Serene Highness (*Durchlaucht*) Prince Malte von Putbus, a young gentleman, had been a cornet in our horse-guard, but when, during his officer training, he was required to groom his horse and clean out the stable, the service did not seem to him to be princely, so he returned home to his castle, where he was of course exempted from shovelling manure. Both gracious and kind, he was much beloved.[8]

The old feudal castle and its surroundings were reminiscent of the Middle Ages, but the interior showed the sophisticated taste and artistry of today.[9] In the galleries,

---

7　Putbus was the seat of the House of Putbus, which had been elevated from noble to princely status by Gustav IV Adolf in 1807.
8　Wilhelm Malte I, Prince of Putbus (1783–1854) joined the Swedish Life Dragoon Regiment as a *kornett* in 1800 at which time officers and non-commissioned officers had to undertake a two-month probationary period of education and training, termed *gradpassering* before they could be accepted into in the Swedish army. His military service was short-lived, and he became a royal chamberlain to Gustaf IV Adolf in 1802. He was appointed by Karl Johan as Governor-General of Swedish Pomerania following its re-occupation in 1813, and continued in this role after the territory was ceded to Prussia after the war.
9　Although originally a castle dating from the fourteenth century, a three-wing palace was created at the start of the seventeenth century which was in turn almost completely rebuilt during the eighteenth century in baroque style but retaining a Gothic wing.

the connoisseur could admire paintings and other works of art, which I did not understand, whilst, on the other hand, the armouries and hunting equipment aroused my delight.

The season only offered hunting for woodcock, which were now on their migrations north and were being shot for gun dogs to retrieve, and then I had to stand by and be ashamed at the rapid flying shots that the German hunters were capable of and which I could not emulate. These delicious game-birds were served daily in such *haut goût*[10] that no Småland farmer would eat them without an accompanying drink, but one gets used to many things, and in the end, rotten woodcock tasted pretty good.

That Rügen is a fertile land could be observed by its large but oafish peasants, who probably never got

Wilhelm Malte I, Prince of Putbus (1783–1854). Nineteenth-century German engraving. (Public Domain)

to warm themselves beneath a sooty roof beam, because the island has no forests. Thus, the Prince derived considerable income from the crack willow – *Salix fragilis* – that were planted along roads and field boundaries. A proportion were cut back each year and the wood sold was rather expensive.

The colossal loaves which the peasants ate were baked with a quarter straw, otherwise potatoes of excellent varieties constituted their main food.[11] I must describe a national dish, much enjoyed here as well as all over Pomerania. A large cooking pot would be half-filled with prunes, which grow here in abundance. The other half comprised dumplings of wheat flour, eggs and milk together with a couple of pork bellies. Well cooked, this stew should last for a week. The dish is called *Klützen* or *Klüt*. Worse fare could be had!

We longed to see the much-talked-about city of Stralsund, so praised by older comrades. We finally got to see its towers and ramparts, ferried across by way of Alte Fähr, marching in with martial music sounding. We were inspected front and back

---

10 From the French, literally 'high taste' meaning a taint of decay typical for game, gaminess.
11 Straw bread (*halmbröd*), like bark bread in Sweden, was considered a famine food. Setting aside the impact of war, harvests had been poor across much of Europe in 1813–1815, largely through a strong El Niño event, and there was a pan-European famine during the immediate post-war years 1816–1817. But the description suggests the situation in Rügen was not bad at this time. (Patrick Webb, 'Emergency Relief during Europe's Famine of 1817 Anticipated Crisis-Response Mechanisms of Today', *The Journal of Nutrition*, Volume 132, Issue 7, July 2002, pp.2092S-2095S).

Stralsund, looking west across the harbour from Dänholm island, 1830s. Lithograph from *Borussia Museum für Preußische Vaterlandskunde* (Dresden: Pietzsch, 1838). (Sächsische Landesbibliothek – Staats- und Universitätsbibliothek, Dresden)

by army bigwigs, who could not deny their approval of 'His Excellency's Regiment.' The commander-in-chief had not yet arrived, but one had to be careful at street corners not to bump into one of the many excellencies, generals and foreign diplomats who were waiting for him. Guard duty was somewhat challenging, because one needed a nose like a gundog to know all the strangers who would have a right to pass.

Certainly, Stralsund was magnificent, but it did not live up to my expectations. The houses appeared ashamed because their gable ends faced the street, a peculiarity of all older German towns. But the fortifications were reasonably maintained and repaired such that, in the event of a defeat, we would have a bolthole.

At last the Crown Prince arrived, and we received this man, who would care for us like the most affectionate father, but would yet carry our Swedish banners victorious in the fields where they had flown under the great Gustavus Adolphus. One could with eagle-eyes behold the hero of the moment – we felt that a soldier's hand had grasped the reins.

Our honourable and esteemed von Döbeln, always keen to be where danger presented itself, at the behest of foreign diplomats and against orders, or rather without orders, sent forces to Hamburg, for which action he was placed under arrest and sentenced to death. More difficulty ensued in trying to keep him alive, for he could not be persuaded to plea for mercy, but his sentence was commuted to a period of imprisonment at Vaxholm.[12]

---

12 Following the precipitate evacuation of Hamburg by the French under *Maréchal* St Cyr on 12 March 1813, the city had been 'liberated' by 1,500 Russian Cossacks under General Tettenborn on 18 March. In mid-May, with *Maréchal* Davout's Corps approaching and in response to

Plan of Stralsund, etching circa 1803. (Sächsische Landesbibliothek – Staats- und Universitätsbibliothek, Dresden)

Ankarsvärd, who disliked the way events were unfolding and had the impertinence to put his concerns in writing in his famous letter, was sent home in ignominy,[13] as

---

appeals for support, von Döbeln, commander of the 3rd Division deployed in Mecklenburg, on his own initiative sent four battalions of Swedes who arrived there on 19 May. After Crown Prince Karl Johan had landed at Stralsund the same day and learnt of this action, he countermanded the order, and the Swedes were withdrawn on 26 May. For his actions, von Döbeln was court-martialled and sentenced to death, but the Crown Prince commuted this to a year's imprisonment. Tettenborn abandoned the city on 29 May, Davout re-occupied it the following day and would remain there until after Napoleon's abdication in 1814.

13 Carl Henrik Ankarsvärd (1782–1865) was appointed commander of the Närke Regiment for the 1813 campaign. In somewhat youthful ignorance, he wrote a plain-speaking letter to the Crown Prince in which he strongly criticised the war and Sweden's politics, and in particular the alliance with Russia and the risk of betrayal by an untrustworthy Tsar. Karl Johan did not react well to this, and also being fearful of another conspiracy arising, immediately dismissed him from service and sent him home.

Georg Carl von Döbeln (1758–1820). (Finnish Heritage Agency Historical Picture Collection)

Karl Henrik Anckarsvärd (1782–1865). Portrait by Fredric Westin (1782–1862). (Nationalmuseum)

a lesson to others in the nobility not to play games with the Lion,[14] and that revolutions can succeed with madmen and cowards, but not with better folk.

During field exercises, the Crown Prince would sometimes march as right marker with the infantry and on occasion took charge of an artillery piece, showing that he also had experience of service in the ranks. Sometimes he patted soldiers on their cheeks, so that those who were used to physical and verbal abuse asked if this really was their Prince who made himself so 'common.' It was fun to see him walk past a guard post – he could be in a hurry, but as soon as the drum sounded the slow parade-march, he immediately took pace thereafter, observing form and posture as if he were in the ranks. And when the standard dipped, he dutifully doffed his bicorne hat, nodded kindly and might sometimes call out, 'Very good'. It was thus clear to see that he had learned to obey the drum, and was thereby qualified to command, and that he was not raised on tea and *ölost*.[15] We longed to show him what we could do and that we were devoted to him.

New regiments arrived and we were moved away to make room for them, entering into quarters in and around Damgarten. The 3rd Battalion was billeted in the town, which was quite pleasant. In Stralsund we had already been thoroughly inspected and

---

14 The Lion being the symbol of kingship; Gustavus Adolphus was famously known as the Lion from the North.
15 *Ölost* (literally *beer-cheese*) was popular in Sweden, Norway, and Britain, where it was known as *posset*, a hot drink made of milk curdled with wine or ale, often spiced, and considered to have medicinal properties.

approved so we were not occupied with drill and, since a truce had been concluded to mediate for peace, we had no enemies to fear.[16] We could thus attend to our pleasures. We had only five subalterns in the battalion. One of them, Ensign von Nackreij, who died during the war, lived most comfortably, and with him we had our gaming club in the afternoons, where many acts of folly and adventure occurred.[17] One such incident I must relate, although it may not amuse anyone but me.

Tobacco was poor and expensive in Germany, the Continental System prevented foreign imports, and the local product was comparable in both taste and smell to the rubbish that our old mountain men had to put up with. Nackreij had, as it happened, sneaked in two packets of Swedish tobacco, which was being rapidly consumed.[18] In particular, a large and rather coarse companion by the name of Henning, fondly known as 'Bornholm', would belch out smoke from his wooden pipe, which he always carried with him, and which could hold a large amount of tobacco.[19]

The host lamented over the demand for his fine tobacco and daily asked Henning to use a smaller pipe, but he just carried on smoking and playing. One afternoon, when I came to see Nackreij, a man who was quiet and steady, and rarely made a fuss, I found him engaged in cutting leaves, straw, spruce needles and the like with a pair of scissors. And when I enquired as to what purpose this would serve, he replied that it would become tobacco for the large wooden pipe, whereupon I, as you can easily understand, helped, and we then mixed the ingredients with some of the real thing.

But while Nackreij was busy producing these materials, I noticed his own tobacco box in the window and a musket cartridge next to it, which he used to improve his tinder, because matches were not available in those days. I reckoned that he too could benefit from some processed tobacco, and therefore emptied the cartridge into the box.

Our third man arrived, and we drew him into our confidence, the gaming table was set, and everything was prepared, and Henning came in with his big wooden pipe under his arm. We bade him to sit and play cards, and to save time, the host politely offered to fill his pipe.

---

16 Following major battles involving Russian and Prussian allies at Battle of Lützen (2 May) and Bautzen (20/21 May), the Armistice of Pläswitz, signed on 4 June, provided a welcome breathing space for both sides in the campaign, and lasted until 16 August (some sources state 10 August).
17 Carl von Nackreij (1793–1813) from Västerlösa, 20 kilometres west of Linköping, was appointed *fänrik* in the Jönköping Regiment in March 1812 and died on 11 November 1813 in Wismar during the campaign in Germany.
18 Sweden had a flourishing tobacco industry and the State had encouraged tobacco cultivation since the seventeenth century.
19 Henning Svante Schmiterlöw (1794–1853) was born in Askeryd, 50 kilometres east of Jönköping, appointed *fänrik* in the Jönköping Regiment in March 1812, reached the rank of *kapten* before leaving the army in 1827. *Henning* was a name indigenous to the local area around Stralsund and Rügen, which is where the noble family Schmiterlöw originated. Use of the name 'Bornholm' is a little curious since the island of Bornholm, which is situated 120 kilometres north east of Rügen but only 40 kilometres off the southern Swedish coast, was Danish territory.

Soldiers playing cards. Watercolour by Carl Johan Ljunggren (1790–1852) dated 1818. (Nationalmuseum)

The game began, and Henning smoked with relish, though it sputtered, crackled, and stunk enough to smoke out fox cubs. We looked at each other and made faces, but he was so engrossed in the game that he did not notice anything amiss, until the steward, an old soldier, came in and began to search in and under the beds, amongst chairs and clothing, wondering if a fire had started somewhere, because of the terrible smell. Then our supressed laughter finally erupted. Henning looked down at his pipe, heard its crackling, and finally perceived the smell. So he went to the stove, knocked out the pipe and examined the contents, then muttered 'rogues' while he opened the previously mentioned tobacco box and refilled his pipe himself. There was not enough to fill the bowl, so he added more from the packet in the bureau, after which we sat down again to continue the game. I alone anticipated the coming explosion and kept myself at a safe distance.

Suddenly there was a loud bang like a gun shot, the plug of tobacco hit the ceiling, the bowl hit the floor, bits of pipe hit the wall and Henning rounded on Nackreij, who protested his innocence and thought all hell had broken loose. We lay on couches and chairs and laughed as Henning mournfully collected the pieces of his beloved wooden pipe bowl, declaring the damage irreparable, and deeply cursing all the world's reprobates. Had he known that it was me, he might have killed me with a bear hug, for he was a strong as a bear. We collected the pieces, got a blacksmith to fix a couple of inch-wide iron bands around them and offered it back to him – but we had almost got it in the neck!

Fate had several singular events in store for myself and Henning. He was my best friend, safe and reliable at all times and an excellent serviceman, with his heart in the right place.

Now, during this present truce, he swore about our inactivity and that we were not engaged in any fighting. I suggested to him that this was not so bad for us, but he replied that we were soldiers and trained for this purpose. Some time thereafter, when we had unexpectedly encountered the enemy and stood facing a fairly sharp artillery fire, a ball removed half the head of a close compatriot so that his brains splattered over Henning's face. I leaned out of the line and saw my friend turn white as a sheet. When we were talking later, I asked him if he still thought fighting was fun, whereupon he avowed himself henceforth to never wish to go into battle again. When such occasions did arise, however, he showed himself to be unafraid.

During the march towards France, we undertook regimental quartermaster's duties together so we always travelled ahead of the regiment and often came across rebellious peasants whom he would calm with his giant strength, which he duly maintained with his intake of food and drink. When we passed taverns – which in Germany are not far from each other – two bottles of French wine were usually ordered, the corks extracted, we then counted 'one, two' and on 'three' we drank and the last to finish their bottle paid the bill. This was capital in the warm weather and could be done without fear.

Poor Henning! He died several years ago of water sickness, although he rarely drank water.[20]

We were now divided into two brigades under Brigadier General von Vegesack's command. The 1st Brigade, commanded by our own General Bergenstråhle, was made up of a battalion of the Småland infantry (today known as grenadiers); three battalions of the Jönköping Regiment; one battalion from each of the King's Own, the Northern Skåne and the von Engelbrechten regiments; a squadron of Cederström's Hussars (now Charles XV's); two squadrons of the Skåne Carabineers – old fellows – and a battery of Wendes artillery.[21]

---

20 *Vattusot* (lit. *water sickness*) means edema, also commonly known as dropsy, which is swelling caused by accumulation of fluid in body tissues, most often in the feet and legs. It is generally the result of a serious underlying health condition such as heart, lung, liver, or kidney disease and has nothing to do with the drinking of water.

21 The Småland Dragoon Regiment Infantry Battalion was formed in 1812 by converting some 500 men from that mounted unit into infantry. The King's Own was an enlisted regiment commanded by Gustaf Reinhold Boije of Gennäs (1769–1836), who was incidentally no direct relation to Hultin's battalion commander, Johan Fredrik Boij. The Northern Skåne Regiment had been newly raised in December 1811 with *Generalmajor* Georg von Döbeln as its first commanding officer. The von Engelbrechten Regiment was an enlisted regiment based in Swedish Pomerania, named after its then current commanding officer, Herman Fredrik Christian von Engelbrechten (1765–1818). Cederström's Hussars only became known as such in 1816; during the Napoleonic Wars it was officially Mörner's, although Bror Cederström was its effective commander at this time, and it was only named after Charles XV between 1860 and 1882 when Hultin was writing his memoirs. The Skåne Carabineers went through several name changes and were only referred to as 'carabineers' between 1805 and 1822, and

The 2nd Brigade, commanded by Mecklenburg General von Fallois, comprised a battalion of the Duke's Guard; two battalions of line infantry; two volunteer *jäger* battalions, one of which was mounted, all Mecklenburgers; a Hanseatic battalion from Bremen; a unit of von Schill's hussars – veritable freebooters; and a battery of Wendes artillery. Later, in addition, a host of Cossacks, whom God knows if anyone had control over, for they were everywhere and nowhere, and cared for no-one but themselves.

So, you can see that it was a mixed company, but, with *'Papa'* Vegesack at its head, it was not to be scorned. This general, who could for good reason be called the Blücher of the Swedes, was quick-witted, resourceful, and courageous to the point of foolhardiness, and beloved by both officers and men.

Other generals would direct their troops movements from an appropriate distance behind the lines because much depends on their lives, and this would be right and proper, but you could be sure to find Papa Vegesack where the fighting was most intense. You could contend that in enemy country he 'plundered', one might call him 'Stål of Holstein',[22] but in the end he suffered hardship and died in poverty. Perhaps the epitaph that Hampus Mörner wrote of himself could be equally applicable:

'Here lies Hampus the hussar,
A poor householder, but a damn fine soldier.'[23]

Possibly he was suspected of being a Gustavian, but to thereby overlook such an excellent general was not reasonable. My own belief (and that of many others) was that amongst all our generals he was the most trustworthy in a crisis.

---

as dragoons thereafter. The Wendes Artillery Regiment was formed in 1794 and was based at Stralsund. It comprised eight companies and a mounted battery and was expanded in 1809 with three companies from the disbanded Finnish Artillery Regiment.

22 A reference to *Fänrik Ståls sägner* (The Tales of Ensign Stål), an epic work by Finland's national poet Johan Ludvig Runeberg which describes the events and heroes of the Finnish War of 1808–1809, published in two parts in 1848 and 1860.

23 *Generallöjtnant* Hampus Elof Mörner (1763–1824) was commanding officer of the eponymous hussar regiment; known for his military prowess, outspoken and humorous, often in debt, he lived a life of debauchery, but also wrote poetry and played the violin well enough to be admitted to the Royal Academy of Music in 1794.

11

Mecklenburg (August–December 1813)

With the ending of the Truce of Pläswitz on 16 August, both sides resumed hostilities, aiming to implement their respective strategies. Maréchal Davout's XIII Army Corps immediately set out from its positions in and around Hamburg to march towards Berlin in support of Maréchal Oudinot's advance on the Prussian capital from the south. Vegesack's Swedish division was part of Wallmoden's Corps which was assigned to cover the right flank of the Crown Prince's Army of the North and thus oppose this movement. Davout's offensive was however short lived: when he learnt of the defeat of Oudinot's Corps by the Crown Prince at Großbeeren on 23 August he ordered his forces to retire to re-consolidate around Hamburg.

The Prince of Eckmühl (Marshal Davout) had occupied and fortified Hamburg and had advanced outposts at Dassow, Lübeck, Möllen and Ratzeburg, and we occupied positions at Wismar, Grevesmühlen and Rena. With the ending of the truce, our eager general probably wanted to push forward, but had been ordered to co-ordinate manoeuvres with General Wallmoden, who had a strong army corps positioned around Lauenburg, and he must have known from experience that Davout was not to be trifled with, and he did not want to get his fingers burnt.

I now took command of the battalion jägers and got to do the rounds of our outposts and observe the chivalrous Frenchmen.[1] Yes, they could justifiably be called chivalrous. They never shot at our vedettes or other individuals, as our Scandinavian brethren the Norwegians did when we got there, and often would warn our outposts of an impending advance. This happened to me once when I visited the line one morning, and an officer called out to me, 'Pull back your vedettes, for we intend to carry out a reconnaissance.' This was shouted in pure German, so he was probably from Westphalia or Württemberg.

Of course, we sometimes had petty squabbles with them over the scavenging of chickens and geese from nearby villages, but these usually went off without casualties, for the weaker side would immediately beat a retreat.

Davout's soldiers were drawn from the last conscripts that Napoleon called up – generally small lads aged just 18. When out foraging, we sometimes made prisoners

---

1 Jäger (Swedish: *jägare*, literally 'hunter') was a common term in European armies for light infantry. In the Swedish army at this time, each battalion had a jäger company nominally 58 men strong, operating as skirmishers in battle and undertaking scouting and guard duties.

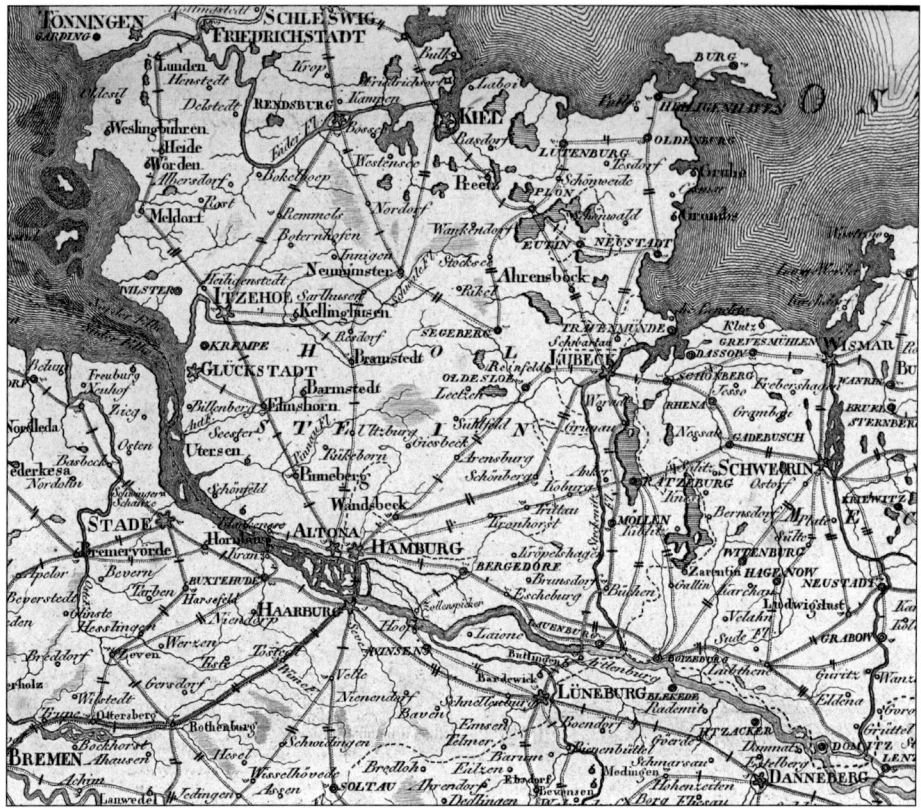

Holstein and west Mecklenburg – extract from 1814 map by J.E. Knittel, Nuremburg. (Leibniz-Institut für Länderkunde, Leipzig)

of them, and then our men would wring their hands and exclaim, 'Lord Jesses,[2] do we fight against children?' But these children would occasionally display fighting spirit.

We often had Cossacks with us on sentry duty, and then it could be considered safe enough lay down and sleep. Their like is not to be found – they have a sense of smell like dogs, hearing like hares and they could crawl and hide like cats. And although we did not understand each other, they fully understood what was being required of them. When visiting the line, one might come across a horse idly grazing on the grass but would fail to see the Cossack until he crawled out of a bush or ditch, from which he would observe the French lines at close quarters. Then he whistled for his horse, which would come to him like an obedient dog, and called out '*dobra*'[3] – the only word we understood. We viewed their horses with astonishment. Skinny,

---

2   A contemporary euphemism for Jesus to avoid a blasphemy, equivalent to 'Jeez' or similar terms in modern English.
3   Assumed to be a phonetic form of the Russian word доброmeaning 'good' or, more colloquially, 'OK'.

Cossack allies in the 1813 campaign. Watercolour by Carl Johan Ljunggren (1790–1852) dated 1823. (Nationalmuseum)

shaggy, goat-necked and with protruding hips,[4] these wretched creatures seemed barely able to walk, but they were indestructible – no river, no terrain hindered them. If the rider was so drunk that he tumbled off, the horse stood wide-legged over him. If he lost his horse and had instead to ride one of the great German dromedaries, this would be unfit for service within a month. They were clothed and armed as they pleased, some with an old pistol, some with a rusty sabre or dress-sword, but they all carried a lance. Of course, they could never be used as regular troops, but in pursuing a beaten enemy, taking prisoners, foraging, and murdering, they were champions. Although they were safe and good comrades, it was necessary, however, to look out for one's equipment and supplies when they were nearby.

These observations apply only to the irregular Cossacks, for there were many regular cavalry regiments in the Russian army which could be compared with or surpass any other cavalry in equipment and demeanour.

How and who had found them is incomprehensible, for they were everywhere, and the Germans used to say that the worst thing Napoleon did was when he marched up to and opened the stable door, for to drive the Cossacks back from whence they came was not so easy.

---

4   Hultin uses the word *koländade*, an obscure term from an early nineteenth century book on horse care, meaning deformation of the lumbar, such that the hip bones are sharp and broadly protruding.

The overall outpost commander was Captain Barck of the Jönköping Regiment.[5] As an ensign, during the war of 1805–1807,[6] he had gained renown as our most successful partisan,[7] for which he was decorated with the Order of the Sword. Now, as a jäger commander, he twice surprised and captured French pickets, despite them being twice his number. Our jägers thus acquired French muskets,[8] which they kept for themselves and were used despite being of carbine calibre, so that we sometimes had trouble getting hold of suitable ammunition for them but they performed better than our army issue.[9] On one occasion, he was ordered to do a reconnaissance with a jäger battalion and a squadron of hussars to observe the enemy's position and strength.[10] We marched for about five kilometres, and as the road then entered a beech forest, we halted there while half the hussar squadron under their lieutenant's command – their captain was sick – was sent ahead to investigate.

They had been gone for about half an hour when a couple of gunshots were heard, and immediately thereafter, the *piff-puff* of pistol shots. And then our hussars reappeared at the gallop, with lancers hard on their heels, who stopped short when they caught sight of us and heard some of our musket balls whizzing past.

---

5   Johan Adolf Barck (1776–1822) eventually reached the rank of *överstelöjtnant*. His father was a Småland parish priest and botanist who collaborated on a work with Carl Linnaeus, 'the father of modern taxonomy'.
6   The original text states '1804–05' and there is reference again later to 'Gustaf Adolf's crazy war in 1804' in relation to *Fänrik* Barck, so this does not seem likely to be a typographical error, but Sweden was not at war until 31 October 1805 when Gustaf IV declared war against France as part of the Third Coalition and, in addition, the Jönköping Regiment (one battalion) was only sent to Stralsund in the summer of 1805. The so-called Pomeranian War effectively ended with the Swedish surrender (under very favourable terms) and evacuation from Rügen 7 September 1807, leaving Pomerania in French possession. Thus, the text has been amended to read 1805–1807. Neither the 1954 or 1955 editions pass comment on this, or other instances of erroneous dates.
7   The Swedish word *partigängare* is usually translated as 'partisan' but in this context refers to actions undertaken in small groups of regular troops – raiding parties and the like – rather than insurgency or guerrilla warfare which the term has come to mean, and particularly in relation to the details of a raid jointly led by (then) *Fänrik* Barck which resulted in the capture of Wismar in April 1807.
8   Hultin uses the Swedish word *gevär* which in modern translation means rifle; but the word originally meant any kind of weapon and came to be applied more specifically to flintlock muskets from the eighteenth century. True rifles – firearms with rifled barrels – were rare in Napoleonic armies. The Armémuseum publication *Between the Imperial Eagles* notes that Sweden's specialist jäger units were rifle-armed but that 'Infantry *jägare* probably had ordinary muskets, not rifles' and Hultin's account would appear to corroborate this. See: Fred Sandstedt (ed.), *Between the Imperial Eagles: Sweden's Armed Forces during the Revolutionary and the Napoleonic Wars 1780–1820* (Stockholm: Armémuseum, 2000).
9   The French Charleville musket is generally reckoned a better weapon than the imported British Brown Bess in widespread use by the Swedes, although of smaller calibre (0.69 inch against 0.75 inch). Its success can be gauged by the fact that it was copied during the Napoleonic Wars by the Russians, the Prussians, and the Dutch, and after the war it was used in America as the basis for the 1816 Springfield.
10 As was common practice on campaign the individual battalion jäger companies within the brigade had been combined into a separate battalion. The hussars must have been Mörner's since this was the only hussar squadron assigned to the 5th Brigade. At this period a cavalry squadron was nominally 100 men.

I never saw the calm Captain Barck angered more than once. He ran up to the lieutenant and reproached him for such a disorderly retreat, which dishonoured our best cavalry, but the cornet – von Horn – led the other half of the squadron forward, without awaiting orders, to chase off the lancers. I witnessed a hussar take a hack at a lancer only to hit his upright lance, yet with such force that the man tumbled off his horse, and we took him prisoner, completely unharmed.

After a short while, the cornet returned and reported that numerous infantry as well as cavalry were rapidly approaching us, in consequence of which we were ordered to about face and fall back at the double, for we had a large field to retreat over where we could easily be cut down by cavalry. We managed to get through a hawthorn hedge, and there, as true jägers, we were able to open fire, which their cavalry did not appreciate, and so fell back themselves. A couple of infantry battalions did then appear in the field, but they did not pay any attention to us. In this incident we had one man and a few horses injured by pistol bullets and one jäger twisted his ankle.

For this action, which in the bulletin was described as a reconnaissance at Karlow and Klocksdorff, Barck, our oldest jäger officer, was promoted to major and awarded a medal.

After 14 days outpost duty, we were relieved, returned to our original quarters in Rena and vegetated but fared well. Together with a few others, I was housed with an old Jew, considered the richest in town. The host and I got along well enough, but his household and especially the steward – a dancing master[11] – were not quite so pleased, perhaps because they were short of schnapps. Once, when I returned for dinner, I found the entire Jewish family assembled in the street outside the house in tears and gnashing their teeth. The patriarch met me with a handkerchief over his nose, complaining miserably, 'Oy vey! Lieutenant, sir, your men are roasting pork in my house, it is against my religion, I cannot remain in there!' Of course, I did not want to deprive him of being seated at table with Abraham, Isaac, and Jacob because he had smelled pork, but I could not forbid our men to prepare their provisions as they pleased, which is why I advised him to allow them their pork if they ate it raw, and this brought about mutual tolerance of religion.[12]

A couple of times we had alarms when shots were heard from the outpost lines, but this was mostly the aforementioned chicken and goose wars, until mid-August, when the situation became serious, and adjutants came running to inform us that we were being attacked, and this time the news-bearers were right.

Davout considered Hamburg to be over-crowded and that we were impertinent neighbours who had no respect for chickens, so he sent out a strong army corps to teach us manners.[13] Wallmoden gave orders to retreat and Vegesack swore. All the jägers had been despatched to reinforce our outposts; we saw one deep column after

---

11 Hultin is most likely using this in the sense of a mischief-maker rather than literally as a dance teacher.
12 Minced raw pork, known as *Hackepeter* in Northern Germany or more commonly *Mett*, remains popular today, albeit considered as a delicacy.
13 As noted earlier, Davout's XIII Army Corps was in fact setting out to support *Maréchal* Oudinot's advance on Berlin.

another approaching, and the skirmisher fire had begun to smatter on either side, when we received the order to retreat, which was reluctantly obeyed. But the French tirailleurs, voltigeurs and other devils were so hot on our heels that we had to move pretty sharpish. And occasionally, when they got too close, we turned around, and with a volley enquired if they wanted more? Upon arriving back at Rena there was not so much as a Swedish cat still there, the troops were retreating on to Wismar and we would follow their example, however, we first had to delay the enemy as much as possible. We held positions in the town for an hour, which cost us several killed and wounded, but finally, to the dismay of the citizens, we had to leave and sought to catch up with our columns. These set off again upon our arrival, and for a long time we did not get any rest; before the enemy came within range of our vedettes we retreated, though we were not hotly pursued. In the evening we arrived at Wismar, where we remained undisturbed for two days, and we hoped that the dance would end, but on the third day the retreat resumed, to which we were now well accustomed.

I had the honour of serving on guard duty and thus, according to the custom of the time, wearing white trousers. Of course, the guard had to bring up the rear so I could not catch up with the baggage wagon with my knapsack in it and thus I had to march through smoke and dust and lie on the ground in white trousers, so that upon arrival at Rostock, where I could change, they qualified as only fit for a seaman!

That night we lay in and around Neu Bukow and reached Rostock the next day, where we dared not take quarters but remained on the streets with muskets at the ready, thanking God that we had the road open to Stralsund, within whose fortifications we should be able to defend ourselves. We were awakened by the drum on 28 August,[14] and although many swore at those who slaughtered calves but did not consume the skins,[15] they were, however, fully attentive when they heard the command, 'Open right column', and Papa Vegesack's voice, 'Now, lads, let us go forward.' A cheer that shook the city's foundations was the answer, and we marched out through the same gate through which we had entered the previous evening. We subsequently had an explanation for this. When the French corps moved a little too far from Hamburg in the process of driving us away, Wallmoden had approached from Lauenburg. He was about to fall upon their rear and thus place them between two fires, whereupon they now retreated, as far as they were able, during which we would snap at their heels.

For about five kilometres we marched peacefully, singing our usual soldier songs, when, unexpectedly, we heard a cannon shot ahead of us which caused our ears to prick up and jaws to drop. I said to a marching companion, 'That shot must have been fired by mistake?'

'Well, a fine mistake,' he replied. 'Didn't you see that the ball bounced twice and I believe it has hit the King's Battalion.'

---

14 Hultin's memory for dates seems (understandably) rather unreliable. He gives the date as 13 August, which was just after the Pläswitz armistice expired, but goes on to describe the action at Retschow which took place on 28 August.
15 Hultin is referring to drummers.

At that same moment, our artillery came racing past us, unlimbered on a rise, and started firing. It received a bold return fire, but we could not see from where because we were in a depression.

But the poor King's Battalion had halted just at the top of a sunken lane. They fared badly. In addition to many being killed, many more lost legs, for some balls struck them along the sunken lane whilst others were hit by balls that were intended for the artillery, which had deployed in front of them. Orders came to advance, and we caught some of the plentiful fire, but in general it was directed at the artillery. Miraculously, a shell struck and exploded between the legs of the battalion commander's horse, without injuring either the major, his horse or anyone in the battalion. A spattering of musket fire commenced around the Mecklenburg Brigade, and our hussars appeared from there.

The exchange of fire continued for maybe half an hour, not to our particularly great delight, because standing idle under cannon fire and taking punishment into the bargain rapidly becomes disagreeable. We were stood so close to the artillery that I heard the commander, Lieutenant Colonel Elfving,[16] shout to the general, who was of course in the heat of the action, 'I think our opponents are starting to get unsettled and tired of this sport, how does the general command me to act?' and received the answer, 'The Lieutenant Colonel shall manoeuvre the artillery as he considers best, but seek to make it respected.'

At the same time, the enemy was seen to abandon his position and retreat. Now we could see what the Wendes artillery was capable of. The trumpet signalled, the battery sped off, so that the horses would be sheltered by the ground, the cannons bouncing like chariots. The enemy had been only a few hundred paces from the position where ours had unlimbered, opened fire, and caused, as we then saw, carnage. Men, horses, dismounted cannons, limbers and shot-up ammunition carts lay in piles amongst each other. Many poor wounded souls were left to be cared for by us, all the more pitiful as they only spoke Danish, because the artillery which had acted against us was Danish.[17]

A cavalry troop made a demonstration to strike at our splendid artillery, but by then we had advanced into musket range, and our carabineers, who were certainly not skilled riders, but in close order with their big horses and big men were not to be trifled with, dug in their spurs, and burst upon them like a thundercloud, driving them away.

I was ordered to have the wounded delivered to the surgeons who carried out their bloody handiwork some distance away, and met our field priest who, like us, had exposed himself to the enemy's fire.[18] This particular friend of mine was in many ways nurtured by the regiment. He knew the service just as well as any officer, and

---

16 Finnish-born Samuel Elfving (1760–1837) initially served with the Finnish Artillery Regiment but when it was disbanded, he transferred to the Wendes Regiment.
17 The Danish battery was 3-pounder horse artillery whilst the Wendes battery had 6-pounders, so the Danes were heavily out-gunned. Accounts are sparse and conflicting but suggest the Danish battery had three guns destroyed.
18 Johan Karlsson (1777–1833) served as the Jönköping Regiment's field-priest from 1808 to the end of the Napoleonic Wars.

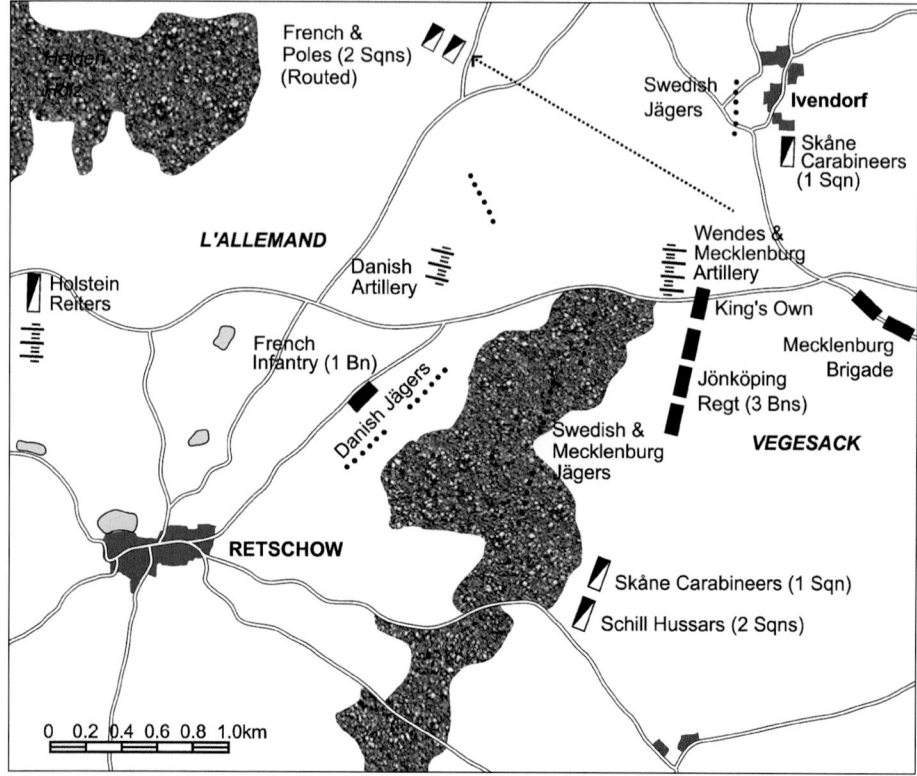

The Battle of Retschow, 28 August 1813. Positions after initial cavalry action. (Author's map)

was a good companion, but never forgot that he was a priest. When I now reproached him for participating in affairs that did not concern him – that we, for our sins, must be there, but he should not, he replied earnestly, 'Well, my brother, it behoves me to be present when there are many who need my comfort and my counsel, and I am here on higher authority than yours.' I had always loved the man; now I revered the priest.

The jägers began firing, and the voltigeurs, who had been hunting us, were now hares themselves, and we pursued them. Nevertheless, we had to keep our distance, for they had Danish cavalry on the flank, riding as skilfully as stable-masters, and to send our fine capital fellows against them was not advisable, for in dispersed formation we could not oppose them. In addition, the Danes were well-known and particularly esteemed as flankers by the French, who called them '*grandfathers*.' Had we had our hussars, the pursuit would have gone faster but they were engaged on the left wing.

The Smålander is fond of his kinfolk, and even under fire he retains such feelings for his compatriots. When we went forward passing by the slain of the King's Battalion, we were somewhat indifferent, but a little further on lay a soldier of the Småland Regiment, causing a murmur, 'Lord God, there is a Smålander'. One fellow sprang forth and turned him over to see if he recognised him, fearing this would be more lamentable than anything else.

How training and experience can have an effect even in death was shown by an elderly soldier who received a wound to his head such that he rolled over several times, but he got up, re-took his place in the line and a few seconds later fell stone dead.

Although one could not be truly attuned for amusement, we did however, laugh at a poor peasant who was tested like the confession of faith before Pilate.[19] He was driving an ammunition wagon, and when he saw that the situation was getting serious, he led his horse behind the wagon and crouched down, but when a shell set the wagon ablaze, horse and peasant bolted, but each in opposite directions.

This battle was known as the affair at Retschow, perhaps the fiercest we had, and garnered several awards and much praise. A medal was struck by the Duke of Mecklenburg which he liberally presented to his own officers, who behaved perhaps less well than we did, but he could not afford the same for us, not even for our artillery, which, however, deserved it.

At Neu Bukow, the enemy stood for a couple of hours and gave us a bloody nose. They then retired quickly to Wismar, where we expected stronger resistance, but the town was evacuated, and we met again old acquaintances and our former hosts, who welcomed us.

The enemy had been harsh with them, imposing significant contributions and levies, but they had not been plundered, which was considered strange, since Napoleon was most embittered at the Duke, being the first to defect from the Confederation of the Rhine.[20] The small town of Rena had to pay 6,000 guilders, which my aforementioned pork-Jew advanced in one go, anticipating future recompense and charitable interest rates.

Returning from our travels, which had been no vacation, we reoccupied our former quarters and outposts. The French had now concentrated more around Hamburg and withdrew their most advanced outposts, so that the chicken wars ended, and we were left in peace.

Our diet on outpost duty would, from a physician's perspective, be considered poor. There was not much to be found in the villages, and what little there was, the Cossacks sniffed out and whisked away. One morning, when I was on guard duty, one of them, probably some sort of commander, came up and moaned at me. I only understood 'hunger, kaput, comrade,' but concluded that he was hungry and told my man to give him some liquor, which he did unwillingly, since our supply was small and he had rather kept it to himself. The Cossack drank, said '*dobra*' and looked pleased when we gave him some bread and cheese, after which he put his index finger in his mouth and gave a shrill whistle. A companion came forward and lifted a haversack from the pommel of his saddle, which he opened, took my headgear, and

---

19 1 Timothy 6:12–13: 'Fight the good fight of faith … Christ Jesus, who in his testimony before Pontius Pilate made the good confession …'
20 In 1806 following his defeat of Russia and Austria at Austerlitz, Napoleon formed 16 German states, formerly part of the Holy Roman Empire, into the Confederation of the Rhine. It later expanded to comprise 35 states with a population of 15 million at its height in 1812. However, the Confederation rapidly collapsed after Napoleon's defeat in the 1813 campaign. The Duchy of Mecklenburg-Schwerin under Duke Frederick Francis I (1756–1837) was one of the last states to join and the first to leave.

dropped into it a couple of handfuls of sugar candy, which he handed to me and then set off shouting '*dobra*, comrade.' Doubtless he had come by it through plundering some poor confectioner.

A Cossack rode into Rena past a shop outside of which, as a form of sign, hung a splendid ham, which the Cossack took a fancy to. He looked around to check if he was being observed, stuck his lance in the ham, pulled out a knife and cut it free, gave the horse a rap and took himself off with the lance held aloft and the ham on the end, like a French eagle, so that the shopkeeper could do no more than swear and spit after him.

But they were not difficult to get along with. In a village where I was quartered, I had placed our ammunition cart in a street at a secluded spot, instructing a sentry to guard it and not allow anyone to approach with any naked flame. That evening, a Russian was heard arguing and causing a commotion, so I went over to see him. He seemed much agitated and shouted, 'Swedish comrade, Russian comrade kaput', and much more, whose meaning I could not understand. However, a corporal came up to me and reported that a Cossack horse was stood in the street with its rider lying beside it. I immediately went over and asked the sentry what had happened. He then told me that two Cossacks, one with a smoking pipe in his mouth, wanted to ride past, and, despite his warning, kept on coming and were about to knock him down when he struck one of them on the head with his musket so that he fell to the ground. Concerned about this incident, which had potential to cause much unpleasantness and trouble, I had the man carried indoors, bathed his head with cold water and placed some paper moistened with schnapps over his face. He had scarcely smelled the liquor, when he opened his eyes and shouted, '*karascha*' (nice) then took a stiff drink and departed in all friendship.

As I said, we did not always fare well in the outposts, but did much better in the towns and in the manor houses. We youngsters enjoyed the German diet well enough, but the older soldiers, who were accustomed to a *brännvinsbord*[21] with its regular shots of spirits, found it topsy-turvy. Dinner always started with a meat soup, then a meat and fish course with various vegetables, then a dessert of walnuts, prunes, raisins, almonds, and fruits, and finally cheese, butter, and some third-rate brandy, which was sipped in small glasses. A bottle of red wine was provided for each place-setting and was often entirely consumed, which could be done safely, being no stronger than our own small beer.[22] Bread and butter were seldom more than a day old, herring and salted meat dishes were rarely seen, milk could only be obtained on request, but excellent small beer was found everywhere, and it was necessary because there was a shortage of good water. Chicory coffee with cane sugar or beet sugar was drunk by the gallon.

It is said that potato cultivation spread through Sweden during Adolf Fredrik's Pomeranian War.[23] This present war added fresh fish to our diet through fish farming

---

21 A *smörgåsbord* with schnapps/brandy (*brännvin*).
22 *Svagdricka*, (lit. weak drink) was a sweet, dark, malt beer with low-alcohol content, still brewed in Sweden today.
23 The Pomeranian War (1757–1762) between Sweden and Prussia was part of the wider global conflict known as the Seven Years War and took place during the reign of Adolf Fredrik

which the Germans taught to us and our compatriots, and which in my youth was unknown. One might wonder where fish might be caught in a land in which rivers and lakes are so scarce. But in manor house gardens, more often than not, there were ponds, which looked like our cess pools, into which a small net could be thrown and pulled out full of Prussian carp (*Cyprinus gibellio*) and tench (*Tinca vulgaris*), from which the edible ones were selected, and the rest thrown back. In many places there were ponds where common carp (*Cyprinus carpio*) were systematically cultivated, but there was still no knowledge of artificial insemination.[24] In Lake Schwerin, I saw them catching handsome perch.

In the small town of Grevesmühlen, I was housed with a clergyman named Bardolin. I am now old and not worth powder and shot, and many acquaintances have fallen from memory, but this patriarch remains there vividly. He resembled the portraits I have seen of Melanchthon.[25] When I said prayers, I would always see his pale, bald head – the first evening, tears had run down his hollow cheeks as he embraced me and sobbed, 'God bless you and your people! I can imagine myself watching the soldiers of the great Gustavus Adolphus, who also prayed and sang *A Mighty Fortress Is Our God*[26] as they fought for our faith and our freedom and scattered Tilly's troops and Wallenstein's wild hordes.'

Both morning and evening prayer aroused great interest. Several hundred local people might gather around us. Many of our hymn tunes were known to them and were sung with German words. No other nation's armies availed themselves of such priests or prayers. In general, the Lutheran priests were exemplary. They rarely visited entertainments or public amusements, and when conducting a funeral, they followed the procession to the house, but rarely went in to partake in the reception. They did not consider this contrary to their doctrine, but discomforting to themselves, subjecting them to reproach by Catholics who would freely abuse and condemn them. One fared well if quartered with Lutherans, but with a Catholic priest, as often happened during the march to France, one was assured of wretched and foul accommodation. These poor souls have to live unmarried, and if they were conscientious and wanted to avoid suspicion, had ugly and unkempt old crones as housekeepers. Napoleon had also restricted their livelihood, so that they did not have

---

(1710–1771), the first king of Sweden from the House of Holstein-Gottorp and father of Gustav III.

24 Fish farming was in fact practiced in manors and rectories in Sweden from the seventeenth century and Carl Linnaeus had been inspired by carp cultivation he had seen in Scania around 1750. He and others had tried to encourage aquaculture in Sweden from that time but increased agricultural productivity and low margins for aquaculture meant that what little there had been declined further, with ponds infilled or becoming purely ornamental, and interest was only revived again around the mid-nineteenth century. A detailed study can be found in Bonow, Olsén and Svanberg (eds.), *Historical Aquaculture in Northern Europe* (Stockholm: Elanders, 2016). G.C. Cederström, *Små-plancher till ledning vid fisk-odling (Small plans illustrating the management of fish farming)* (Stockholm: J.F. Meyer, 1859) includes references to artificial insemination.

25 Philip Melanchthon (1497–1560) was a close friend and associate of Martin Luther, who became the spokesman of the Reformation after Luther's death.

26 *A Mighty Fortress Is Our God* is one of the best-known hymns by Martin Luther, who wrote the words and composed the melody, circa 1528.

much to eat themselves.[27] However, a degree of elegance could sometimes be maintained where their households were headed by a so-called relative, like an adopted nephew or niece, or by *lusu naturae*[28] who were not so gruesome. These priests were generally not as fanatical as one might think. You could even encounter freethinkers amongst them who doubted the infallibility of the Holy Father, ate meat on Friday and were partial to a glass – when it was offered.

We had not quarrelled with the French for so long that Papa Vegesack decided to take the initiative. Except for Lübeck, which was strongly held, their most advanced outpost was at Ratzeburg, and this he deemed unacceptable, in consequence of which Barck was ordered to carry out a reconnaissance with a jäger battalion and drive them away if possible. This small town is on an island which from our direction was reached via a long bridge. We had been there several times before and observed their defence works, which were not so easy to circumvent. We advanced in line up to the lake shore and commenced firing, although the distance was too great, and we received an ineffectual response, with no cannon fire, from which we concluded that they had no guns available. Storming was decided upon. Our line concentrated behind a hill near the bridge, and the troops were instructed that a successful assault was now down to our ability to run; that if the enemy really had cannon, we would wait for shots at the start of the bridge, but that the crossing then had to be effected with such speed that they would not have time to reload and fire again. So, we set off at a dash and with a cheer, as fast as our legs would carry us. We immediately received a weak salvo of small arms fire, which did little harm, but then everything went quiet, and when we reached the rampart, we found it abandoned, and we were told that the Danish garrison, comprising an officer and 50 men, had immediately taken themselves off to Hamburg.

Thus, our victory was easy, but the town was nevertheless taken by storm and, as a result, entitled us to subject it to plunder, wherefore the mayor and councillors appeared in procession and begged for mercy. We responded that Swedes would never behave in such a disagreeable and shameful manner, but on the understanding that in return they would treat our men well, which they implemented so thoroughly that half the men were completely inebriated by nightfall, whilst their officers looked the other way. Our restraint was praised, and a couple of jäger squads were posted in the town.

Ratzeburg belonged to the Duke of Mecklenburg-Strelitz,[29] whose domain was no larger than many of our own well-to-do *rusthållare*,[30] and it was said that his contingent in the national army, when it was placed on a war footing, comprised a

---

27 Napoleon had in fact eased the restrictions that had almost destroyed Catholicism during the Revolution; but it was merely tolerated, remaining fully under state control. See e.g., Gemma Betros, 'The French Revolution and the Catholic Church', *History Today*, Issue 68 December 2010.
28 Literally 'game of nature', meaning a person with a physical disability.
29 Charles Louis Frederick (1741–1816), Duke of Mecklenburg-Strelitz from 1794 until his death. He had been Governor of Hanover 1776–1786. His sister Charlotte was the wife of King George III.
30 A *rusthållare* was the owner of a *rusthåll* which supplied a cavalryman to the army under the Allotment System, in return for exemption from taxation.

View of Ratzeburg from the north. The Swedish jäger assault was across the narrow Langenbrücker bridge to the left (east); the main entrance to the town was via the isthmus and bridge to the right (west) and the main defences faced in this direction. (Illustration from Friedrich Wilhelm Alexander Nay, *Holsteen & Lauenborg* (Copenhagen: Baerentzen, 1859))

one-eyed drummer. This potentate was seldom seen; he lived like a recluse and was said to be an old man, with a mummified court, and thus the complete opposite to our friend, the Duke of Mecklenburg-Schwerin, who had generals and guards, played, caroused, hunted, rode horses to death, was often broke and was reckoned to be the father of one in eight of his faithful subjects!

Wallmoden had encircled Hamburg, so that we were safe from that direction. But a French corps had approached the Elbe and needed to be observed, which is why we were moved to Boizenburg and Möllen, which are close to this river, and entered into quarters.[31] Here we dwelt peacefully until one evening we heard a couple of shots and found a mischievous young officer with some jägers engaged in shooting at three French officers who were walking along the opposite riverbank. Certainly the distance was considerable,[32] but if the balls had hit, they would probably have caused injury. The Frenchmen, however, did not show concern, for at each shot they turned, doffed their hats in thanks for the salute, and continued their stroll. We took our sharpshooters to task over this, and this was observed with polite compliments on both sides.

---

31 Boizenburg is on the right bank of the Elbe five kilometres upstream of Lauenburg and 20 kilometres from Hamburg; however, Möllen (Mölln on modern maps) is situated at about the mid-point of the fourteenth century Stecknitz Canal which runs north-south between Lübeck and Lauenburg and was intended to be Davout's forward defensive line in front of Hamburg.
32 The Elbe is typically 200–300 metres wide here.

The small town of Möllen is remarkable only because Eulenspiegel is buried there, standing on his head.[33] Out of appreciation I made a pilgrimage to his grave, which one can perhaps understand and consider to be in order.

I must tell of a noteworthy event that occurred here. A Russian regiment marched through the town, and one dared not let those folk tarry in inhabited places in allied land, for they would readily appropriate whatever the Lord would bestow upon them. One is always curious about foreign troops. We were standing in a group in the square, observing the passing Russians, amongst whom was a tall handsome officer who marched alone. With us was Lieutenant Klingspor, who commanded the Södermanland jägers. He remarked, 'Bless my soul, but how that Russian has a Swedish countenance!' The Russian turned, fixed upon him, and exclaimed, 'Do you think it so strange, my dear Klingspor?' His name was Bergenstråhle; they had been cadets together at Haapaniemi, and he had a better memory than his former comrade![34]

A similar thing happened to me a couple of times. When we advanced into Holstein and arrived hungry in Segeberg, I asked where I could find a baker in order to get some bread. When I came to the house, out came a Mecklenburg soldier, whom I asked in German if a baker lived here, to which he replied, 'Yes, of course a baker lives here, but he has no bread' – in perfectly pure Scanian. He saw by my uniform that I was Swedish.

In Aachen, Henning and I were quartered in the same house and ate at the same table as four Russians. One of them, a cavalry captain named Düroch, a decent man, spoke German like a native, another had a smattering of French and the other two were simple Russian peasants with neither education nor manners. In talking about these gentlemen, I and my comrade would often make not exactly the most tactful remarks. One day, when I was not feeling well, I passed the wine bottle untouched to Düroch, whereupon he asked in Swedish, 'surely not?' I asked if he understood Swedish, and he replied, 'Yes, of course I do, I live in Finland, my wife is Swedish,

---

33 Stories of Till Eulenspiegel, a peasant who travelled throughout the Holy Roman Empire in the first half of the fourteenth century, first appeared around 1500. He is depicted as a practical joker, but one who exposed medieval society's vices and wrongdoings. He is said to have died of the Black Death in Mölln in 1350. Tradition has it that he was buried vertically, because at the funeral the coffin fell into the grave and stayed upright. Eulenspiegel, 'the most famous fool in the world' remains a popular figure in Germany today.

34 These officers are likely to be Carl Gustaf Klingspor (1786–1833) and Per August Bergenstråhle (1787–1843). Klingspor enlisted in the Södermanland Regiment in 1797 and was a cadet at Haapaniemi military college in southeast Finland 1804–1807. He took part in the Finnish war 1808–1809 including the retreat from Åland and the Västerbotten expedition; participated in the battles of Großbeeren and Leipzig in 1813 and the invasion of Norway in 1814. He continued in service until 1831 reaching the rank of *överstelöjtnant*. Per August Bergenstråhle was the son of *Överste* and *Generaladjutant* Johan Bergenstråhle, one of *General* Gustaf Bergenstråhle's brothers. He was a cadet at Haapaniemi 1801–1805 and later served as a staff adjutant to his father, but he left Swedish service as a *löjtnant* in July 1810, subsequently enlisting with the same rank in the Russian 1st Neva Infantry Regiment in March 1812. The Neva Regiment fought during Napoleon's 1812 invasion and the 1813 Leipzig campaign when it was part of Baron Winzingerode's Russian Corps under Karl Johan's overall command of the Army of the North.

Russian allies in the 1813 campaign. Watercolour by Carl Johan Ljunggren (1790–1852) dated 1823. (Nationalmuseum)

and my children cannot speak any other language.' We subsequently became closer acquainted with him, and I reproached him for eavesdropping so subtly on our remarks about the Russians, to which he replied, 'What has that to do with me, you can readily perceive that I am not a Russian, although I wear the uniform.'

Two officers of the Småland Dragoons had a worse experience. The jovial and not easily surprised Gösta M-r was one of them.[35] They were being accommodated with a priest in Holstein, and there, at the dinner table, two unusually beautiful daughters presented themselves, to whom our young gentlemen took a fancy. They began to make plans of conquest and to agree on how, without getting in each other's way, they would share the spoils, when M-r's servant came in and reported that the horses would not eat the hay that they had been given. The priest turned to the servant and said, in perfect Swedish, 'Tell the stable boy that he can take hay lying at the gable end of the barn which is usually given to the sheep.' It is claimed that even Gösta M-r was taken aback!

The French withdrew from the Elbe, and we took up positions in the vicinity of Lübeck, which we aspired to take. There, in Mecklenburg, we felt at home, and we

---

35 Hultin does not identify this officer beyond the abbreviated form 'M-r'. At that time, 'Gösta' was a nickname, a variant of Gustaf. A likely candidate for this officer is Carl Gustaf Hjalmer Mörner (1794–1837) who was appointed as a *kornett* in Småland Dragoons in 1810 and was employed on *General* Skjöldebrand's staff during the 1813 campaign and was present at Großbeeren, Dennewitz, Leipzig and Bornhöft. He was the nephew of the then commander of the regiment, *Överste* Axel Otto Mörner. He went on to become a well-known artist. But it could be his cousin Nils Gustaf Mörner (1793–1843) who was also a *kornett* in the regiment from 1812, having transferred in from the Mörner hussars.

felt good. It is a fertile country, and not, like a part of Germany, so flat and barren as to weary the eye and cause the northerner to become homesick. In Mecklenburg one can see lakes and beautiful deciduous forests, in which are to be found red deer, roe deer and wild boar, managed by numerous, well-paid, and knowledgeable gamekeepers. The people were prosperous, and it often happened that a farmer would have a group of officers quartered with him, who all got to eat their fill. All hunting was the preserve of the Duke; the peasantry were never permitted to handle guns and gunpowder.

In August and September, a number of hunting grounds were opened and hunted on behalf of the Duke, and large quantities of game of all kinds were being brought to market in the town squares. Once, whilst I was staying with a chief forester, I had the pleasure of such a hunt. He had all his staff assembled, and they were many, although mostly youngsters who, if I remember correctly, were apprenticed for five or six years, for, besides hunting, they would plant, assess and mark trees to be felled. Many peasants were mobilised as beaters, but the weather was wet and unsuitable, so that, in the opinion of the forester, the hunt was not a success, but I had never seen so much wildlife in one place. The old man was in a bad mood, contending that some people misfired or only their priming powder ignited because they did not have their equipment in good order, and claimed that such a thing could never happen to him. After they had eaten, target shooting commenced, using a bottle hanging from a tree. Some hit, but most of them missed, and the old man swore. Last to shoot, he took aim with his double-barrelled gun which misfired on one barrel and only burnt off the priming powder on the other, at which he threw the weapon to the ground and went to his carriage, accompanied by the restrained laughter and derisory faces of those he had upbraided.

In Lübeck there was a strong Danish corps, well entrenched such that attacking them would be too costly. They only made one sortie, but we received it so warmly that they lost any desire for more. Thus, we merely maintained our positions, until the end of November, when we were ordered to advance to the south of the city, where, instead of the enemy, we found 50 battalions of Swedes in battle array, and could hear cheering and thereby understood that our beloved Crown Prince was at their head. We had not seen him since Stralsund, but had cause to hear of his actions at Großbeeren, Dennewitz and Leipzig, and we could hardly control our men before they got to see him. He is now gone, but never forgotten by the few still with us, whom he always called 'my children.' Concerning those who have criticised this great man, one can reasonably say, like Wallenberg in 'My Son on the Galley':

> A lion falls under the lance,
> And rats play with the tail.[36]

---

36 'My Son on the Galley' (*Min son på galejan*) was a humorous travelogue written by ship's chaplain Jacob Wallenberg (1746–1778) based on his voyage to the Far East on the East Indiaman *Finland* 1769–1771. The couplet quoted is from an earlier composition inspired by a visit to Helsingborg, reminiscing on Sweden's victory over the Danes in 1710 and is a reference to the death of Charles XII and its aftermath. In the poem he rails against the King's detractors and in particular Voltaire's treatment in his 1731 book *L'Histoire de Charles XII*.

The Danes were called upon to surrender Lübeck, but they had to be persuaded, so our jägers commenced firing, a large number of storm ladders and fascines were brought forward, and Vegesack's division was ordered to be prepared for storming. These arguments were difficult to refute and brought about a capitulation.[37] The city was to be evacuated the following day, and the Danes were to retreat to Holstein and would not to be pursued until 24 hours had elapsed. The next day we entered through one of the customs gates while the Danes marched out through the other. We thus got to see the old Hanseatic city which played a role in our history; but we saw little of it, for scarcely had 24 hours passed before the cavalry and Vegesack's division were ordered to hunt down the Danes, at a rapid pace.

37 Lübeck was surrendered to Crown Prince Karl Johan on 5 December 1813 by French *Général de brigade* François Antoine Lallemand who commanded a Danish brigade.

12

Holstein and the Fall of Denmark (December 1813–January 1814)

Following Napoleon's defeat at Leipzig, 16–19 October, and with Davout besieged in Hamburg, Crown Prince Karl Johan's Army of the North was free to pursue the Danish forces through Holstein and back into Denmark aiming to knock them out of the war. Occupation of Holstein would also strengthen Karl Johan's hand to ensure he secured the agreed prize of Norway.

As mentioned, we saw little of the old Hanseatic city of Lübeck, its magnificent buildings and fortifications, and of its works of art only pictures, except for the Holsten Gate, in front of which stood the statue of Mercury, Roman god of merchants. It seems wrongful that the malicious Romans also made him patron of thieves!

We set off on a forced march and arrived at Segeberg the next day. The Swedish cavalry had got well ahead of us, but this caused us little inconvenience; the small towns and villages had been evacuated, their inhabitants having fled with their most valuable possessions, but houses and homes stood untouched so that one could see that we were a civilised enemy. We crossed the fields at Bornhöft, where the Swedish cavalry showed what it was capable of against the Danish corps, who stood with artillery, cavalry, and considerable infantry, which it attacked, cut down and took many prisoners. It is true that the attack was considered rash, and General Skjöldebrand (my former commanding officer), who commanded there, had been ordered to employ the cavalry with care, but he did so like a soldier.[1]

One or two anecdotes from that action may be of interest. A squadron of Cederström's hussars was in danger of being out-flanked on the left wing, so the general ordered a right-turn, but this was not obeyed. Astonished at this indiscipline from our best cavalry, he sought to inform them that the intention was not to retreat but to take up a better and more secure position, when one of the adjutants reminded him that this regiment was commanded in German, and when he repeated the order in this language, it was instantly obeyed. Raised in Pomerania and paid for by the

---

1 A 700 strong Swedish cavalry force under Skjöldebrand, comprising 12 squadrons from the Mörner (Cederström), Schill and Skåne hussar regiments and the Skåne Carabineers, engaged a mixed force some 2,500 Danes in confused fighting in and around the town of Bornhöft on 7 December. Casualties were relatively light, around 60 dead and wounded on each side, but the Danes were forced to retreat.

Hultin's most memorable sights in Lübeck: the statue of Mercury on the Puppenbrücke Bridge and the Holsten Gate. (From E. Bollmann, and C. J. Milde, *Lübecker ABC* (Lübeck: Selbstverlag des Herausgebers, 1857), Staats- und Universitätsbibliothek Hamburg Carl von Ossietzky, CC BY-SA 4.0)

The Mörner Hussars at Bornhöft, 1813. Watercolour by Carl Johan Ljunggren (1790–1852) dated 1815. (Nationalmuseum)

Pomeranian state, this lively regiment took orders in German, although nowadays there are few Germans in it.

I have mentioned a number of times our Scanian carabineers or so-called 'gentlemen' that there is reason to give a more detailed account of this unusual unit. His Excellency Count Toll was their commander;[2] he had a free hand to direct them as he pleased, and they did not want to lose him as their leader. He was old and selfless, he wanted his men to be like him, and thus many remained in service beyond their time. A young man was a rarity among them; their ranks comprised corpulent old men, and we often made fun of them and their Scanian language and inexperience. If the street was full of carabineers and you shouted out 'Bennet,' you could be sure that many of the old men would look around in surprise to discover where the caller was. The reason for this was not known for sure but we conjectured that men with that esteemed name, and in general their eminent officers, have always been numerous in this regiment.[3]

Incredible stories were told and made up about them. For example, that when a trooper came home from service and handed his weapons to the armoury, the *rusthållare,* observing that the original stoppers were in the pistols, praised him for looking after them so well and took out a stopper from the muzzle, whereupon

---

2   Count Johan Christopher Toll (1743–1817). It was Toll who negotiated the favourable surrender of Stralsund to *Maréchal* Brune in August 1807 which allowed his 13,000 men free passage home with all their arms and equipment; and it was Toll as commander of the army in Skåne to whom Gustav IV intended to flee during the 1809 coup. However, he did not take part in the 1813 campaign, retaining a home-defence role with a small force in Skåne.
3   Descendants of a Scotsman, James Bennet, who entered Swedish service in 1650 and was ennobled for services rendered in 1675.

Skåne Carabineers and a Mörner (Cederström) hussar during the 1813–1814 campaign. Illustration from Ljunggren, Carl Johan, *Minnes-Anteckningar under 1813 och 1814 Årens Kampagner, uti Tyskland och Norge* (Stockholm: Adolf Bonnier, 1855). (Armémuseum)

the carabineer exclaimed with astonishment, 'Oh! my life and soul, I thought those things were hollow!' When one who had been placed under arrest was asked the reason by his comrades, he replied in pure Scanian that flies had fouled his pistols, which his corporal had got wind of and informed his lieutenant. If an ungainly old soldier had to dismount during an exercise, it was said that he would ask for a younger comrade to help him remount. These and other such follies amused even their own commander.

They were dressed and equipped just as during Charles XII's time: a short tunic with a yellow belt, from which hung a large broadsword with a basket hilt, which projected so far behind that chickens could sit on it; yellow leather breeches, tall bucket-top boots and a bicorne hat with a straw cockade, which was often nibbled by the horse when it was hungry.

To be sure, these old men might have trouble mounting their fine horses (they had excellent horses), but once they did, they would sit as if held fast and draw their swords, then a breath of Charles XII's spirit would come over them, and in close formation they were irresistible. At Bornhöft, they struck like a hurricane and crushed all resistance, though they were roughly handled.[4]

---

4   Mankell, *Anteckningar rörande svenska regementernas historia*, notes that two squadrons of the Skåne Carabineers were present at the battle, forming the reserve of the first line. One squadron, attacking through a gap in the embankment on the left wing, 'inflicted heavy loss on the Danes.' Götlin records the Carabineers' losses as five killed and 14 wounded, see L.E. Götlin, *Anteckningar under Svenska Arméens Fälttåg 1813 och 1814* (Notes on the Swedish army's campaign 1813 and 1814) (Uppsala: Palmblad, 1820), vol.3.

After returning home, General Stierncrona was appointed as lieutenant colonel of the regiment to reorganise it and was often subjected to His Excellency's whiplash. On one occasion he wanted a captain removed. His Excellency not being so inclined asked to know the reason and when Stierncrona remarked that he was too old and infirm, His Excellency replied, 'I know nothing else wrong with him other than that he cannot dance.' It is worthy of note that Stierncrona was the most outstanding dancer in the army. At the camp in Skåne in 1819 I saw this regiment operating as dragoons and probably on a par with the best of our provincial cavalry. Count Toll had since passed away and Stierncrona was now in command. This shows what a commander with the strength of will and confidence can accomplish in a short time.[5]

So far everything had been going well, at night we had had a roof over our heads, and supplies could reach us; but between Segeberg and Neuenmünster we travelled along a road where Wallmoden's corps had passed before us, and then we experienced misery. Under steady rainfall, often with sleet, the roads were so churned-up that we waded in mud and walked like toads. Fallen horses, broken-down supply and ammunition carts, worn-out footwear and clothing were strewn on and beside the road. Houses were burnt or wrecked, for everything that could burn had been removed, and since the remaining building materials consisted of clay and straw, walls and roofs collapsed as they lost their support. Of course, the occasional stone building remained standing, but doors, windows and all the wood were gone, and many windowpanes broken with bayonets, being a pleasant pastime for the Germans. I was reminded of the Swedish proverb and saying, 'He who shall truly torment a peasant must be a peasant.'

Wallmoden had under his command the so-called Russian-German legion (Germans in Russian service).[6] These were the worst perpetrators against their countrymen and excelled in misdemeanour. Even our normally good-natured Mecklenburgers did not hold back. In the vicinity of Segeberg I shared quarters with one of their officers. The house was intact, but the occupants had fled and only an old woman remained, who sought to give us all possible comfort, but despite this he intended to search and plunder the property. I took issue with him that he should be ashamed of such an act and assured him that nothing like that would happen with Swedish troops; and that since I happened to have a few more men than he, I would surely prevent this action which would have dishonoured us both.

Not far over the border we passed a dairy, where a woman stood crying, and the yard was full of soldiers. When asked, she replied that they were wrecking the house.

---

5   *Generallöjtnant* David Henrik Stierncrona (1786–1845) had commenced military service as a cornet in 1805. In 1813 he was a *major* in the Skåne Carabineer Regiment and recipient of the gold medal for valour in the field. He was appointed as regimental commander and *överste* in 1817. In 1819 he was promoted to *generaladjutant* on the general staff and ultimately attained the rank of *generallöjtnant* in 1843.

6   The Russian-German Legion was recruited in the summer of 1812 from native Germans opposed to French hegemony and included prisoners and deserters from Napoleon's Grand Armée. In the 1813 campaign it numbered around 9,000 men and amongst its ranks was the military theorist, Carl von Clausewitz. From July 1813 the Legion had been financed and re-equipped by Britain.

I went in and found the soldiers occupied with the milk bowls, some drinking, some skimming cream with their hands. I would have gladly treated them to the milk, but through their ill-discipline they wasted more than they consumed; moreover, we were ordered to respect individual property except in the direst emergency. At my exhortation 'Get out of here!' those who belonged to our regiment obeyed well enough, but those from other regiments did not respond in this manner and likely thought, 'that loudmouth neither knows us nor will he be able to find us.' Just then, a Captain Boraen of the Kalmar Regiment arrived, the happiest soul there was. He immediately spotted one of his own company in the crowd with a milk bowl, drew his sword and said, 'so, Pol, you drink milk too, do you? Wait and we will get you a little ginger to add to it.' But Pol, who knew and did not like the spice, jumped out of a window, and as Boraen was about to intercept with him in the yard, he slipped and fell backwards in the mud, whereupon, with sword held aloft, Boraen exclaimed, 'I will find you enough to fill your dog's belly!' By then a crowd had gathered, and everyone laughed heartily, the cheerful Boraen most of all.

During the day's march, a young pig was spotted which had escaped the Germans and now stood in a field. The jägers, who thought that a little pork would be a treat, sought and obtained permission to appropriate it. A few of the men removed their packs and headed off towards it, but the animal had probably been chased before, so it could not be caught. Instead, we permitted it to be shot, with the proviso that the men took turns in carrying it to our overnight halt. This went well enough at first, but by the evening, when they were tired, they would have discarded the animal had they not been prevented from doing so by word of command. The pork tasted good, even without mustard.

The abysmal roads did not allow for long day marches, however hard we strived. For provisions to reach us was near impossible, so in the evenings each company received a cow that was slaughtered, butchered and cooked in the field cauldrons, as well as our sparse fuel supply would allow.[7] Eating meat without bread or vegetables, and often without salt, is all very well, but you do not eat more than is necessary to satisfy the worst of your hunger. Usually, I took some tongue but did not eat much of it. The officers drank a little of the broth, but the soldiers, who ate their soup thick with flour and grits, snivelled at this. One might occasionally stumble across a forgotten goose, which by avoiding attention had become so wild that it had to be shot in flight, but when cooked it turned out worse than the beef. Smålanders are resourceful however and they secured some variety in their diet. Beekeeping flourished in Holstein, and since bees were now dormant, beehives were looted, the bees picked off, and canteens filled with honey to provide a delicious dessert to accompany the unseasoned beef. Of course, one or two bees occasionally slipped through, and the gourmand got stung so that his tongue hung like a sock out of his mouth, but this only gave rise to laughter and raillery.

---

7   Based on a full-strength infantry company of 150 men and a typical yield of 350–450 pounds of meat from a cow this would equate to 2.3–3 pounds per man. In the contemporary British Army 3 pounds of beef was considered a complete substitute daily ration, see R.W. Adye, *The Little Bombardier and Pocket Gunner* (London: W. Blackader, 2nd edition, 1802), p.225.

Arriving in Neuenmünster we found the town abandoned and looted, and we lodged in empty houses, cursing the Germans who could not leave a single window intact, for now the winter cold began and although it only rarely dropped below four degrees, it bit sharply on the open plains. This was the last time during the Christmas period that we were housed beneath a roof; from then on, we had to bivouac in the open.

Soldiering in dry weather is passable: you dance, you lark about and develop many inventive ways to keep the body warm and the mind alive; but when one is soaked, frozen, bitter and downcast, with no dry clothing available or opportunity to change, but must endeavour to rest in wet clothes, then one discovers what a man is capable of and whether he can get by without his dear mother. True, army officers today are better educated, more knowledgeable, more strategically minded, but they are brought up in nightgowns, smoking caps, fur coats and lined boots. They may be able to fight better than we did, but a winter campaign can easily make any man ill and hospitalise him when he is needed most.

We acquired overcoats for ourselves, because uniform coats were not available and could not readily have been carried, unless you were willing to be the packmule yourself. In each company, one man was assigned to look after the baggage cart, which was sufficiently loaded with knapsacks for three officers and four non-commissioned officers together with their associated seven shako-boxes, field kettles, axes, shovels, etc., so that the horse could barely endure, so whilst not devoted entirely to the officers, they encouraged the baggage-driver both verbally and physically to purloin grain and hay to maintain body and strength of such an important member of the company. They never seemed to tire. However, for ammunition wagons and carts, farm horses were taken, and used for as long as they could. Their poor owners would accompany them for as long as possible in the hope of regaining them, but they were often disappointed and had to abandon their emaciated and weakened animals to their fate.[8]

From Neuenmünster we trudged off as best we could and after a couple of days we were in the vicinity of Rendsburg, when we unexpectedly heard ahead of us the roaring of cannon and rattling of musketry. We understood that Wallmoden sought to prevent the remaining Danes from Bornhöft from ensconcing themselves in the fortress. Papa Vegesack rode to the fore, calling out 'step up the pace lads, and we'll hit them' but we arrived too late.[9] From a hill barely a cannon-shot from the battlefield, we saw two squadrons of our Mecklenburg mounted jägers force a defile which the Danish infantry defended from behind hawthorn hedges. They advanced with great loss, but a battalion of the Russian-German legion, who were

---

8   The Armémuseum's *Between the Imperial Eagles* notes that per the 1807 regulations each company should have a one-horse pack cart which should carry six shovels, six axes, six cooking pots, a scythe, a tent for company officers and a tent for muskets, plus the company officers' valises. One man from the company was appointed as driver. Commandeered horses would generally be accompanied by and remained in the care of their owners.
9   Vegesack's Swedish infantry had arrived just too late to intervene in the Battle of Sehestedt, 10 December 1813. The Danes under Prince Fredrik of Hesse numbered around 10,000 men as did Wallmoden's corps, which came off much the worst in the encounter, and enabled the Danes to reach the security of Rendsburg fortress.

Napoleonic one-horse pack cart. Sketch by Pehr Eberhard Cogell (1734–1815). (Nationalmuseum)

supporting them, took flight at the Danes' first salvos and abandoned our determined Mecklenburgers, so that most were cut down and the remainder taken prisoner. One of the Mecklenburg princes, a pleasant and amiable youngster, who, as a captain, led one squadron, was badly injured, including losing two fingers on his right hand, and became a prisoner but, as a relative of the Danish royal house, was immediately released.[10] However, we were glad to see the treacherous Russian-Germans pay the price, for the Danish cavalry chased after them and they were deservedly beaten. As we advanced, we saw their officers sitting on tussocks and rocks with defeat written across their faces. We comforted them that the Crown Prince would soon follow and hang the cowardly knaves who had so readily deserted their comrades.[11] We were so much more embittered at their shameful behaviour since we always had the Mecklenburgers in our division and we knew almost every officer and especially the fair prince. This brigade, the best equipped one could wish to see, consisted of volunteers who equipped themselves, and it was said that a non-commissioned officer owned a horse for which our Crown Prince offered 100 Louis d'or.[12]

However, the Danes fell back into Rendsburg, which was then diligently encircled by Vegesack's and Wallmoden's divisions. Our brigade was placed near

---

10 Gustav Wilhelm von Mecklenburg (1781–1851) who was the second son of Frederick Francis I, Grand Duke of Mecklenburg-Schwerin.
11 Hultin's judgement on his allies' performance may be a little harsh; accounts of the battle indicate that Wallmoden had ordered the Mecklenburg mounted jägers forward to cover the retreat of his surviving infantry *after* the Danish cavalry attack had cut many of them down when they failed to form squares in time.
12 The Louis d'or was a pre-revolutionary French gold coin.

the village of Bovenau, which was deserted and had been plundered. Any leftover wood that could be broken loose and any plain furniture that was found, including a broken pianoforte and some items of mahogany, probably from the parsonage, was used to feed our campfires and cook our meat. Among other things, we found a small backgammon set in the form of a box which was saved and then followed us throughout the campaign all the way back to Sweden, and you could always hear it rattling during bivouacs and rests, but it was played with two dice, for there was a longstanding agreement that gambling should never be allowed between comrades.[13]

We now camped on the plains for five days. Six-inch deep snow covered the ground, and the temperature was four or five degrees below zero. Fortunately, there was plenty of straw in the plundered village, as the houses were covered with it. The straw was carried out, the men bedded on the snow, and those who had warm bodies and calm minds, got to sleep the sleep of the righteous for half an hour, after which they would have to get up to dance, run and leapfrog about until they had warmed up. Most pitiful was our eminent brigade and regimental commander, who for all his great ability was, however, an incarnate cabinet-chamberlain,[14] who breathed a great deal into court atmosphere, but was now lying on a bundle of straw and appeared to be of little worth. We covered him well with as many soldier's coats as we could spare, but it was of little help, he still had to go up to the fire from time to time to be roasted on one side and frozen on the other. I do not know what he ate; he could not be living on meat, for he was as thin as a rake. One or two of our young gentlemen one would also consider pitiable, but they danced with the others until they forgot about the comforts of home.

The soldiers suffered badly and since they, quite rightly, regarded their officer as an older brother who should have advice and remedies for everything, I often heard their lamentations and, for that reason, have to go back a bit in my simple story. During the time that we were faring well in Mecklenburg, one fine day a deputation came to me and complained about their host, who served them buttermilk. Of course, fresh milk was generally not much used, but I, who knew my jägers' tastes and knew that an oat cake and a tub of sour milk was a festive dish for them back home, put them to shame and foretold that they could do worse. As they now complained about their beef and honey *ambrosia*,[15] I could not help but ask if they 'would not now lick their lips for some Mecklenburg buttermilk?' at which they walked off muttering to their comrades, 'He still tastes that buttermilk in his throat.'

---

13 Playing backgammon with two dice means that the doubling cube which denotes the stake is not in use.
14 A *kabinettskammarherre* was a serving royal chamberlain at the court who personally watched over the king.
15 Hultin uses the phrase '*den lösa maten*' (lit. loose food) which is a reference from the 1858 comic opera *Orpheus in the Underworld*, a Swedish version of which was published in 1861. Quoting from the US English edition of 1868, in Act 2 Scene 5, the gods complain to Jupiter, the king of the gods: Diana: No more nectar! Cupid: That beverage sickens my stomach! Venus: No ambrosia! Let these victuals be no more served to us. Pluto: A revolution among the gods! In the Swedish version, Pluto refers to nectar and ambrosia as '*den lösa maten*'.

We had in the brigade an unusual man, who had joined in the present sport in a unique way. This was Colonel von Platen of Silenz,[16] who was over 70 years old. In his youth he had served under Old Fritz in Prussia,[17] and then as a major in one of our German regiments, from which he resigned many years ago, and then settled peacefully in his estate in Pomerania. Two of his sons in Prussian service had fallen during the War of Liberation and had been buried in the family grave; but during the French invasion, soldiers had broken in and looted and violated the corpses, which so enraged the old man that he applied for a position and was appointed commander of a battalion of the von Engelbrechten Regiment, which he led with acclaim during the war. This esteemed veteran was our meeting point. As soon as the old man sat down, he was surrounded by a crowd who listened to his advice and laughed at his anecdotes and stories, of which he had an inexhaustible supply, often so ridiculous that Cato himself would have laughed.[18]

I would like to quote a couple of them, although they lose a lot in transcription, lacking the old man's mimicry and half German, half Swedish language.

Three students, who were venturing into Berlin, wanted to have a little fun with the guard. To the officer's question, who they were, the first replied, 'I am von Goethe,' the second, 'I am von Schiller,' and the third, 'I am von Wieland.' The officer, who appeared flattered to be making acquaintance with persons of such high renown, exclaimed happily, 'Welcome gentlemen, please be so kind as to step into the guard-room,' and added, as he produced a fine hazel cane, 'This is Herr von Klopstock who has been waiting for you for a long time!'

Some young men in Berlin had a friend named von Viereck (meaning square but literally four corners), living outside the city who, on penalty of a forfeit of several bottles of champagne, promised to meet at a specified time at a particular inn. They figured out a plan to get their friend to pay the fine. Three of them went out of town, hired horses, and one by one returned to the guard at the Brandenburg Gate. To the guard's question, the first answered, 'My name is von Eineck' (lit. one corner) and was allowed to pass; the second, 'I'm von Zweieck' (two corners) and was also allowed to pass; when the third declared himself to be von Dreieck (three corners), the officer became a little suspicious and mumbled, 'Eineck, Zweieck, Dreieck, that's odd,' but he too was allowed to pass; finally the properly-named Herr von Viereck arrived, at which the officer realised that he was being made a fool of and put him under arrest. Observing this from a distance, his friends waited until the clock struck the appointed hour, then went to the guard, confirmed Herr von Viereck's identity, revealed their plan, and invited the officer to join them in drinking the champagne.

---

16 Von Platen was an extensive noble family from Rügen and Pomerania. Silenz is an estate in the present-day municipality of Kluis on Rügen.
17 'Old Fritz' meaning Frederick the Great.
18 Another indication of Hultin's classical education, a reference to the Roman republican senator Cato the Younger (95–46 BCE), a follower of the Stoic philosophy, who features in Dante's *Divine Comedy* as the guardian of purgatory and was celebrated as a martyr to republican causes as depicted in Joseph Addison's 1713 play, *Cato, a Tragedy*.

Rendsburg fortress viewed from the north, prior to its demolition 1854–1862 and essentially as it appeared in 1813. Lithograph by Anton Ludwig Meinung, circa 1862. (Royal Library, Denmark)

A saying originated from old von Platen, which was much used in the army, and for which I must mention the reason. During the siege of Glückstadt, the old man sat down by a campfire one evening, surrounded by his usual circle of listeners. The soldiers collected all available materials for maintenance of the fire, and stood attentively, listening agape, and although they did not understand all of the old man's lingo, they nevertheless joined in the bursts of laughter. Cannonballs, which the fortress fired across daily, were collected and put on the fire, for they retained the heat. By chance, a live shell had been brought, so that having been placed, it exploded. Fire, flames, and smoke erupted, most everyone sprang up and ran away, imagining their ultimate demise. But the old man sat still, looked around and said calmly, 'Children, children, what are you doing?' and this then became a saying, which was often repeated, when something went wrong. Fortunately, no one was injured.

Rendsburg was a strong fortress, which at first proved stubborn, but seemed less so as the cold increased. The general's adjutants, von Düben and Vegesack, departed as negotiators to summon the fortress. It was said that they were treated inappropriately, and this seems likely, for the Danish officers of that time considered themselves superior. However, the adjutants were observant and noticed that the defensive ditches were ice-covered and would soon be practicable to cross, so that when they received audience with the commander (the Prince of Hesse) they drew his attention to it, and also suggested that it would not be good for them to make an enemy of Papa Vegesack, which had the consequence that they received a letter requesting a truce; a good sign, for he who negotiates is usually ready to capitulate.[19]

---

19 Following Bornhöft, Prince Fredrik of Hesse (commander of the Danish Auxiliary Corps in Holstein) requested a two-week truce which was concluded on 15 December, but it excluded

This negotiation had the happy consequence that we had to leave our plundered village and take quarters in Kiel, where no troops had yet been, and where we felt so good that when I toured our quarters on the first evening, I came across some jägers sat around a table replete with coffee pots, tobacco and clay pipes, peeling and eating apples. I myself was accommodated with a rich wholesaler and ate at table dishes other than soft-boiled cow tongue and honey with grilled bees!

On old runic calendars you see the drinking horns upright and full as long as Christmas lasts, but when it is over, the horn is turned upside down and empty.[20] So it was now with our halcyon days in Kiel, they were not many, and we barely had time to get used to a civilised diet and real warmth, when marching orders arrived. We were no longer needed in the vicinity of Rendsburg, but Glückstadt was a serious nuisance that required our attention.

The siege corps was commanded by General Boije, who probably deserved his own ballad, if only it could be sung to a pleasant enough melody.[21] He was the jolliest, most decent, and agreeable of our generals. He gambled, drank, hunted, danced, courted, etc., all with immense pleasure and had only the fault of having holes in his pockets – for coins never stayed in them. It was said that after Glückstadt's capture, he received, in addition to a lieutenant general's commission, 5,000 ducats from the Crown Prince, but it was also alleged that by the following week he was gambling on credit. He, like Vegesack, had certainly not had much opportunity to excel on the battlefield but from his quickness, his resourcefulness, his generalship at Glückstadt, one could conclude that only opportunity was lacking, and that he could be gainfully employed anywhere. But this excellent general ended up bankrupt. Karl Johan tried to help, but it did not work; the victor at Glückstadt had to expatriate, lived for a time in Hamburg, then in Finland, and would often have suffered distress if his old comrade, Baron J.C. Adelswärd of Åtvid, had not supported him.[22] In Norway, where he was my brigade commander, I often had the pleasure of being in the company of this excellent general on the hunt, and I will never forget his cheerfulness bordering on levity.

With regret we left Kiel and approached Glückstadt. Anyone who had a sense and ear for the music of cannon fire could dance to it here. Our batteries played the principal part, the heavy cannon of the fortress the second, two English frigates with their 36-pounders the bass, an English rocket battery whined the alto and the

---

the fortresses of Glückstadt and Fredriksort which then became Karl Johan's priority. Meanwhile, peace talks continued at Karl Johan's headquarters in Kiel, and the truce was extended until 6 January.

20 Runic perpetual calendars were very common and had been in use in Scandinavia since the Middle Ages. They took the form of a staff with two lines of runic characters together with symbols (which Hultin describes) representing special days such as Christian holidays, equinoxes, and the like. Adoption of the Gregorian calendar in 1753 rendered existing staffs redundant.

21 *Generalmajor* Gustaf Reinhold Boije's brigade reached Glückstadt on 18 December 1813. He was subsequently heavily reinforced by Russian, Prussian and Hanoverian allies and was also supported by the British navy and a Royal Artillery Congreve rocket battery; the Danish garrison capitulated on 5 January 1814.

22 Baron Johan Carl Adelswärd (1776–1852), then Cabinet Chamberlain (*Kabinettskammarherre*) to Charles XIII.

Glückstadt Fortress, 1813. (Royal Library, Denmark)

occasional skirmisher shot snapped along to the beat; all this without pauses, so that from a distance one imagined they were hearing a drumroll. I could not collect any laurels or anecdotes here, for I was not destined to remain for long; however, I want to mention a remarkable cannon shot. We had a patrol route over a footbridge within cannon range of the fortress, so that during the day it was not a good position to be in, but every night a reconnaissance patrol crossed the bridge to observe if the enemy might be preparing for a sortie. One night a squad set off from the Kalmar Regiment. On the footbridge, which was narrow, they had to proceed in single file and they were in the middle of it when a cannon was fired from the fortress. The officer, small in stature, was leading and the ball went over him without causing injury; the corporal, who was second in line, had his hat knocked off; the next man lost half his head and the following man was completely decapitated; the shot then proceeded to strike the neck, chest, abdomen, thighs and legs of those behind, so that eight men were killed by the same ball, all from the same company and almost all from the same parish. The fortress probably knew about the patrol route and had aimed the cannon at the bridge during the day and fired when they heard the enemy's approach at night.

I had now to leave the fortress unconquered and part with comrades and friends.

13

Lübeck (January–February 1814)

Hultin only spent a short time at the siege of Glückstadt, having been given an assignment which took him and a select few men from the regiment back to Lübeck, a city which he had earlier lamented not having time to get to know. Whilst there, on 14 January 1814 the Treaty of Kiel was signed which ended hostilities between Denmark-Norway and Sweden and Great Britain. Amongst its terms were that Norway was to be ceded to Sweden Demark would receive Swedish Pomerania in compensation (together with the return of captured territory), and that Denmark should provide a force of 10,000 men to support the Allies in return for a £40,000 subsidy from Britain.

The regiment had a large number of *sans-culottes*,[1] who were not presentable to Napoleon, whom we now intended to face in decent attire. Setting up a workshop in enemy territory was not possible, because tailors need heat, light, irons, and snuff.[2] Therefore, I was ordered to leave with one non-commissioned officer and 16 men of the regiment, selecting the best artisans, to travel to Lübeck to have 300 pairs of trousers made ready for the regiment's arrival. Feeling dejected, I set off with my caravan on Holstein haywains and comforted myself by occasionally singing:

'It pleases me down to the ground,
that sixteen tailors weigh a pound …'[3]

The roads were now incomparably better, we rode quite comfortably on the straw in our wagons, tall as siege engines in the Old Testament, and after a few days we entered, without military honours, old Lübeck, where I reported to the commander, Colonel Holst (a Norwegian), was given accommodation for my tailors and a larger room for our workshop. I myself was accommodated with a merchant named Stanau

---

1 A term borrowed from revolutionary France, meaning the poorer/lower classes of society but perhaps also here reflecting its literal meaning without trousers/breeches.
2 The British Government *Report on The Sanitary Condition of the Labouring Population* (London: Clowes & Sons, 1842), p.100, notes that in the tailoring profession, snuff was much used as a stimulant, and a substitute for smoking, and that men believed it had a beneficial effect on their eyesight.
3 The Swedish Music archive (*Musikverket*, <musikverket.se>) records this to be a dance-song (*dansvisa*) from Ursult, Kronoberg County, Småland. It appears to have been a popular four-line ditty, still known today, and can be sung as a round.

on Fleischhauerstrasse, No.8, where I then lived for almost two months. I arrived late in the evening to find that my hosts had already retired, but food was served in my room. I have always had and still maintain the habit of not being able to fall asleep without some reading, so I asked the maid if my hosts were asleep yet, which she thought not. I therefore begged her to fetch me something to read, in any language and on any subject, except religion. She returned and placed two books on the table, I opened them and could hardly believe my eyes when I saw *Fredman's Epistles* and *My Son on the Galley*.[4] The occurrence was easily explained when I met my host the following day to find that he spoke Swedish as well as I did. As a young man, he had lived in Sweden for several years and made annual trips there in connection with the timber trade.

After I got the tailoring workshop up and running and solemnly installed the non-commissioned officer as elder of the guild, I had plenty of time to stroll and see the sights of the

A Swedish infantryman on campaign in 1814. Contemporary watercolour by Carl Johan Ljunggren (1790–1852). (Nationalmuseum)

remarkable old town; but to describe it would be pointless since so many better pens than mine have already done so. All told, I had fun, lived well, ate well, had a young and pleasant hostess, and one cannot ask for more. The town was full of officers who had been wounded, some at Rosslau, where Sandels fought for the sake of it,[5] and others from other lesser actions, so that company and gaming were not

---

4   *Fredman's Epistles* was a collection of songs Carl Michael Bellman first published in 1790. Bellman (1740–1795) was and remains a hugely influential Swedish composer, musician, songwriter and poet. See earlier footnote at the end of Chapter 11 regarding *My Son on the Galley*.
5   The action at Rosslau took place on 29 September 1813. Sandel's entrenched force of circa 4,200 repulsed *Maréchal* Ney's 7,000 men attempting to drive the Swedes from their

lacking. Dances with good music were held and attended twice a week, where our liberals could find their utopia, for greater equality is not to be seen in humanity. In the large, well-lit hall, the waltz was danced and if you stood in the middle, so you could see pass by, as if in a shadow play, a blond Swede, a bearded Russian, an oafish Englishman, a half-drunk, arrogant Prussian, a stiff, white-coated Austrian, a red-coated Hanoverian, a handsome Cossack, a meandering sailor, a tall grenadier, a short jäger, an upright musketeer, a flamboyant hussar, a 15-stone cuirassier, a guards officer, a knight with two chivalric orders and a commander's sash, a well-fed commissary, an old and doddery captain, a swaggering ensign, a drummer, a musical director, all with their hats on, many with their swords and clay pipes (cigars were not then known). Ladies were plentiful and at least outwardly were beautiful, although they had big feet typical of the German. Had flat-nosed Tartars and trouser-less Bashkirs also been present, and not as Muslims considering dance to be disgraceful to man, one would have had a cross section of the entire Allied army. The entrance fee was not ruinous, only four shillings, and anyone who showed his ticket at the counter in the restaurant also received a drink and a sandwich into the bargain. The musicians would play waltzes for half an hour, then break for a quarter of an hour, when one would find our courteous cavaliers accompanying their winsome, sweaty ladies to the bar to cool off with a dram, a sandwich and a couple of glasses of beer, without arousing attention. The house rules stipulated that for each waltz that was danced you should pay a half shilling and the musicians went around during the breaks with plates and reminders but usually reaped a poor harvest.

In general, good neighbourliness prevailed and fights were rare and only occurred on the stairs and in the entrance hall. Unexpectedly, I was once involved in such an affray when I was about to enter the ball in the company of an officer from the Uppland Regiment. We heard squabbling and swearing in German and Swedish, then saw one of our hussars walking backwards whilst taking heavy blows from a swarm of Hanoverian hussars who pursued and manhandled him. He fought back, swearing, but descended into the entrance hall, where we had side-stepped into a corner, and exclaimed, 'If I dared to draw my sword, I would probably whip these red dogs!' My comrade, who was a lively youth and always keen for adventure, then said, 'so draw your sword, comrade, and defend yourself.' The hussar looked towards the nook where we were standing, and cried out, 'There speaks a Swedish officer!' Immediately swords clashed, and I took my comrade by the arm, reproaching him for his recklessness, since we might be held responsible for the consequences. The next day we were indeed called to the commanding officer's inquiry, which was held at the hospital, where the man, badly cut, had been treated, but he had next to him three Hanoverians whom he had served even worse. The fellow was acquitted, but my friend was sentenced to 24 hours confinement for his friendly advice.

One day the local newspaper advertised a ball at the theatre-house, but we would discover that the Germans were somewhat lax in describing a forthcoming event.

---

bridgehead over the Elbe, but then counterattacked contrary to the Crown Prince's orders. The Swedes lost some 350 killed and wounded; the French two to four times as many. The fighting had minimal strategic impact on the campaign.

As the entrance cost was one riksdaler without a brandy and sandwich, we were expecting something special, but we had been duped. Those of us who were going to attend donned our parade dress uniforms as usual; but when we arrived to see the city's gentlemen in overcoats and frock coats, we immediately retraced our steps, put on our own uniform frock coats and thereafter danced soberly; for if one tasted their punch, one was tempted to exclaim, as the Disciples of the Prophet, 'There is death in the pot!'[6] Nevertheless, no disreputable ladies[7] were allowed to enter, whilst the most beautiful were the daughters of the bourgeois (and, perchance, the higher echelons) of the Free Imperial City.[8]

The Germans did not value their women for a variety of reasons. The constant contact with foreign soldiers, especially with the debonair French, had so depraved high and low born, rich and poor, married and unmarried, beautiful and ugly, that to find an honourable woman was an exception. For the most part, they were pretty but somewhat foolish.

We often attended plays and they deserved to be seen, for members of Schröder's troupe from Hamburg performed with an artistry which showed that they were trained by this German Garrick.[9] As foreigners we had great freedom, because if one bought a parterre ticket one could go anywhere,[10] even the theatre boxes, where there was room and one might hope to strike it lucky. Many matches were settled here, for better or worse; for example, one poverty-stricken lieutenant got engaged and after the war married a filthy-rich wholesaler's daughter after an acquaintance in a theatre box.

A Scottish infantry regiment was garrisoned in the city,[11] unusually handsome fellows, whose recruits and appearance aroused astonishment, *non plus ultra*;[12] but how these sons of the free and proud Albion could submit to the iron-fisted discipline that prevailed among them was wondrous. Roll calls were held four times a day, when each man was inspected from head to toe, everything scrutinised and the slightest disorder brought, not as with us a couple of strokes of the cane, but prolonged confinement. For major infringements, the cat o' nine tails danced, a

---

6   2 Kings 4:40: 'so they poured out for the men to eat. And it came to pass, as they were eating of the pottage, that they cried out, and said, O thou man of God, there is death in the pot. And they could not eat thereof.'
7   Hultin uses the term *kameliadamer*, a reference to the novel *La Dame aux Camélias* published in 1848 by Alexandre Dumas *fils* (son of the author of The Three Musketeers) about a love affair between a bourgeois and a courtesan.
8   Lübeck's more formal designation, the Free Imperial City of Lübeck
9   A reference to the famous English actor, dramatist and manager and director of the Drury Lane Theatre, David Garrick (1717–1779), whose influence spread across Europe during the eighteenth century.
10 The *parterre* means the area accommodating a standing audience, a parterre ticket typically being the cheapest available, and therefore mostly attracting the lower social classes.
11 Most likely the 4th Battalion of the 1st (Royal Scots) Regiment of Foot which had embarked for Stralsund on 2 August 1813 and in mid-December advanced to support the Crown Prince on the Elbe. The battalion halted at Lübeck on 24 December and remained there until 17 January 1814 when it was ordered to join the British force under Sir Thomas Graham in the Netherlands.
12 Literally 'nothing further beyond'; the ultimate, the peak of perfection. High praise indeed!

whip with nine strands and three knots on each strand, from which up to 48 lashes could be applied to the bare back, perfectly corresponding to our now fortunately abolished 40 *par spö*.[13] I became acquainted with some of their officers and had the opportunity to see the contrast that prevailed within these man-machines. In everyday life they were quiet, sluggish, distracted and suffered with boredom, but when they had opportunity to celebrate, they became so hilarious and wild as to be almost life-threatening. The first sign would be throwing of plates and dishes out of the windows, and when the rum punch (always with plenty of lemons and nutmeg) was finished, the bowls would follow, perhaps accompanied by one or two pieces of furniture. If the landlord came in and protested, they would retort, 'Get out, the room is ours, we have hired it, just give us the bill and we will pay!' They usually remained overnight where they lay upon this field of battle like the Viking berserkers of old and awoke full of remorse.

I had to witness an unpleasant execution here. A regiment of French defectors and prisoners of war had been raised, called the Royal Suédois.[14] Lavater would have found among them the archetypes of all southern villainous physiognomies,[15] for there were French, Italians, Spaniards, Portuguese, Germans, and even Corsicans, mostly of a character that one would rather treat them as enemies than as friends. Of these, a Spanish non-commissioned officer and several men had committed insubordination and openly incited mutiny. They were put on trial, as our articles-of-war dictate. Three were sentenced to death, and after a brief conversation with a Catholic priest, they were shot in front of the town hall wall, but this was so poorly carried out that one remained alive until a jäger blew out his brains with a fresh shot. It was awful, but that is the nature of war.

Occasionally we received news from the army in Holstein. Glückstadt had been taken, but now the victors rested on their laurels. Our diplomats hankered after Norway, a matter which would stick in their throats, for our two-timing allies seemed to have forgotten their promises to our master, as they were now secure and free from restraint.[16] However, we did receive a pleasant and cheering announcement. Our beloved prince, who understood what a soldier desired, who did not forget that we had suffered during the siege and wanted to put dressings upon our wounds, rewarded us with double wages for the month of February.

---

13 The Swedish corporal punishment *40 par spö* (lit. 40 pairs of rods) was abolished in 1855; 40 strokes were inflicted on the bare back using a pair of rods typically about 0.8–1 metres in length and made from willow. Usually after every three strokes the rods were replaced with new ones.
14 The Royal Suédois Regiment was raised in Pomerania in the autumn of 1813; it served in the Norwegian campaign and was disbanded in December 1814. Not to be confused with the more famous 'Régiment de Royal Suédois' which served in the French army having been formed from Swedish prisoners of war in 1690 and which was disbanded in 1791.
15 A reference to Johann Kaspar Lavater (1741–1801) best known for his work in the field of physiognomy i.e., how a person's facial features or expression may relate to his ethnicity or character.
16 British and Russian support for Sweden's annexation of Norway was the condition under which the Crown Prince had committed Swedish forces to the Allies 1813 campaign.

The Royal Suédois and jägers of the Life Regiment Grenadier Corps during the 1813–1814 campaign. (Illustration from Ljunggren, Carl Johan, *Minnes-Anteckningar under 1813 och 1814 Årens Kampagner, uti Tyskland och Norge* (Stockholm: Adolf Bonnier, 1855)). (Armémuseum)

A number of ships were frozen in the Holstein ports, and were declared prize goods, to our benefit. Karl Johan could follow his magnanimous inclination, for he had no miserly state treasury to 15 times turn and thumb every penny at the regent's disposal. No objections were raised, and we made fitting use of the proceeds.

* * *

Since a truce had now been concluded,[17] the higher command had nothing to do in Holstein, so many headed to Lübeck, where they could better look after, groom and brush themselves, and General Brändström was among the first.[18] This general, commonly called 'Peder Brännare' (Peter the Firebrand), an honest, able and good man, found great pleasure in dealing with ignorance, especially amongst his friends, but in such a good-natured and humorous way that no one took offence, despite being delivered in rather forthright language. During a major field exercise outside Wismar, he had a laughable affair with his adjutant, Ensign Fredensköld, a brisk lad and, ordinarily, his golden boy.[19] He was dispatched to one of the wings with a movement order. Whether Fredensköld or the battalion commanders themselves

---

17 The Treaty of Kiel.
18 Baron Pehr Brändström (1771–1833) had commenced military service in 1788. In 1813 he was a *generalmajor* and *överste* of the Västmanland Regiment and had recently taken part in the battles at Großbeeren, Dennewitz and Leipzig.
19 Anders Vilhelm Fredensköld (1792–1841) had joined the Västmanland Regiment as a *fänrik* in September 1812 after graduating from the Karlberg Military Academy.

had misunderstood the General's order, a confusion arose, which it was feared that the Prince would observe. Peder Brännare rode across, and as soon as he met Fredensköld, he began to swear as an introduction to a diatribe to suit the occasion, but the adjutant did not wait to hear it and instead turned his horse about and fled. The General dug in his spurs to catch his fleeing adjutant, shouting and swearing; but Fredensköld, who had a good horse and feigned deafness, got clean away after a long chase. The whole brigade, who witnessed this sporting hunt, laughed; whilst the General, returning, laughed the most and was in a brilliant mood the whole evening. On reaching the city, the adjutant left his sword on the General's table and retired to his room but suffered neither arrest nor reprimand.

Baron Pehr Brändström (1771–1833). Miniature by Jacob Axel Gillberg (1769–1845). (Nationalmuseum)

We had another general, later His Excellency, C.H. Posse, who was notorious for his scolding, but in a completely different manner, for it bit to the bone. Nevertheless, he had the good quality of keeping in with his regimental and battalion commanders, whose training he frequently honed very well, but he left the nurturing of their company officers up to them. I had a kind of kinship with this excellent general. During the war in Finland in 1788–1790, he commanded the same company with which I subsequently served for 14 years. At Savitaipal he made a brilliant bayonet attack with this company but was captured. Gustav III had his portmanteau sent with an envoy to the enemy in which he personally placed the Royal Order of the Sword upon his tailcoat, which was on top – one can by such action recognise *The Enchanting King*.[20]

The man who packed and carried that bag, whose name was Ljung, still served during the first few years that I was with the company, employed as a steward, water carrier, etc., and in such a way that he never appeared in the ranks more often than necessary, as in musters and the like. At camps in Skåne and elsewhere, where he was to meet General Posse, my man, Ljung, had to put on uniform and was dressed, scrubbed, combed, washed, and brushed under the watchful eye of the officers, in order to appear properly dressed for his old company commander. When his

---

20 'The Enchanting King' (*Tjusarkungen*) was a nickname for Gustav III.

comrades asked what was going on, he would answer gravely, 'I am going to visit General Posse.' The adjutants would recount the tale of a meeting of the old comrades. Ljung came in, stood to attention, so that the floor trembled, after which he exclaimed, 'God save the General!' and was greeted in return, 'Oh, you old pimp, have you not drunk yourself to death yet?' 'No,' replied Ljung, 'it is not today as it was back in our time, and I have a captain who is much more irascible than the General.' 'Here, take this,' said the General, handing Ljung some money (usually a tenner), 'so

Carl Henrik Posse of Säby (1767–1843). Miniature by Giovanni Domenico Bossi (1767–1853). (Nationalmuseum)

that you can offer your captain a drink, he should then be more amenable.' 'God save the gracious General!' And so Ljung trudged home, took off his dress uniform and exhibited his reward. When he was congratulated by his comrades, he replied, 'It is not too much, for it was I who delivered him his Order of the Sword.' Poor Ljung, he died as a minor church official in Färgaryd, but was buried with military honours.

For further characterization of General Posse, I must anticipate the future. When the Småland brigade with 60 sharpshooters went to Norway in 1821 to peaceably put a stop to the Norwegian veto, General Posse was in command.[21] He quarrelled with and hectored one of the senior Norwegian commanders, which Karl Johan, who courted the Norwegians to some degree, came to hear about, and therefore ordered him to apologise. He swore but had to obey, so he approached the Norwegian, kept his hat on and announced in his harshest tone, 'The king has ordered me hither, for otherwise I'll be damned if I would have come.'

As I said before, we had a unit of von Schill's hussars in our division. They were in Prussian service and comprised a disorderly rabble which plundered friend and foe alike. Many of my readers will probably know that during Prussia's earlier war with Napoleon, whilst peace talks were taking place to which Major Ferdinand von Schill was opposed, he revolted with his hussar regiment and supporters from other units, which the French chased to the north. They fought as long as they could, but were finally trapped in Stralsund, which was stormed. Schill was cut down, his officers

---

21 Karl Johan was proposing significant constitutional amendments to the Swedish-Norwegian union and put pressure on the Storting (the Norwegian parliament) to accede by arranging military manoeuvres close to the capital while it was in session.

The death of *Major* Ferdinand von Schill in Stralsund, 1809. (Illustration from *Die Gartenlaube Illustrirtes Familienblatt* (Leipzig: Ernst Kiel,1860))

put on trial by French courts-martial and shot. All of Germany canonised Schill and regarded him and his companions as martyrs.[22]

He had a brother, about whom one could say, 'that his words were Jacob's but his actions were those of Esau', for he bore the name but lacked the spirit.[23] Nevertheless, he was made use of as a figurehead by our commanders, and the name Schill still attracted all the world's adventurers. Although much employed on outpost and reconnaissance duties, the new Schill was not cut from the same cloth as his brother, which he also demonstrated when after a meeting with Vegesack he rode back to his unit outpost (probably drunk), got lost and was captured in the middle of a gap in the French lines.[24]

In this unit I met a notorious countryman by the name of Wästfelt, born in Östergötland, who had been an officer in the Life Grenadiers but, after a duel with his captain, joined Schill's hussars and was now the most senior regimental

---

22 Much has been written about Schill's 1809 rebellion and its impact on German history. See, for example, Sam Mustafa, *The Long Ride of Major von Schill* (Boulder: Rowman & Littlefield, 2008).
23 Genesis 25: Esau was the first-born son of Isaac, son of Abraham, but gave up his inheritance birth right with its attendant responsibilities to his younger twin brother Jacob in exchange for a bowl of stew.
24 *Major* Karl Johann Heinrich Alexander von Schill (1766–1845) was captured near Lübeck. He was released in 1814, and subsequently took command of the 1st Silesian Landwehr Cavalry Regiment and took part in the Waterloo campaign.

officer.²⁵ Since von Schill had been captured, Wästfelt should, of course, have taken command; but he was overlooked and a native officer was given the position, which angered him so much that he was thereafter most often to be found skulking in taverns and billiard halls.

Another officer had a rather comical but hazardous adventure with Wästfelt. He was an adjutant at the time, and in response to a sortie from Glückstadt he was instructed by the commanding general to direct a squadron of Schill's hussars to intercept the impertinent Danish troop. He fulfilled his mission, but Wästfelt carried out his orders so promptly that he set off at a gallop and took the adjutant with him, who did not therefore have time to get away but took his place in the line and fought like an ordinary hussar.

Lübeck must have been a prosperous community, since, despite exploitation by the French and the Danes, it still seemed able to bear the burdens of the war. Passing troops would be housed and fed. A couple of hundred serving or sick officers had board and lodgings there for long periods, several hospitals had to be set up and maintained, requisitions for transport, fodder, provisions, medicines, etc., were delivered, and still one heard little complaint; only the desire to be left in peace for a couple of years, whereby they should sufficiently recover.

The Jews, of whom there were many and wealthy families, provided generous accommodation, and their beautiful daughters tolerated non-Jewish officers quite well. Wholesalers lived frugally, poring over their account books, and did not flaunt their wealth with fine carriages and footmen in livery. Craftsmen sat at their work, content with moderate reward, and in drinking sessions one never heard them talk of deposing or appointing their leaders. The lower classes did not drink as heavily as in our larger cities. The government was certainly patriarchal, for contemptible police were not to be seen, and the fat-bellied high and mighty left their arrogance at the town hall – the same town hall where our great Vasa requested and received assistance.²⁶

My prescribed assignment in the art of tailoring had been completed, and I longed for the arrival of the regiment, for one can also grow weary of idleness. Troops began to arrive from Holstein, first among them the portly Cardell at the head of the artillery, and we viewed with astonishment that a horse could bear this inhuman mass of flesh.²⁷ That he was the most eminent of our generals is known well enough, and that he deserved this recognition could be seen in our Swedish artillery which his iron

---

25 Bleckert Adolf Wästfelt (1782–??) who was a *fänrik* in the Life Grenadier Regiment in 1797, taken prisoner at Lübeck in 1806, then went into French service as a *lieutenant* in a jäger regiment in 1808 before joining Schill's Hussars.

26 Gustav Eriksson Vasa (1496–1560), who in 1519 had escaped from Danish captivity and sought refuge the Hanseatic city of Lübeck; the city's support was also instrumental to his election to the Swedish throne in 1523 as Gustav I, the first of the Vasa kings.

27 Pomeranian-born *General* Carl Friedrich von Cardell (1764–1821) entered Prussian military service in 1780 and transferred into Swedish service in 1789. He was instrumental in establishing Sweden's mounted artillery in 1793. From 1797 he was commander of the Royal Wendes Artillery Regiment and as an artillery commander he participated with distinction in the 1805–1807 campaign, the 1808–1809 war against Denmark and the 1813 the Leipzig campaign.

hand had shaped into a unique model for the time.²⁸ But he had brought this about and implemented it with the most harsh Asiatic despotism, for he respected a human life less than a horse, his own perhaps least of all. His pointed head resembled that of a cannibal, his fat lower lip and flabby cheeks suggested sensuality and egotism, his firm, legs-apart stance seeming to brave the thunder and say, 'Beware, boys, I speak with cannons.' It is alleged that when he inspected the French square which he had shot down at Dennewitz in just a few minutes, he stood with legs apart and laughed out loud.²⁹ While he was exercising, typically in the afternoons, both the general and his horse became blood-spattered, for, when his spurs did not suffice, he punished the horse with his sword, often with the sharp edge.

General Carl Friedrich von Cardell (1764–1821) in the uniform of the Wendes Artillery Regiment, circa 1815. Portrait by C. Hellström (1841–1916) after original by J.R. Way. (Armémuseum)

How he was regarded by comrades can be understood from an incident in Kristianstad, perhaps unheard of in military history, when, as commander of the Wendes artillery, he was driven away from a guard parade by his own majors, von Geist and von Gerber, declaring that they would not stand in line with him. However, the matter was kept quiet, neglected, and forgotten after a couple of years.³⁰

---

28 Horse artillery was common, but Cardell's innovation was for all the crew to be mounted, rather than some riding on the limber/gun carriage, allowing faster movement.
29 At the Battle of Dennewitz on 6 September 1813, the Prussian, Russian and Swedish allies won a major victory over the French forces of *Maréchal* Ney.
30 *Major* (later *Överste*) Carl Gustaf von Geist (1769–1835) was a veteran officer who had enlisted in the artillery as a cadet in 1781, fought in the Russian War 1788–1790 and served in the 1813 campaign as commander of 3 mounted batteries, part of Cardell's reserve artillery division. He was badly wounded at Leipzig but remained in service with the Wendes Regiment until 1820. The second officer is assumed to be Karl Vilhelm Daniel von Gerber (1772–1860) born in Lübeck, from German nobility, who moved to Sweden in 1789 and married into the Swedish noble family Gustafschöld in Kristianstad in 1808. The biography of Cardell by Len Jacobson in the *Swedish Biographical Lexicon* ('Carl Friedrich Cardell', *Svenskt biografiskt lexicon*, <https://sok.riksarkivet.se/sbl/Presentation.aspx?id=16360>, accessed December 2023) notes that before the war of 1805–1807 (then) Staff Captain and Battery Commander Karl von Gerber had become an 'implacable enemy' of Cardell. Both officers were recipients of the Royal Order of the Sword.

Wendes Mounted Artillery, from an 1825 lithograph after original by Alexander Clemens Wetterling (1796–1858). (Armémuseum)

He would subsequently use the same motto as the pirate-supreme, 'the enemy of the whole world,'[31] and as such, regardless of circumstances and considerations, bring about a formidable re-organization of our artillery, especially the horse artillery, which he trained to become proper centaurs.[32] He was born a German, where there were fine horses, and one would rarely see better teams than he had for his guns. One of the mounted batteries had four white parade horses which he had purloined from a countess in Holstein, with whom he had been quartered; but on this occasion he had made a serious error, for either the countess was known to the Prince or she had acquired channels to him. She reclaimed the horses and Cardell was ordered to hand them over, which he did, accompanied by full-blooded oaths. When one encountered this barbarian, one would have believed him interested only in the cannonball and the sword, but his artillery reforms were popular and appreciated at the time, and his iron will created Marieberg where so many officers were trained to the nation's credit.[33] It was strange that such a colossus so often weathered hails of bullets without coming to harm, and many considered him to have a contract with the devil.

The Crown Prince arrived and brought with him our new Minister of War or, as he was then, Adjutant General of the Army, Björnstjerna. If Cardell had a pointed head, Björnstjerna's would be described as flat, but there was a mastermind within, to the extent that he was also an author, although perhaps lacking in classical underpinning. We did not have a more capable, enterprising, and fair Minister of War during my time in service. Damage from 'bedroom influence' and intrigue worked against and upset him. He had shone in the 'Little War' in Finland and his reconnaissance

---

31 A reference to Søren Norby (d.1530), pirate and commander of the fleet of Christian II of Denmark, who styled himself as 'Friend of God and enemy of the whole world'.
32 A fitting allusion to the training of horse and rider to act as one, as the mythical half human-half horse Centaur.
33 Cardell founded the Higher Artillery College (*Högre Artilleriläroverket*) in 1818 at Marieberg, Stockholm.

General Magnus FF Björnstjerna (1779–1847) by Johan Gustaf Sandberg (1782–1854). (Nationalmuseum)

Fältmarskalk Curt von Stedingk (1746–1837). Print after original by Lars Herlin (1806–1841). (Nationalmuseum)

at Wittenberg testified that he performed well in his role. Say what you will, but as long as I live, I value him because, although an aristocrat, he was a Swede in heart and soul.[34]

So much has been spoken and written about Adlercreutz that further comment would be superfluous. He was a fearless soldier and a good comrade, especially if one spoke Finnish.[35]

After the Crown Prince's arrival, we were graced with a plethora of generals, ministers and other dignitaries, the amiable and cheerful Swedish army commander, Field Marshal von Stedingk excepted. This veteran was not to be seen at court, standing like a corncrake and graciously nodding his head. He received comrades as comrades, for he considered that in the serious business of war, facing bullet and cold steel outweighed the niceties of rank. He brought to mind old friendships, asked after old acquaintants and recounted anecdotes from his eventful life. They would pay their respects to him with joy and depart with reverence.[36]

---

34 Magnus Fredrik Ferdinand Björnstjerna (1779–1847) was born in Dresden but sent to Sweden in 1793 aged 14 and enrolled as a *fänrik* in the Life Guards. He served with distinction in the Finnish war of 1808–1809 and the 1813–1814 campaign, during which he was *generaladjutant* to *fältmarskalk* von Stedingk. He was present at the battles of Großbeeren, Dennewitz and Leipzig, the crossing of the Elbe at Wörlitz (near Wittenberg) and a reconnaissance in force against Dessau albeit criticised by the Crown Prince for its unnecessary boldness. He was Swedish minister in London from 1828 to 1846.
35 Adlercreutz was then Chief of Staff of Karl Johan's Army of the North.
36 Curt Bogislaus Ludvig Christopher von Stedingk (1746–1837) graduated from Uppsala University in 1763 and then joined the Royal Suédois Regiment in France, becoming close

The Guards Brigade, which included the Life Regiment Grenadiers, arrived, and if anyone wished to view a grand spectacle, they were now given the opportunity with no entrance fee. The freshly uniformed Guards were much admired. No foreign army generally had sufficient men of the requisite height, but to a large extent comprised shorter specimens, comparable to our drummers. When now a couple of thousand men, mostly six-footers, appeared in tall grenadier helmets, which made them even more imposing, the Germans shrank back in fear at these tall sons of the Nordic Vikings, but amused to see that Gustav Adolf the Great's spirit and discipline still resonated amongst the Swedes.

---

friends with Louis XVI and Marie Antoinette, and he performed meritorious service in the American Revolutionary War, the Russo-Swedish Wars of 1788–1790 and 1808–1809, as well as commanding the Swedish forces at Großbeeren, Dennewitz and Leipzig. He also served two terms as Swedish ambassador to Russia in St. Petersburg.

14

To the Rhine and Belgium (February–April 1814)

With Denmark defeated and Norway secured by the Treaty of Kiel, Karl Johan took the army south, supporting the Allies' final advance on Paris. He was however keen not to take his forces into France itself, since he still harboured some hopes of gaining the throne of his native country.

The regiment finally arrived.[1] My comrades overwhelmed me with their ignorance in thinking that I had stayed in a fattening-house whilst they had had to toil, but I set them to rights with my 300 pairs of trousers. We had to rest for a couple of days before embarking on the long march, to Paris we hoped, where we could learn *savoir-vivre*[2] and French. During this interlude, I had to act as a guide to the city which was unfamiliar to my comrades.

Railways were unknown at that time, so we had to use Shanks' pony,[3] a mode of transportation with ample hardships. The officer, who mostly has it easy, suffers only when challenged by idleness, but the poor private with his knapsack or so-called *calf* on his back, on top of it a rolled-up cape, a cartridge case with 60 rounds, a heavy musket and often a few days' provisions, struggles under the burden like a pack-ass, and cannot other than in exceptional circumstances be exerted too hard; he must be encouraged with chatter and especially with singing. One then experiences language and songs which would not be considered appropriate in our domestic parlours. Most exhilarating are improvisations which characterise not only rank and file but the officers too, for, as god-fearing as they are otherwise, they must, however, tolerate such free expression. Character defects, mishaps and weaknesses would be presented in verse and melody, and often the improviser would be rewarded with loud bursts of laughter, even from the subject himself. I had amongst my flock Number 89, *Kron*,[4] known as the worst of gluttons both at home and on campaign; he could knock back half a gallon of boiled potatoes, a couple of herrings

---

1 The Jönköping Regiment had been in Kiel since 18 January having returned there following the fall of Glückstadt and then set out for Lübeck on 26 January.
2 Literally *knowing how to live* – knowledge of the world and the ways or usages of polite society.
3 The Swedish idiom Hultin uses is *apostlahästar*, lit. Apostle horses.
4 The recruit's number (within his company) and his soldier name.

and half a loaf of sour bread for breakfast, a bowl of peas with accompanying tit bits was a meagre lunch, and other meals in proportion thereafter. Reflecting on this, a voice was raised from the ranks and sang to our marching tune:

> Eighty-nine, his name it was Kron,
> He ate all the porridge for the battalion.
> Hey falleralla,
> Ho falleralla,
> Hi falleralla,
> Hello!

Which was so expressive that we laughed for a long time and forgot our exhaustion.

After every five kilometres we would rest for half an hour, where it was pitiful to see officers' and baggage horses put out to graze in the cornfields.[5] We took the familiar road to Boizenburg, greeted our old hosts, getting to know once again their predilections, thoughts and opinions which had likely changed during our absence, then crossed the Elbe on barges at Blekede and had a couple of rest days with obligatory dances in Lüneburg.

To now account for all the locations where we had either good or bad quarters would be as instructive as a description of innkeepers' lodgings during a trip through Småland, so as a general rule it may only be stated that if we were quartered in towns and cities, and there are many such in Germany, and we had a day off, a ball was part of the regime for the day. Dancing ladies with big feet, drinking rum punch and *'negus'* (a drink of port, tea and sugar), were ever present; for if a comrade was lodged in a house where there was an adult daughter, he only needed to inform her of the event and she would immediately send messages to her acquaintances, and these to theirs, so that we had more ladies than we could attend to. Mothers, aunts, and chaperones were rare, for the French and the Allied armies had emancipated the women. These balls cost us barely 50 *öre* per man, because venues and music were provided gratis. When we bivouacked in the countryside, we danced to another tune, for as soon as the men had eaten and rested for a couple of hours, they were asked if they wanted to hunt, and they gladly did so, partly for the sport, partly because it could bring in brandy. They undertook game-drives, always catching hare and often deer, which were roasted in camp by creative stewards, and it was good to find on the march communal tables set up by the roadside where non-hunting gentlemen would trade liquor in order to sample the delicious game. In this way we passed through Ülzen, Zelle, Hanover and Minden, where the monotony was interrupted by a little adventure.

We had a day off in the Prince of Schaumburg-Lippe's domain, near his capital Bückeburg. The principality was no larger than a couple of our own farmsteads, but was ruled by God's grace by a *doudesfurste*,[6] who must have been a great hunter

---

5 Pitiful behaviour presumably both because of the damage to crops grown for human consumption and failure to provide the horses with proper fodder.
6 Literally *dozen-prince*, meaning a prince over a very small country. Schaumburg-Lippe joined the Confederation of the Rhine and became a principality in 1807, Georg Wilhelm Lippe (1784–1860) became its first prince.

Cartoon from the weekly German satirical magazine *Fliegende Blätter* in 1848 concerning the number of small states and associated customs tollgates that existed before the adoption of a customs union. The caption translates as 'You see, Herr border guard, that I have nothing to declare, because what's on the back of the wagon hasn't crossed the Lippe border yet, there's nothing in the middle, and what's on the front is already over the Lippe border again.' (Universitätsbibliothek Heidelberg Digital Library, <https://doi.org/10.11588/diglit.21330049>)

on behalf of the Lord, for when the peasants were asked if there were hares, they lamented that hares ate their cabbages and fruit trees; but it was even worse with the deer, which grazed and trampled down their grain, so that at night they had to keep watch. Consequently, they would bless us if we could kill all the game that was to be found!

Although quartered in a village with only my jägers, I considered my 50 men more than a match for the Prince's soldiers, if any such existed, so I deployed them in a perimeter around a forest grove of oak and beech at the direction of the farmer, who would not join in the hunt because it was practically a death sentence for them to touch the animals. The sergeant-major and I were the only shooters. He had an infantryman's musket loaded with buckshot and I carried a small double barrelled piece, one barrel of which was loaded with a single ball and the other with birdshot.[7] Our game-drivers had not been long gone, when an animal, which I could not distinguish in the bushes, passed close to me, at which I discharged both barrels, seemingly without effect, and immediately afterwards the sergeant-major shot a roe deer. When I inquisitively ran over to him, I spotted two red deer and five roe deer barely 20 paces from us, who now stood with empty weapons, outsmarted. But we were happy with our one kill, and when the drivers arrived, arrangements

---

7 Swedish musket cartridges mostly contained a single ball (*passkula*) to suit the bore (18–20 mm), but there were alternative cartridges with two balls; with one regular ball and three smaller bullets (*rännkulor* (buckshot), typically 6–8 mm diameter); or just buckshot, for use at close quarters. Hailshot or birdshot (*hagel*) for hunting comprised much smaller pellets.

were made to transport it, when a soldier, who had been cutting withies to bind its legs together, shouted, 'Bless my soul, here lies an animal that is much larger!' We hurried over and found a large deer in its death throes. My shot had just penetrated its hide, but the bullet had lodged in its lung. Overjoyed, we cut off the head and removed the entrails to be able to transport this heavy quarry, when four of the Prince's jägers, who had heard the shots, arrived and protested, promising that those who harmed the Prince's animals would be broken upon the wheel,[8] but I indicated that the Prince would have his share in the great head and the delicate entrails, which could probably be used in his sausage factories.[9] But if they wanted something further, I could throw a flogging into the bargain. They left without so much as a thank you!

From here we proceeded through Herford, Bielefeld, Münster and Dortmund to Duisburg, where we crossed the much-sung, hero-generating, castle-strewn River Rhine, about which the Germans wrote, spoke, and sang more than any mortal had time to digest in his lifetime. Anyone who has seen the rivers of Norrland, however, would consider that the Rhine was not so extraordinary. The water was muddy, and the banks were bare; but then in compensation we reached Düsseldorf, which is not a big city, but is the most beautiful I have seen.

Of course, German was the common language, but the spirit of the inhabitants was quite different from that of the enslaved Germans. French sympathies were apparent in them through clenching of their teeth if they were alone; but if they were gathered, especially at night, we would often hear *'Vive l'Empereur,'* which we ignored, for many of us might have wanted to sing the same song; it was also best not to defy public opinion too much, for French heroism and rage could easily be ignited.

In a small town I got into a quarrel about a carriage ride with a citizen-official, corresponding to our *hållkarl*,[10] and, being used to inviolable behaviour in Småland, I threatened him with a boxing about the ears; but he straightened up, stepped back and said gravely, 'Monsieur, I was once a French grenadier and such a gesture is unworthy of both you and me; but if you want to engage in cold steel, then I am your man.' I was forced to back down, for according to our customs I could not cross swords with a *hållkarl*.

The North German army under the Crown Prince's command, 70,000 men, now began to concentrate and we came into contact with our allies, among whom the Prussians were the most unpleasant. They had forgotten Austerlitz and Jena, considered themselves invincible, claimed that our forces had been withheld and conserved too much, that they alone could decide the war with mere braggadocio. If one were quartered with them, one could be sure of duels and brawls in the days that

---

8 *Stegel och hjul*, being broken on the wheel, was a barbaric form of capital punishment still in use in Germany in the early nineteenth century and remained on Sweden's statute books until 1841.
9 *Lungmosfabriker, lungmos* (lit. lung mash) meaning a dish of ground lungs or heart, liver, and lungs together (also known as pluck) mixed with barley.
10 A *hållkarl* was a post-master in the original sense of one who hires out horses to travellers from post-houses and inns.

Prussian allies in the 1813 campaign. Watercolour by Carl Johan Ljunggren (1790–1852) dated 1822. (Nationalmuseum)

followed. I myself fared ill, for a Prussian cut me right well, although I repaid him in equal measure. It may seem strange, but our traditional enemies, the Russians, had become our best allies.

We marched to Aachen, albeit with due caution, for we had an opponent in Antwerp who was not to be trifled with. The famous revolutionary and fortress engineer Carnot was commander there with a considerable garrison.[11] He was asked how he was minded. Showing his hat, whereon was set the white cockade, he replied, 'What France does, I do, but this fortress I defend for France; poke your fingers in here and they'll get burnt' and that old man was known to keep his word. Thus only an observation force was left there, with which a small affair took place; for when a French troop which was in Maastricht, was ordered to Antwerp, it encountered two squadrons of the Småland Dragoons under Captain von Schantz, who struck the

---

11 Lazare Nicolas Marguerite, Count Carnot (1753–1823) had been appointed Governor of Antwerp in January 1814 with a garrison of about 10,000 men and successfully defended the city until the end of the war following Napoleon's abdication.

French with such impetus that they were routed.[12] It was said that the trumpeter attacked most fiercely and was so captivated by the clash of sabres that he could hardly be persuaded to sound the recall.

At last we came to Liège, which supplies the world with double-barrelled shotguns.[13] That a couple of score of these found their way into the regiment is certain; and had we had more money, there would probably have been more, for some were so beautiful that Sunday-hunter gentlemen might even pose with them *'at weddings and at balls.'*[14] In the gun factories the machinery was so complicated that it would take half a year to understand it.

For the first time I had the pleasure of seeing heretical Catholics, for I was accommodated with a canon, in whose company I went shooting larks on a Thursday, with which we treated ourselves at Friday dinner, and when I remarked that his reverence broke the Fast, he still took a bird, drank a full glass of Rhine wine and declared, 'Fasting is for the masses, who cannot eat, having nothing to eat.' The city was so large that one could get lost therein and was so full of well-fed priests and monks, images of saints and other blasphemies, that *pax vobiscum* whirled about one's ears.[15]

* * *

In Aachen we were quartered for almost a month,[16] and there our footsore young men had the opportunity to bathe and to drink blood-purifying decoctions. Here I had an argument with the commandant, a Prussian major, and was getting into difficulty. As acting regimental quartermaster, I had travelled ahead to arrange our accommodation, and whilst stood in the square I saw a patrol of the Saxon Guard, who were garrisoned in the city, bring an arrestee in Swedish headgear to the commandant. As there were no other Swedish troops in the city, I surmised that the man was one of my assistant-furriers,[17] so I hurried across to meet the officer who was engaged in boxing the detainee's ears in a courtyard. I stepped forward and announced that the man was under my command and that if he was to be punished, that should take place through me, according to Swedish martial law, and not by his boxing him about the ears, which is only suitable for thugs. He then turned towards

---

12 Johan Christian von Schantz (1781–1846) had enlisted in the Småland Dragoon Regiment as a corporal in 1796, becoming a *ryttmästare* in 1809 and retired from service in 1830 as the regiment's *överste*.
13 Liège had long been a major international supplier of small arms, and during its 'golden age' grew from 36 manufacturers in 1816 to 195 in 1909.
14 A line from the aforementioned Fredman's Epistles, No.15, My Dearest Theophile.
15 The common Catholic farewell *pax vobiscum* meaning 'peace be with you.'
16 Regimental records indicate that the Jönköping Regiment arrived in Aachen on 7 March and departed on 24 March and thereafter only briefly passed through Liège (Hultin refers to it by its German name, *Lüttich*) on their way to Brussels, so the preceding brief description of Hultin's time in Liège appears chronologically out of place.
17 Furrier's assistants (*furirskyttarnas*) supported the furrier (*furir*) who was the company non-commissioned officer responsible for selecting the company campsite or accommodation and receiving and distributing the company food supplies. There were six *furirskytt* in each company.

me, exclaiming, 'I am the commander and punish as I see fit and you, who argue with me, I will place under arrest.' I lost my temper, grabbed my sword, went one step closer to him, and stated that I might not be able to prevent such a thing, but if he continued to strike the man, I would defend him, as long as I had the wherewithal. He calmed down and agreed that the detainee should be taken in for questioning and promised to notify me. I followed the frightened man to the guardhouse and requested the officer to give him a fair hearing. The matter was investigated, and it was found that he had quarrelled with a reluctant host over our scouting party's requisitioning. Thus, the issue was insignificant and mundane.

At noon the regiment arrived, and our commander had barely settled into his quarters, when I stopped by and reported the matter. This excellent officer,[18] who both could and would support his subordinates when needed, was so upset that I, who had never seen him other than calm and level-headed, became truly fearful. He blushed, turned pale, and shook, such I thought he was having a stroke. When he was finally able to speak, he said, 'The Lieutenant's own sword is the guarantee to me that you shall not be permitted to be placed under arrest by anyone other than your regimental commander. Now go straight to the commandant and tell the detainee to report immediately to General Bergenstråhle, then we will settle the matter.' In the afternoon the Crown Prince arrived and had not been in the headquarters for many hours, when a special General Order was issued, that since the Prussian commandant, Major von Suchow, had allowed himself to arbitrarily punish a Swedish soldier, he would be dismissed from command. With this, I considered the affair over, but the next day the orderly came with an order that I should report to my commanding officer. He was then back to his usual self and said, 'From what I have heard, the Lieutenant railed against the deposed Major in the heat of the moment; therefore, go and ask him if he has anything personal against you? If not, you and your compatriot are at his service. Should he look down upon you, then say that your commanding officer is ready and willing to take your place.' The Major was surprised by my subsequent visit, talked about friendship, morality, camaraderie, erroneous reporting, heat of the moment, misunderstanding etc., and thus the matter ended. Many officers do not have such sympathy for a poor subaltern, 'for they are made to be sacrificed.'

The inhabitants, especially the priests, were more fanatical here than anywhere else. At a ceremony, when an image of the patron saint of the city, I believe it was Saint Ursula,[19] was carried in procession, everyone walked with bare heads, singing, and making fools of themselves. I stopped on the sidewalk, gaping at the ghostly idol, when a priest came up to me and asked why I did not bare my head to the saint, and when I replied that I was a Protestant, he invoked papal bulls, synods, mandates and ordinances, which imposed the showing of due reverence for Catholic

---

18 The aforementioned *Överstelöjtnant* Christoffer von Hartmansdorff, who was effectively regimental commander since *General* Bergenstråhle now commanded the brigade.
19 Ursula is a legendary Romano-British Christian saint, supposedly one of many (up to 11,000) virgins martyred in Cologne in the fourth century. The Basilica of Saint Ursula in Cologne holds the alleged relics. The Diocese of Aachen is one the six dioceses in the ecclesiastical province of Cologne.

ceremonies, so that the mob began to crowd around us; but when I informed him that we did not bare our heads during our own services, not even for our king, he went on his way. Certainly, I felt a twitch in my right foot to hasten the priest along, but I resisted the temptation. It was worse for another zealot, who stepped forward and tried to remove the headgear from an orderly of the Second Guard Regiment, for he received a blow to his consecrated ear.

Their worship was beautiful, their singing excellent, but the Latin Mass, which they bellowed in a French accent, often in tones that could frighten our Lord from heaven, certainly did not arouse religiosity. Their auricular confession seemed particularly bizarre. In the churches, which remained open day and night, there were confessionals, similar to our market stalls, but so small that only one person could be accommodated. There sat the priest, and at the level of his ears were small dense lattices of braided rattan, and below on the outside was a stool, whereupon the penitents knelt and whispered their sins in the priest's ear, without being able to be seen. Some were dismissed quickly, others might remain for half an hour, girls often the longest. Whether these latter were the greatest sinners or whether they interested the fathers the most, is difficult to say. I would have liked to have acted as a sinner in order to hear the priest's technique and method of redemption, but since my pronunciation could betray the heretic, I did not dare to act a Catholic and receive absolution free of charge.

Images of the Madonna, strewn with flowers, ribbons and pieces of glass, stood in kiosks in the streets. In the evenings they were illuminated, some with several torches, some with just a tallow candle, which the orthodox would light during hymns in praise of the Virgin and prayers for assistance. Among other things, you could hear groups sing *'ora pro nobis.'*[20]

The baths, where in the summer half of Europe seeks remedy for tapeworm and gout, were then empty, and for a few *öre* you could splash in pools, where otherwise only crowned heads would bathe, without feeling better or worse for it. Both ordinary and sulphurous springs were numerous, but were used sparingly by us, who preferred to drink wine.[21]

The people, who spoke reasonably pure German, were kindly and typically keen on secret societies, for we came into contact with Freemasons, who were enthusiastic and numerous, and freely granted us degrees, which, however, were not of strict observance.[22] Gustaf III, who during his stay in Aachen often visited their lodges, had masonic panegyrics and eulogies hung upon his walls, both in verse and prose, from which we derived credit.[23]

---

20 Pray for us.
21 Since Roman times Aachen had been famed for its thermal springs.
22 The Rhenish masonic lodges, particularly in Aachen and Cologne, were closely affiliated to France; only a small percentage of members at that time were recorded as German; but about one fifth of the membership were of undeclared origin and likely included many Germans who wished to keep that information secret. See Michael Rowe, *From Reich to State: The Rhineland in the Revolutionary Age, 1780–1830* (Cambridge: University Press, 2003).
23 Gustav III famously visited Aachen in 1791, ostensibly to take the waters for his health, but unofficially to rendezvous with the French royal family on their escape from the Paris following the revolution and to seek to mobilise an army to overturn it.

With my 50 jägers I was ordered to guard Ordingen castle, five kilometres from the city, belonging to a Count d'Arschot, who was staying in Paris and was probably known by the Crown Prince, who offered a troop to protect the property from Prussian and Russian pillage.[24] The large castle was uninhabited except for a steward who occupied a wing and fed me and my troop abundantly. Here I could have thoroughly studied Zimmermann's dissertation on the effect of loneliness on the heart and mind,[25] if I had had it, for to dwell alone in an entire floor of an old castle with its ghosts, ghouls and goblins can only interest spiritualists. The library was closed off with secure locks, and what I had brought with me (exercise and service regulations) was sleep-inducing. Hunting could only be carried out exceptionally, for the steward indicated that the Count was protective of his animals. Our duty was thus dull. Fortunately, the distance from the city was not too great so that I could sometimes travel in to meet comrades, and they would occasionally come out to visit and congratulate me on having some 30 rooms at my disposal.

One day the steward came up and said he had received a letter from the Count, who thanked us for the good order we kept and sent 10 ducats to be distributed amongst the men. I refused the gift because the articles of war forbade it. He opined that the Count would be upset by this and asked if he could not reward them in some other way. I have previously remarked that herring was not farmed much in Germany, but here it was never seen, and I had often heard our men long for it, for the Swede seems to need salt fish. I therefore asked if the steward could obtain some herring for us. Immediately an order was sent to Antwerp, which yielded us several firkins of Dutch herring. My men went half mad with joy, immediately broke open a firkin, helped themselves to the fish and showing them to each other, exclaiming, 'Jesses, such a feast this is!' and then ate herring morning, noon and night and drank small beer, so that they could barely take a breath.

A company of the Uppland Regiment relieved us, and I then had the opportunity to take a closer look at the remarkable old city. The remains of Charles the Great,[26] together with a few dozen skulls, bones and teeth, around which candles burned day and night, could not make me holier, who considered our own great Charles XII more outstanding, although we had neither counsel nor mind to illuminate his remains.

We were now assigned to General Boije's brigade, which consisted only of Småland regiments, and met with so many acquaintances and countrymen that if you spoke in the vernacular, you could get an answer in that province's dialect.

---

24 Ordingen castle is some 80 kilometres from Aachen on the then main road between Liège and Brussels; if Hultin was posted here it cannot have been when the regiment was in Aachen, and, furthermore, Flanders Heritage Agency (*Onroerend Erfgoed*) records show that it was not in the possession of a Count d'Arschot. The most likely candidate for the Count may be Louis Engelbert (1750–1820), 12th Duke of Aarschot and 6th Duke of Arenberg whose son was married to a niece of Joséphine Bonaparte.
25 The widely translated multi-volume work *Über die Einsamkeit* ('On loneliness') by the Swiss philosophical writer, naturalist and physician Johann Georg von Zimmermann (1728–1795).
26 *Karl den store,* Charles the Great, the emperor Charlemagne (748–814). The ornate shrine (*Karlsschrein*) containing Charlemagne's remains in Aachen cathedral was completed in 1215. Aachen also holds remains of the early Christian martyrs Saint Corona and Saint Leopardus and the Holy Roman Emperor Otto III (980–1002).

In the Kalmar Regiment there was a man who lived not far from my hometown, and to whom I had the honour of being personally known. His rise to high office bore, in miniature, a certain resemblance to Karl Johan and his story deserves to be told. The then Lieutenant Colonel Karl Klingström was born on a soldier's croft, became a very young volunteer, corporal and non-commissioned officer, rose through all the ranks, both non-commissioned and commissioned, and ended up as major general and commanding officer of that same regiment.[27] He was capable under all circumstances, hardworking and strict. It is strange, but one often finds that those who have risen from the lower ranks tend to be the strictest, even barbaric, with their men. So too was he, and when his friends drew his attention to this behaviour, he replied, 'I know best their tricks and dodges, I who lived amongst them.' I think he knew every man in the regiment. I once heard the major tell him, 'That one, he does not fear a flogging,' and when the company commander asked how he should be punished, Klingström replied, 'To give that man 50 lashes' (the highest a major could impose) 'he would merely laugh; flog him as much as he can stand.' When he was far from the drums during manoeuvres, his harsh voice was often heard to call out, 'Whoever is closest, give the drummer a blow on my behalf!' or, 'Whoever gets the chance, give the third rank a stroke every now and then, so they end up better!'[28] This behaviour notwithstanding, he was, for his strict justice and husbandry, cherished by the nation, but for a young ensign he was an ugly brute. He placed such great value in able non-commissioned officers that he often said, 'It was good that so-and-so became an officer, because he was no damned use to me as a non-commissioned officer.' Of course, his upbringing meant he was self-taught, such that he could barely read and write; but he dictated to his adjutants with a clarity and knowledge which made all his dispatches excellent, although the adjutants had a hard time maintaining their countenance, as he pronounced French words, such as captain, lieutenant, battalion, etc., in a Småland accent, rather than in the court style of the time. When someone behaved too ineptly, he always used to spit and exclaim, 'Are you a peasant?' and this was often the case at the Royal College of War, which for the most part he was at odds with and where he peddled his ignorance. He was not married and lived in an official residence which he likely had held as a non-commissioned officer; he had with him a literate battalion adjutant, to whom he dictated his orders and dispatches, and for company usually an old comrade, a former non-commissioned officer. One could say about them, like Runeberg about von Konow and his corporal, 'Most of the time they bicker.'[29] You could often see the General going out into the yard for firewood and lighting a fire himself, because it was 'so damn cold.'

---

27 Karl Klingström (1770–1834) was acting commander of the Kalmar Regiment during the 1813–1814 campaign, and its official commanding officer 1826–1832.
28 Swedish infantry normally formed in three ranks, although briefly experimented with two-rank lines per revised regulations in 1806. However, jägers retained the two-rank formation.
29 Paraphrasing the final lines of the poem *Von Konow och hans korporal* from J.L. Runeberg's *Fänrik Ståls sägner* (Tales of Ensign Stål): 'As dear friends you often see them, And almost as often they bicker.'

The adjutant once informed him that a stranger had arrived. 'Be damned!' he said and when the adjutant informed him that it was a woman downstairs, the General exclaimed, 'That's even worse!'

Despite this cynicism, he was valued and respected by both higher and lower ranks for his honesty and ability. When he applied to resign from service and was asked by Karl Johan for the reason, he replied, 'I am too old.' The king then said, 'I am older, and since I can still be king, you can still be commanding officer; go home.'

Generalmajor Karl Klingström (1770–1834). Lithograph by Johan Elias Cardon (1802–1878). (Wein Museum, Vienna)

* * *

Nothing certain was heard, only rumours that the Allies were deep in France and that Napoleon was gathering troops to make them pay the price, and that the Crown Prince had stated that no Swedish soldier would cross the French border. So farewell Paris and French education! Napoleon's forces aroused no fear in us, for even if he came driving the Allies in front of him, we had plenty of time and a familiar route to fall back and ensconce ourselves in Stralsund, but we were worried about our prince, who was said to have designs to personally go to Paris and was probably restrained from so doing not so much by the French as by us. Orders came, however, to advance, and I was ordered, as usual, to proceed ahead to Herve and settle accommodation. Upon arrival there, what I found confirmed what I had been told, that this was a miserable little backwater inhabited by the most inveterate French Jacobins. At the accommodation office they were unhelpful, refused to accept placement of troops and claimed that they did not have enough to eat themselves, let alone be able to satisfy voracious soldiers. I then asked if it would be more convenient for our commander to assign quarters to our men at his own discretion, for quarters we would have. As we argued, an adjutant rode up with orders for to me to return and cancel quartering arrangements for the time being. A town clerk immediately ran out into the street, which within a few minutes was full of people, shouting '*Vive l'Empereur*' and making threatening gestures. I ordered our weapons to be loaded, but a troop of four non-commissioned officers and eight men did not impress much, as the allied army was thought to be retreating, and when I requested transport, they kindly offered that the Emperor would likely provide for us, so after less than polite parting words on both sides we set off on foot. I told them, like Napoleon in Leipzig's city square, '*Adieu Saxons – au revoir,*' and promised to settle both the transport and accommodation matters the next time we met.

As luck would have it, we did not return, but the next day took the road to Louvain via Saint-Trond and Tirlemont, where we had a couple of rest days. This old university town is now only remarkable for its beautiful town hall dating from the Middle Ages, its ruined fortifications, its carillons, and its unusually polite inhabitants, with whom you would get on well, if you understood and could talk to them. They speak broken Dutch, and since no honest man understands even pure Dutch, we would have been lost had not every other person spoken French. Our soldiers assisted themselves with sign language, which the whole world understands. So, for example, one, housed with a widow, wanted to get more substantial food than pancakes and salad, so he got up on a chair, flapped his arms, crowed like a rooster, clucked like a hen, and then squatted down into an egg-laying position, which she understood and then served him eggs. I was quartered with a couple of unmarried ladies who were engaged in the clothing trade. The danger to either side was not great, for they were moth-eaten and mature. Although they over-provided me with confectionery and sweet-dishes, I felt good with them; but they had a couple of younger brothers, real carousers, who grumbled over our monastic life and for a change would take me out to secular inns and coffee houses, so that I sometimes had difficulty finding my lodgings, whilst they took quarters under tables and benches.

Passing through the fertile and beautiful regions that characterise Flanders, we finally marched into Brussels.

To try to describe this city would be to bite off more than one can chew. It is large and has a similar population to Stockholm, it has regular streets and excellent buildings, but, unlike Stockholm, lacks a castle. In this labyrinthine anthill, finding their way around and locating their officers' and comrades' quarters strained the Smålander's sense of direction. As a rule, I needed to find my way to the main square in order to locate my quarters, which I would otherwise have innocently walked past. When I mention the square, I cannot forget one thing, which proves what artistic pleasures one can miss in the absence of an aesthetic foundation which was almost universally lacking in the soldiery of that time. I often searched out and admired works of art, but in this square, which I passed through many times a day, there stood upon the town hall tower one of the greater works of art: the statue of the Archangel Michael by Michelangelo. I never saw it and now must sit back and curse my stupidity and ignorance.[30]

---

30 Hultin's description suggests he is referring to the gilt weathervane of Saint Michael the Archangel (patron saint of Brussels) atop the spire of the Gothic Town Hall on the Grand-Place, which is barely visible from the ground; but it is not by Michelangelo. The original was made by Maarten van Rode in 1455 and is now in the city museum, replaced by a copy in the 1990s.

We had good quarters, although the men sometimes remarked that they were fed 'salad' i.e., raw cabbage. Our duties were not onerous and guard patrols seldom undertaken more than once a week, but then we were kept busy, for there were constant fights between Prussians and Belgians, which patrols and detachments had to try to prevent; and often, especially at night, dead and injured were found in the streets. There were also troubles with a variety of detainees from a range of social classes and professions, and under varying circumstances, many of whom aroused sympathy. On one of my shifts, I had the company of a valet of General Björnstjerna who had been arrested. He was born in my hometown, where we played together as children, and when I asked what action had merited his detention, he explained that the General had been angry that he had been absent for a period, but that he would soon be released, for he was indispensable to the General. Meanwhile he had been assigned to picket duty together with an English non-commissioned officer also under arrest. Then an orderly of the Horse Guards appeared with a note for the duty officer with orders to regale the General's valet with five lashes and then have him accompany the orderly, in other words to punish him then let him go. For the layman, it should be necessary to remark that the articles of war permitted such treatment of officers' servants, as often as needed. I read and showed him the note, and he declared that he would not submit to any flogging. I explained to him that the duty was mine to fulfil, and advised him, since he had done wrong, to submit to the punishment with forbearance, which, given our old acquaintance, would not be severe, but which I, as a result of the necessity of orders, must carry out. He threatened to drown himself, which I said I could not prevent – but only after I had executed the punishment and handed him over to the orderly. So, the punishment was carried out, leniently, and it was amusing to see his companion, the English non-commissioned officer, call him a 'most honourable gentleman'. He spat, snorted, and shouted expletives repeatedly. Many years later, I had the pleasure of meeting with the former valet socially. He was then a well-to-do, dignified watchmaker, who told of his glorious memories better than I now tell mine, yet he always neglected to tell of his calamitous guard-duty in Brussels.

Henning and I were quartered with a wholesaler by the name of Mettenius, considered one of the richest in the city, and who became a representative for it thereafter. Herr Mettenius was a young, decent German and Reformed, but his wife was a lively, capricious, and highly coquettish Parisian, who was a Catholic and mannered to observe fasting, which is why problems often arose at the dinner table. A sumptuous meal was served at three o'clock which usually lasted a couple of hours; however, we had our duties to attend to and in addition not so fluent in French as to be able to properly court Madame, so we asked to eat in our room at more suitable times; but Madame undertook this service so ungraciously that she put us on a pauper's diet. For a whole week our dinner consisted of clear thin broth with old over-boiled meat, and other meals similarly poor, so that Henning, who could perform an eating role on any stage at any time, became depressed and wanted to complain vociferously about the diet; but I calmed him down by reminding him of the bottle of fine wine which our host had the steward provide daily. But one day, when Henning was tired, hungry, and angry, and the steward delivered the usual prisoner's fare, he asked if there was nothing else, to which the steward replied that they were gutting fish in the kitchen. This aroused delight in Henning, who loved fish, so that he exclaimed, 'Go down and say that we will have fish – otherwise I will smash the whole house down to the ground.' After a while our embarrassed host appeared and said, 'I am sorry to hear that you complain about the food, and that surprises me, for I believe I keep such a table that you should be satisfied with it.' We then showed him the dishes we had been served, adding that during the week we did not get anything else, but we thanked him for the good wine. Henning looked like Didrik Menschenschreck,[31] Herr Mettenius was taken aback and went out quickly, and after a while fish, steak, vegetables, pastries, and dessert were served, so that we felt ashamed and proposed a toast to our honourable host. Later we felt like mice amongst cheese, and out of gratitude we thereafter kept Madame company in the evenings, accompanying her music, for we both played a little violin.

Getting out into the country to become acquainted with hares, partridges and quails was not so easy, for the city was surrounded by villas, pleasure gardens and factories, so that one had a long way to go to reach open countryside. However, I stole out a couple of times and I think I found myself in the vicinity of Waterloo, not then knowing that higher prey would later be shot down en masse there. I sometimes daydream how instructive it would have been for an old soldier to sit and watch the game of chess which decided the fate of Europe upon this field – but from a hot air balloon, for down below it must have been hell on earth.

Brussels is called, and deserves to be called, Little Paris. Lifestyles, habits, and languages are French. Of course, a '*mynheer*'[32] was sometimes heard and the occasional beer-bellied Dutchman was seen, but in general French was the language in both words and manners. Morality was probably no better than in Germany, but a denser veil covered the lapses. Even in a state of humiliation, the Frenchwoman maintained a certain decorum, which the simple German could not acquire. With traders and dockers, which in Germany were most responsive to the cane, one could converse more amicably here. Religiosity was not as strong as in Liège and Aachen, probably because the Encyclopaedists had whittled down the flock.[33] Certainly, the occasional image of a saint was to be seen on street corners, in front of which in the evenings hymns could be heard sung in nasal French, but traders' stalls stacked with decorated eggs and other dishes from the *brännvinsbord* were many times more numerous and much more popular.[34] Among other things, there was a surrogate

---

31 The title character, a swaggering soldier, in a theatrical comedy by Norwegian playwright Ludvig Holberg (1684–1754), first performed in 1724. The usual English translation is *Diderich the Terrible*.
32 *Mynheer*, from the Dutch *mijnheer*, a polite form of address to a Dutchman, equivalent to 'sir'.
33 The Encyclopaedists were the many contributors to the *Encyclopédie, ou dictionnaire raisonné des sciences, des arts et des métiers* (a Systematic Dictionary of the Sciences, Arts, and Crafts) published in France between 1751 and 1772, a publication challenging of religious belief which was notably banned by the Catholic church.
34 Decorated eggs assumed to be prevalent due to the regiment having arrived in Brussels on 7 April 1814 and with Easter Sunday being 10 April. The *brännvinsbord* (lit. brandy-table), was the term for a starter meal, similar to the French *hors d'œuvre* and a precursor to the *smörgåsbord*, which was common in eighteenth and early nineteenth century Sweden, on which would be served a variety of bread, butter, cheese, fish and meat dishes alongside two or three varieties of spiced brandy.

for oysters in the form of a small edible snail called the *Kleephuysen* (Helix), which was very flavoursome. Rabbles and rogues played a game of chance with decorated eggs; they fought against each other with the victor winning the broken eggs, which is why you could sometimes see a lucky player with his hat full of eggs but often in such a liquid form that they could be used as a pomade.

Old man Thunberg[35] is probably right when he says, 'Water is the element in Holland that makes travel swift and comfortable,' because ships and boats of various shapes and designs travelled the canals incessantly in all directions; one saw floating inns with grand restaurants and staging balls *comme il faut*,[36] as well as taverns where fighting and debauchery were commonplace, and sometimes one might see a belle dancing alone on a small boat to the music of an out-of-tune guitar, which, if you did not hear the faint music, looked rather absurd.

The magnificent Royal Palace, now uninhabited, located at the eastern edge of the city, was surrounded by avenues, parks, and gardens, garnished with tavern-stands, where Prussians and Belgians tried to out-do each other. This was also a gathering place for pleasure-seeking, amorous couples. The upper classes made pilgrimage to the Palace of Laeken, a short distance from the city, where Napoleon used to reside during his visits, taking the air in the shady avenues; and there you could see thoroughbreds, both people and horses; there you saw blue, green, white, black, red, and yellow uniforms, and irregulars in chainmail, cuirass, and reindeer skin kaftans. Music, mostly from barrel organs, tormented all around, but one could also hear wandering virtuosos, who dressed and looked like our Filikrom,[37] perform sonatas and overtures so artistically that they could merit a place in our Royal Court Orchestra.

Rumours now began to circulate that the Allied armies were in Paris, that Napoleon had abdicated, that the Bourbons, 'who had learned nothing and forgotten nothing,' had been invited back only to be later driven away again.[38] These rumours were plausible, for bookshops and windows were full of the most dumb and vile caricatures of the greatest man of the age; but as a result we hoped to start singing, 'soon we shall return to our fatherland.' However, such hopes proved unfounded, for the regiment was ordered to remain and was placed under the command of the English General Graham, a decent and brilliant man who caused such little bother that I only saw him once, in a theatre box where he was enjoying a quiet sleep or was perhaps overcome with the grog.[39]

However, it was very sad to see comrades departing for Scandinavia like migratory birds and to hear them comfort us saying, 'The scoundrels will follow well

---

35 Presumably the naturalist Carl Peter Thunberg (1743–1828) who was born and grew up in Jönköping.
36 According to formal rules of social behaviour.
37 Filikrom was a former guardsman who was a renowned street musician in Stockholm during the 1810s.
38 Paris had surrendered to the allied forces on 31 March; Napoleon abdicated on 6 April and was exiled to Elba and Louis XVIII was restored to the throne, arriving in Paris on 3 May.
39 General Sir Thomas Graham (1748–1843) had been appointed commander of the British forces in the Netherlands at the beginning of the year.

behind.⁴⁰ As a result, our service became more onerous, guard duties more frequent and troublesome. Two English regiments were garrisoned in the city. One consisted of kilted Scots, one might even describe them as in fancy dress, and so well trained that they always walked perfectly erect – when they were sober. From these regiments, whose language we could not understand, we were assigned men for guard duty and received detainees. To compound our difficulties, both fit and wounded Prussian irregulars arrived, who frequently picked fights with the Belgians, so that we often had the guardhouse full of arrested miscreants. However, we took pleasure in the knowledge that the Swedes were routinely mentioned in connection with order and discipline.

---

40 The Swedish army started heading north on 22 April; the Jönköping Regiment did not follow until 28 April.

15

Back to the North (May–June 1814)

It had become apparent by early March that the Norwegians would not passively accept the terms of the Treaty of Kiel. So, following Napoleon's exile and the restoration of King Louis XVIII, Karl Johan began to move his forces back to Sweden for an invasion of Norway.

After a month, marching orders arrived and we headed for Scandinavia, crossed the Rhine at Cologne, and travelled our now well-trodden road where the men felt at home because the populace now understood the very important word 'schnapps'.

At Minden, the monotony was interrupted. There we met the enemy with whom we had so often played chicken and goose wars. Eckmühl, who had hitherto held Hamburg, now displayed the white cockade, and with his corps was, like us, on the march home, and as this force was numerous, we proceeded for nearly a week before we finally passed it.[1] We took quarters in the same towns and cities, and if we met them en route, we paraded past each other with military honours. If the wind blew toward us, the smell of Eau de Cologne and pomade wafted from their columns, whereas our modest men never used perfume. Their infantry consisted of small sprightly youths, but the artillery and cavalry were excellent; they were remnants of the campaign in Russia and gave good impression of the army that had suffered such devastation.

Their officers murmured about the position in France and the restoration of the Bourbons, assuring us that foreign bayonets could not keep those dunderheads on the throne whilst the 'little corporal' was still alive. Of course, we were curious to see the Marshal, and I did manage to see his carriage. I caught a glimpse of a bare forehead and a rather long nose through the window, but that was all. We were assured that this carriage was priceless, which seemed highly probable, for Marshal Davout, Prince of Eckmühl, was known to supplement what the Lord bestowed, and was not so foolish as to return empty-handed from the Bank of Hamburg.[2]

---

1 Davout only surrendered Hamburg on 27 May 1814, long after Napoleon had abdicated, and only on receiving direct orders from Louis XVIII. His corps numbered about 26,000 men. Displaying the white cockade, the symbol of the Bourbon dynasty, indicates his acceptance of the new authority.

2 On his return to France, Davout was accused (amongst other things) of having taken money from the Bank of Hamburg; all charges were successfully refuted but his reputation suffered for it.

In Hanover we were joined by a small young man, always smartly dressed, clearly cultured and well-mannered. He mostly followed us on foot and laughed at our soldier songs, which of course he did not understand. As I was still undertaking regimental quartermaster duties, I asked him after a few days if he wanted accommodation. He thanked me and accepted tokens, which were easy to give, for some were always available in excess of the effective strength; but he always wanted to lodge alone. We considered him as likely an impoverished student or a political refugee, until rumours began to be whispered that the 'little man', as he was called, was in reality a girl, so we began to observe him as closely as possible, short of a body search. The rumour proved true and, without explaining her circumstances, the 'little man' admitted to being a Miss Knigge, daughter of the well-known writer and *Illuminati* Baron Knigge.[3]

Maréchal Davout, Prince of Eckmühl (1770–1823). (Public Domain)

She followed us over to Sweden and on to Fredrikshald, where she usually ate at the officers' table, was cheerful and happy, perhaps a little too emancipated, but was always treated decently; and we never heard that she entered into a more intimate relationship with anyone, even though many hooks were cast for her to bite at; for, without being really beautiful, she was pretty, lively and at home with German and French literature. People wondered what she wanted. Some considered her a failed Aurora Königsmarck,[4] others took her for a spy or a cheated mistress getting back 'on the right track'. She herself said that she wished to enter Swedish military service, which we often joked about, seeking to become her tentmates. She pointed out that

---

3 Presumably Adolph Franz Friedrich Ludwig Knigge (1752–1796), a member of the Hanoverian lesser nobility, writer, freemason, and a leading member of the Order of the Illuminati. However, his only (recorded) daughter, Phillipine Auguste Amelie (1775–1841), was by this time married with several children, so perhaps this was an illegitimate daughter.
4 Countess Maria Aurora von Königsmarck (1662–1728) was a Swedish noblewoman born in the Hanseatic city of Stade in Lower Saxony (then a Swedish possession) who became mistress of Augustus the Strong, Elector of Saxony and King of Poland.

many women served in irregular units, especially in the Lützow Free Corps;[5] but she had taken a fancy to the honourable Swedes. Of course, the higher authorities laughed at her application and little 'Kniggan', as she was now called, remained in Fredrikshald when we went out into the wilds, but she was still there on our return and stayed with the Kalmar Regiment, but she returned to Germany without having officially served and without a campaign medal.

When one speaks of outsiders, one should not forget those faithful and friendly companions, who, without being suspected of espionage or subversive activities, live on good terms amongst officers and soldiers and always associate with them; I am, of course, referring to dogs. Certainly, most are cosmopolitan, moving from one corps to another; but among them there are exceptions, who hold their friendship sacred. We had one such faithful friend in a large golden bitch that we named *Bataljona*, who had accompanied us from Mecklenburg to Brussels, and now made the return journey with us in the hope of celebrating a happy delivery in the fatherland. Her instinct was surprising; she sometimes got lost and could be away for several days but would eventually return to the battalion, expressing her joy in typical canine manner and then resume her place at the front during the march, where she would call out to seek the attention of any civilians we met. During rests she usually went looking for scraps and when she saw a comrade eating, she would stop, take a bite, then move on to another, and when her scavenging was finished, she would return to the front of the column and lay down beside the drum. When the column stirred, she provided a trombone-like accompaniment and was the first to march. That she had originally belonged to the enemy might be deduced from the fact that she was mostly on bad terms with regimental and senior officers – a bicorne hat was an abomination to her. She had learned on guard duty that when such bigwigs approached, the picket shouted, 'to arms!' and the guards rushed out clutching their weapons, so she thought them a danger to her companions and growled at them when they met.

This is not as strange as it sounds. In my youth there was a pug named Bajocko in the Svea Guard, which was always kept on guard when the regiment was on duty, and which was so well trained that the nit-picking *platsmajors*[6] of that time could never surprise them without Bajocko sounding the alarm and snapping at their legs.

One fine day, *Bataljona* announced a joyous delivery with a litter of hopeful puppies, with whom everyone wanted to get acquainted. Two of the most beautiful we picked up and carried in procession to the priest to ask that he baptise the golden one as *Bataljon* and the black as *Pastor*. Although he complimented our polite patrons, he did not want to do it, as no one would register as the father, and it was possible that they were Catholics and thus did not belong to the regimental congregation; but as they seemed inclined to become impudent puppies, he advised that they be placed on the regimental roll and proposed that for the time being they be listed as unpaid ensigns, until they could bark and anticipate promotion;

---

5   A Prussian volunteer force about 3,000 strong comprising both infantry and cavalry established in early 1813 by Ludwig von Lützow, who had served under Ferdinand von Schill.
6   A *platsmajor* was an officer who served as assistant to a garrison commander having responsibility for guard duties and maintaining order.

which advice concluded both ceremony and patronage. The men, however, were Samaritans, they took the puppies with them and at every rest break they were put with their mother to be fed. Before we boarded ship at Rostock, I believe they were placed in the care of some charitable persons, for only the mother accompanied us to Sweden and she was last seen in Fredrikshald, where she adopted a new master and abandoned us, who were encamped some distance from the town.

We now learned the effect of climate on vegetation through experience, for when we left Brussels, the cherries were ripe and this continued throughout Germany; but when we arrived in Norway, they had only just ripened.

A couple of comrades bade us farewell, to meet unknown fates in the South. One, a Baron F., the oldest lieutenant in the regiment,[7] an unusually decent and educated man, who at Sävar deserved and received the medal for bravery, had on the march out, near Aachen, been accommodated with a wealthy old woman, with whom a young, amiable niece was staying, who was expected to become immensely rich, for, in addition to her old aunt, she would inherit from two uncles, who were considered millionaires. The girl and F. were fond of one other, but the aunt was not of the same opinion, so she guarded her niece as the dragon does its treasure. But he was obliged to follow the drum and replace those millions with fond memories and the opinion that all old women belonged in Blåkulla.[8] Now that we were on our way home, he received permission to visit his sweetheart and return to us along the way. He re-joined us at Minden, depressed and downcast, desiring once more that all old women be consigned to hellish Blåkulla. But in Hanover he received a letter, which he had me help him decipher, which entailed a couple of days' work before we could grasp the contents of this Syro-Chaldaic manuscript from the aunt,[9] in which she told us that the girl neither ate, drank nor slept, and since he was probably the cause of this perverse diet, she considered him obliged to return and prescribe an alternative. Although we all advised him to do so, he did not want to ask for permission in the face of the impending war and perhaps thereby to ask in vain; but our excellent regimental commander, who always cared well for his subordinates, got to know the situation, bade him make the journey if he so wished, gave him leave and promised to take responsibility for it – and so he headed south once more. While we were waiting for ships in Rostock, he returned to us not only engaged but also well-to-do, for he had jewellery of high value and money, so that at his engagement party he employed his friends and comrades, all of whom (and myself in particular) were paid our share. When he returned home after the campaign in Norway, he was given six months' leave, left a letter of resignation with a relative and returned to Brabant, from where he wrote to this relative that everything would be fine and asked him to submit his resignation letter, which he reluctantly did. But after six months, F.

---

7   Fitting the description of *Friherre F.* (Baron F.) and the oldest *löjtnant* in the regiment at that time this would be Carl Gustaf Per Fahnehielm (1771–1834). Hultin must have had reasons for not naming him directly.
8   Blåkulla was a mythological island where witches gathered and the Devil held court. It featured strongly in the Swedish witch hunts of the late seventeenth century.
9   Syro-Chaldaic was the biblical language of Palestine, a mixture of the Hebrew, Chaldaic, and Syraic, also commonly called Aramaic. Presumably meant figuratively!

returned in mourning. His bride had died; one could see that his trip had cost him dear.

For the other comrade who left us, circumstances were worse and more pitiful. He was one of the children of the regiment, his father and uncle were majors, two of his younger brothers non-commissioned officers, all capable men. As a 16-year-old non-commissioned officer, he showed unusual bravery at Sävar, Ratan and Djäkneboda, rescued his lieutenant who had been captured, received a medal for bravery, became an officer at the appropriate age, and was like the whole family a fine serviceman, but very careless in his business affairs and his choice of company, such that we advised him to seek foreign service, which he too desired. He left his letter of resignation, and we made a collection so that his subsistence could be secured for a time, and also gave him brotherly advice as he headed south. Along the way we received a letter saying that he was employed as an officer in the Belgian artillery and had good and high hopes for the future. A few years later he was serving as a Russian cavalry officer, twice decorated; I did not meet him at that time, but I heard from comrades that he was completely Russified, smelled of onions and Russian oil,[10] but was otherwise the same. We never heard from him again thereafter.[11]

We crossed the Elbe at Boizenburg, returned to our old quarters and were welcomed by our former hosts. Some were also greeted by hopeful mothers with babes in arms, but these were generally not so welcome, for they were seeking help in their upbringing.

We now passed places where the Jönköping jägers so often and so happily distinguished themselves during Gustaf Adolf's crazy war in 1805–1807,[12] and because many of them still served, many tales were told about their exploits, which were usually carried out in conjunction with the Mörner hussars, whose speed and camaraderie they kept in faithful memory. For example, during our recent march towards France, one of our jägers had met a hussar at a tavern in Hanover, whom he fixed upon and offered a drink. The hussar drank, thanked, and asked the jäger why he seemed so pleased. 'There is ample reason,' he replied, 'do you remember in 1807,[13] when the French dragoons outside Stralsund chased us? You rode past a retreating jäger, who begged to be allowed to grab your stirrup and you replied, 'Grab hold, comrade, although we will probably both be caught,' but we reached the drawbridge

---

10 *Ryssolja*, a strong-smelling tar produced by dry distillation of bark, branches and roots of birch, etc., which was used inter alia for preparation of leather, and a folk remedy for skin rashes etc.
11 The regimental records indicate that at this time the four *majors* included brothers Johan Fredrik de Maré (1763–1836) and Karl Ludvig de Maré (1766–1819), and one of the *fänriks* (along with Hultin) was listed as Karl Johan de Maré; Karl Johan (born 1793) was one of Karl Ludvig's sons and records indicate that he died in Russia, date unknown, so this must be to whom Hultin is referring. De Maré is an old Swedish family of French origin.
12 As noted earlier, the original text states 1804 which cannot be correct. A battalion of the Jönköping Regiment had been sent to Pomerania in the summer of 1805 and participated in several actions during the 1805–1807 war, returning to Sweden following the capitulation in September 1807.
13 Again, the text implausibly states '1804' although the incident is most likely to have taken place in 1807.

just as it was being hoisted, your horse jumped across and carried me with it.' No doubt the old comrades partook of another glass over this incident.

The story about a surprise attack on Wismar was more adventurous, and we still had among us the one who was the principal contributor to the fortunate outcome, although he was too modest to talk about it himself. Spies had learnt that two companies of French chasseurs were stationed in Wismar and that, as was typical, they had neglected their sentry duties, so it was decided to try to surprise them. The regiment's two jäger companies, each 50 men, were appointed under the command of Ensigns Barck and Lilliecreutz,[14] and brought with them 25 hussars. During a pitch-dark night and with a baker as a guide, they walked around the city in complete silence, stopping near the western gate, splitting off a non-commissioned officer and 10 men, whom the baker had promised to lead through farms and gardens into the city and deal with the guards posted by the gate. In order not to be scattered in the dark, they had to hold on to each other and proceed with feline stealth, until the baker stopped and whispered to the non-commissioned officer, 'Here is the garden gate, the latch of which I greased yesterday – now I shall be on my way.' The non-commissioned officer gathered his men, whispered to them to carefully mark the footsteps of the sentry, which could clearly be heard on the other side of the gate, and, when it was opened, to rush in and over-power him. This succeeded, but as the sentry fell he fired his gun. Immediately the baker came forward and pointed out the door to the guard room, whereat six men took up position with fixed bayonets, and since the guards' muskets were standing outside in the racks, they were caught like rats in a trap. One man then took position at the sentry-post, which was on the street, and the others hurried after the baker to the main gate, but, contrary to expectation, this was locked and barred and could not be opened. The officers, who had heard the shot and were waiting outside, shouted to open for God's sake, for success required the French not waking up and having time to gather. The resourceful baker took a couple of men with him, ran to a nearby smithy, found there a sledgehammer and a couple of axes, with which the locking bar was broken, and, when the gate was opened, the hussars rushed in, divided into three sections and careered up and down the streets, so that, although a drum sounded the alarm in the square, the enemy could not gather. Behind them followed the jägers who took prisoners, most of them taken in houses at the direction of their hosts and city residents. At dawn they were gathered together, but when it became full daylight and the prisoners (over 200 men) saw the tiny force which had captured them, they made an attempt to break out, resulting in some being shot to dissuade the others.[15]

---

14 Baron Peter Henrik Lilliecreutz (1780–1848) was an ensign in the Jönköping Regiment in 1802 and promoted to *löjtnant* in May 1807 following the attack on Wismar. He was made *kapten* and *regementskvartermästare* in 1811 also served as brigade *adjutant* in the 1813–1814 campaign. He reached the rank of *överstelöjtnant* of the regiment in 1815.

15 A French army under *Maréchal* Mortier had invaded Swedish Pomerania at the end of January 1807, driving the Swedish forces under Hans Henrik von Essen back into Stralsund where they were besieged. However, at the end of March, Mortier was ordered to support the siege of Kolberg in Prussian Pomerania and left a single division under Grandjean to maintain the siege. Von Essen took the opportunity to break out and in the space of three days (1–3 April) succeeded in driving the French out of Swedish Pomerania with minimal losses. Over

On this occasion, French muskets, which I mentioned earlier, and which our jägers still used, were taken. Our infantry had English flintlocks, for percussion locks were not then available.

Ensigns Barck and Lilliecreutz were made Knights of the Sword, for at that time this beautiful decoration was not just given for long service.[16] The non-commissioned officer, the main contributor to the success of the operation, who with 10 men entered an enemy-occupied city, overpowered the guard and opened the gate, received just a small silver medal.

There would be much to be said about this non-commissioned officer, an unusual man, and for some 30 years my esteemed comrade. He wanted to remain anonymous but is now dead, so that without offending his modesty I can mention Captain and Knight Carl Johan Westrin, who also excelled at Sävar and Ratan and later became an officer. He had served as a battalion adjutant in the major's service, then as chief adjutant, and finally regimental quartermaster for nearly 40 years,[17] so that he might be considered a serviceman personified, who knew and managed everything correctly and on time. Quiet, calm, and unobtrusive, it was impossible to quarrel with him. Whilst the other adjutants were often treated with solemnity, he was always received with pleasure, even if he delivered the most absurd orders. Most of his time, however, he spent at his desk, so that he claimed that he did not have a good day if before breakfast he did not get to draft a few pages of damned orders to torment us with, as was the fashion at the time. During officers' meetings, however, he would sometimes turn up for firearms practice with his medal and his French musket, which he took with his own hands from the picket post in Wismar, both shining like the sun in Karlstad,[18] and on such days it was certain that we would be treated to neither lengthy orders nor other missives. May he rest in peace!

Whilst such stories are not part of my personal tale, I feel that they can justifiably be recounted by one who was there, and so, while I am on the subject, I want to tell of a similar, though not as happy event, at which I had the honour to be present, but which rendered neither fame nor medal.

When the truce had ended and war resumed and we were near Rostock, General Vegesack was informed that some French companies were in Wismar, which he wanted to surprise and capture, so one evening orders suddenly arrived that a battalion of Småland infantry, two companies of Jönköping jägers, a company of

---

the following week, the Swedes carried out a number of raids west into Mecklenburg (where only a few small French garrisons remained) using small, mobile forces which resulted in the bloodless capture of Rostock on 6 April by a small force of Jönköping jägers and Mörner Hussars under *Löjtnant* de Maré and capture of Schwerin on 7 April by a similar sized force, again with minimal loss, along with the capture of Wismar which Hultin describes. These gains were short lived however, and by 24 July the Swedes were once again besieged in Stralsund which surrendered on 24 August.

16 Although created as an award for commissioned officers to acknowledge both bravery and long service, by the mid-nineteenth century the Order of the Sword had essentially become a long service medal.

17 *Kapten* Carl Johan Westrin R.S.O. (1786–1864) retired from the regiment with a pension in 1850 aged 63.

18 An idiom meaning extremely shiny, based on Karlstad being considered to have a lot of sunshine!

View of Wismar from the south, in May 1813, from Gallows Hill looking towards the Mecklenburg Gate. Sepia wash by *Löjtnant* Michael Gustaf Anckarsvärd (1792–1878). (Uppsala University Library collection via Alvin National Digital Cultural Heritage Platform)

Mecklenburg foot jägers, a squadron of Scanian carabineers and a squadron of Mecklenburg mounted jägers were to circle round Wismar during the night and break into the city from Gallows Hill.[19] The plans were no doubt sensibly drawn up, but we had no Ensign Barck to carry them out. The command was entrusted to a Colonel von Müller, a Mecklenburger, who seemed to have been unfamiliar with the invention of gunpowder. We walked in the dark night through beech forests and sunken roads for about 10 kilometres and thought we were near the city, when a shot was heard in front of us and shouts from the leader, 'Back, back but slowly!' and immediately afterwards more shots, the clash of sabres, horses trotting, shouting and swearing. Convinced that we were being attacked by French cavalry, I called for my jägers to throw themselves into the ditches and to the edges of the sunken road, when a cavalry troop, whose uniform and strength could not be discerned in the dark, passed by and a larger one came shortly after at great speed. Then it went quiet, only a few German oaths were heard in front of us. I called my comrade, the commander of the first jäger company, who was an older officer than I was, and asked what he thought and how we should behave. He confirmed my view, that we had been attacked by cavalry and would probably be captured, those that had passed us would likely come back and deal with us, so it was best to lie still where we were and meanwhile philosophise about our journey to France. When daylight came and we saw Mecklenburgers walking back past us in disorder, we followed them without meeting any enemy but instead met our excellent brigade and regimental commander, who had been concerned for us, had asked after us of everyone he met and received answers that we had been captured. So now we received praise for maintaining our troops in good order, when others came in disarray; and to receive praise from this man was highly valued, for he seldom praised. The course of his career had no deviations, he personified the motto he earned when he later received the Grand Cross of the Order of the Sword, 'Forward march!'

---

19 The *Galgenberg* or Gallows Hill lay about one kilometre to the south of the city, outside the Mecklenburg Gate. The site became a cemetery in 1831.

We never uncovered the full particulars of this inglorious affair. It was said that our still-born Mecklenburg commander did not reconnoitre or establish the situation. The mounted jägers, who were in the lead, came upon an advanced picket of our Hanseatic Legion, who gave fire. They turned about and rode down the foot jägers; our carabineers, who heard those ahead of them shouting 'back!', then also turned around and rode through the Småland infantry battalion, and the whole thing became a frightful turmoil. Fortunately, the defeat was not bloody: one Mecklenburger was said to have been trampled to death and a few were injured, but one poor lieutenant was particularly unfortunate. He, like all of us, thought himself cut off and likely captured, threw himself on a spare adjutant's horse, got away first and reported to the commanding general that the whole force had been scattered and cut down, for which he was disgraced and insulted, was forced to resign and died as a major in the Gotland county militia. The French in Wismar, who had heard the fracas and discovered what had occurred, laughed heartily, and of Colonel von Müller we saw no more.[20]

I should have told this tale in its proper place, but I hope the reader forgives the chronological disorder of the ramblings of an old man and continues to follow his story further.

---

20 As noted earlier, Wallmoden's corps had fallen back as Davout advanced from Hamburg; his two brigades (under von Fallios and Vegesack) fell back separately, passing through Wismar and on to Rostock. Following them the French entered Wismar on 25 August. This incident thus likely took place around this time, and certainly before the battle at Retschow on 28th, not long after which Wismar was retaken. The Hanseatic troops Hultin refers to were not part of Vegesack's brigade so the confusion when they encountered one another is understandable, particularly since Fallois' brigade was still en route to Rostock. There is a suggestion that Vegesack continued through Wismar as a result of a misunderstanding, and that would explain why he may have made a hasty attempt to retake it before the French arrived in strength. See Friedrich Brasch, 'Der Feldzug des Marschalls Davoust in Mecklenburg, im August 1813, In Hinsicht der strategischen Gesichtspunkte dargestellt' (*Maréchal* Davout's campaign in Mecklenburg, August 1813, Presented from a strategic point of view) in Anon. (ed.), *Archiv für Landeskunde in den Großherzogthümern Mecklenburg* (Archive for regional studies in the Grand Duchies of Mecklenburg) (Schwerin: A.W. Sandmeyer, 1862), vol.12, pp.181–214.

16

Return to Sweden (July 1814)

Through July 1814, the Swedish army was shipped back to Sweden from the continent and assembled near the Norwegian border for the invasion, along with that year's conscripts. The remaining reserves were mobilised, and magazines and hospitals were set up.

Finally, we came to Rostock, where we were quartered, met many acquaintances, and awaited the ships which were to take us home. Here we heard a rumour that instead of Småland we would be going to Norway, that the 'rams',[1] instead of uniting with us, wanted to fight; but we found it incredible that such starving Hottentots[2] sought to hinder a thing decided by the European powers, and to resist such an experienced and fully equipped army as ours. Nevertheless, this was confirmed when the ship-of-the-line *Gustaf the Great* arrived with orders to take us over to Gothenburg.[3] The Norwegians had taken themselves a powerless king, and we were invited to witness his coronation.[4] Our young men took the news reasonably calmly and thought it might be fun to dance with the 'rams' in the mountains, but the old soldiers swore and would rather have danced with their wives and children at home. The matter could not be helped, however, for the only relevant instrument, the drum, beats the measure of a dance called blind obedience, so we got ready to board. Old Captain Ridderstråhle was already starting to become seasick, and I was ready to proclaim, like Voltaire, '*Adieu canaux, canards, canailles!*'[5]

---

1 *Baggarna* or 'rams' being a derogatory/slang term used by Swedes for Norwegians.
2 Another abusive term, at this time no longer relating to ethnicity or race per its original meaning but essentially equivalent to 'barbarian'.
3 Although Hultin identifies it as the *Gustaf den Store*, the same ship which had transported them to the continent in April 1813, the regimental diary (see Wieselgren, *Bihang till Ny Smålands Beskrifning*) and other sources indicate it must have been the 74-gun *Uladislaus* commanded by M.M. von Hauswolff. It was of similar size but was a Russian-built ship captured at the Battle of Hoglund in 1788. The Jönköping Regiment boarded on 10 July and arrived in Gothenburg on 17 July.
4 Rejecting the Treaty of Kiel, on 17 May the Norwegian national assembly had signed a hastily drafted constitution and elected as their king the 27-year-old prince Christian Fredrik, cousin and heir to the Danish King Christian VI. Although the first draft of the constitution drawn up in February would have severely weakened the King's powers, the amended version restored much of those powers in order to gain Christian Fredrik's assent.
5 Voltaire's alliterative summary of Holland on his departure from Amsterdam in 1740 after having been cheated by his publishers translates as 'Farewell canals, gossip and scoundrels!'

It should not be without interest at the present time, when every abuse of power is pointed out and severely punished, to hear how a commander of that time could proceed without reproach. To invite a cheeky recruit into the guard house and there be so kind as to treat him to a couple of dozen lashes was not *lèse-majesté*.[6] The soldier could be treated like a dog. We had a comrade, the oldest captain in the regiment, an honest, utterly selfless, and reasonably educated man, but a man who could never tolerate the common soldiery who could neither quit nor abide his authority. He had got it into his narrow mind that all service must be based on strictness, hence, when he served as battalion commander, he would also often lash out at his officers, so that he persistently faced stiff resistance. Fortunately, he was not cruel and seldom punished with the cane, but devised alternatives which in his opinion would be more effective. When we were about to embark at seven in the morning, he found his company bass drummer drunk. The captain, not having the slightest respect for his fellow man's intoxication, was absolutely enraged and asked the petty officer commanding the sloop that would be ferrying us out to our ship if he could borrow a rope. When asked what it would be used for, he pointed to the soldier and said that he would bind the drunkard and have him swim out. But the old sailor was not intimidated and replied in a firm tone, 'Herr Captain! I am the master of this sloop and will not allow any illegal punishments on his majesty's vessel.' The man would otherwise have been dragged behind the sloop out to the ship, which was a couple of thousand yards from land. In Norway he carried out another but less dangerous punishment upon the same soldier. On that occasion he had a small hut made, similar to a dog kennel, put a little straw in it, and tied his bass drummer therein with a pig's hair rope, in order that he would now remain sober. Such was considered humorous. Punishments were cruel, mundane, and entertaining for young gentlemen, until Karl Johan gave the soldier something akin to civil rights and transformed an officer cadre of rascals into educated people. Then the barbarism gradually disappeared, so that during the last years of my own long service, whilst punishment with the cane remained legal, you considered yourself punished if you were willing to use it upon a soldier under your command.

On board the *Gustaf the Great* we were on Swedish territory, although it was made of wood, and, in relation to its size, more densely populated than Peking. When 1,500 men with weapons, equipment and baggage are stowed in a ship, no matter how large it may be, there is not much room to move. Below deck, the troops are packed like sardines on the ship's floors, the officers beneath sackcloth canopies suspended in hammocks which, at the ship's listing, swing and nudge one another so that more often than not lullaby is transformed into profanity. The sailors[7] and marines, with whom on land one might condescend to take a couple of drinks only in the greatest need, are here the masters of their environment. Well-fed lice which

---

Some translations of this famous phrase use the literal translation of *canards* as ducks, but this makes little sense in context; in both English and French, canard can also mean rumour, gossip, or false information.

6   An offence against the sovereign or state.
7   Hultin uses the more specific term *båtsmän* (boatman) which was the naval equivalent to the soldiers raised under the Allotment System, providing manpower to the navy in time of war.

often rained down from the crow's-nest, the misery of seasickness, the suffocating smell of tar and provisions in various forms, stomach-churning manoeuvres which prevent sleep – all these comforts were on offer aboard the Crown's ships. The naval officer himself is not particularly well served, for his cabin has less space than a Lapp's hut, and he has to limit his visitors to a few who can sit on each other's laps.

Nevertheless, some fun was still to be had on deck. Occasionally comrades would receive abuse as if they were suffering from a hangover, and when such an unfortunate sought the rail to evacuate his rebellious stomach, there were often others in good health who would stand beside him and exhort him to retch an octave higher to make the tone clearer! Mischievous, playful lads used to, as it is termed in the sailor's vernacular, 'rouse one another from slumber' by cutting the hammock strap at their feet, whereby in an instant from the deepest sleep and sweetest dreams they stood upright on the floor, groping to bearhug their assailant. Snares were laid out on deck into which an absent-minded comrade was lured to tread, whilst others stood ready to hoist him into the air, from where he was only lowered again on promise of liquor.

In Rostock we had provisioned ourselves with both food and drink, for our previous voyage had taught us that the officers would otherwise dine as in the inns of Småland.[8] Comradeship spiced up the dishes and stimulated one's zest for life. Those who have not experienced it cannot appreciate the camaraderie. The higher ranks, who have served for many years, certainly strut around in public like big goslings, but many of them still maintained the liveliness of youth and often took part in worse mischief than their men, for they too 'had been in Arcadia.'[9] Amongst the subalterns, who are generally of similar age, there is a brotherhood, based on the constant contact they have with each other. You get to know character, inclinations, aptitudes, habits and thereby judge one another; you receive together 'the holy baptism of fire'; you feast and you starve together; if one has money, all have money; when everyone is broke, all curse the economic conditions, the commissariat and their relatives' neglect to write, and hope for better luck in the next mailbag. If your stockings are torn, you borrow or take from another who is better provided. You are like the children of a single family, you make a sworn brotherhood for life, your common home is where the flag flies, security is the uniform, and if it is besmirched, you buzz around like angry wasps; one is judged by one's peers, and in extremis the sword proves the strongest bond. Boasting was never to be heard at gatherings and public meetings because they did not serve for public opinion but served king and country for a pittance.

Such was the spirit of that time. May the reforms which are now forthcoming not suffocate it, for then our army will fight on a mercenary basis, and it could happen

---

8   A reference to the comic poem *Dumboms lefverne* (Dumbom's Life) by Johan Henrik Kellgren (1751–1795), disparaging of the fare obtained in the inns of Småland at that time: '… one may eat well at Småland's inns, if one brings a decent packed lunch.'

9   Hultin applies quotation marks here suggesting reference to the painting *Et in Arcadia Ego*, by French artist Nicolas Poussin (1594–1665). Arcadia, from Greek mythology, is a term for a pastoral utopia and the phrase is inscribed on the tomb in the painting, but its precise meaning remains a matter of debate; one version is interpreted as 'I (the deceased) too lived in Arcadia' and another being 'even in Arcadia, I (Death) exist.'

that when commanded to turn right, they might reply: it says in our constitutional law that we should turn left.

Please forgive these reflections on the state of our army from an 81-year-old man, who now wants to resume his simple story.

Due to a headwind we lay for a couple of days at Rostock's anchorage, and thereby many who could swim now washed away their German sins, for daily one saw two-score heads bobbing around the ship without any other misfortune than that a drunken soldier, who neither wanted nor was able to swim, tumbled out of a boat and was pulled out lifeless but under the doctor's hands was revived and sobered-up.

The ship's commander, an old lieutenant colonel named von Hauswolff,[10] was a genial gentleman, who could probably, if so inclined, log a ships speed with a grog glass.[11] He had distinguished himself in 1789, but later for most of his time he commanded merchant ships and thereby became so experienced that, when his second-in-command wanted to use a pilot for the Flintrännan channel,[12] he said, 'It is not necessary, for if you take all the pilots of the world, you will find none who has passed the Flintrännan as many times as I have,' and proceeded at full sail, so that one could see from the cloudy wake that the heavy ship occasionally touched the bottom, at which the old man simply laughed, to the astonishment of his officers.

On the third day we got a fair wind and set sail, bidding a final farewell to Germany, where we had performed both good and poor service, but left many happy memories. Soon we saw Bornholm,[13] which aroused particular interest and solemn congratulations, which we hoped would prove rewarding, for we had a comrade, my oft-mentioned friend Henning, who, in view of his colossal size, we often called Bornholm, and we assumed that when he saw his worthy namesake, he would celebrate the coincidence and hold a great party; but that heathen had so little sense of family that he threatened every congratulator with a whipping. Out of revenge, we renamed him Bohus,[14] which also displeased him, so that one had to use it at a safe distance so as not to get caught in his vice-like grasp.

The weather was beautiful, so that we could admire the Danish islands with their druidic groves, wishing to make a social visit to our new-found friend and long-standing 'handsome brother', who so often snapped at our heels, and to let him know that we were now on our way to cut the tail off the leopard which so often hankered after our three crowns.

---

10 The Swedish navy at that period included similar ranks to the army; from 1771 to 1814, above the rank of *kapten* were *major*, *överstelöjtnant* and *överste*. P. Wieselgren, *Smålands Beskrivning inskränkt till Wexiö-Stift* (Lund: Berlingska Boktryckeriet, 1846), indicates von Hauswolff's rank was *major* at this time.
11 A ship's speed was measured using a knotted log-line together with a sandglass which was similar to an egg timer.
12 The Flintrännan channel is the narrow navigable channel through the Sound (Øresund) between Sweden and Denmark, a length of about eight nautical miles.
13 The strategically important Danish island of Bornholm lies well to the east of the route from Rostock to Gothenburg; presumably this close approach was due to prevailing winds.
14 Hultin is comparing the large and strategically important island of Bornholm with the small and no longer important fortress of Bohus (and its county) on the border with Norway, ceded to Sweden in 1658, then in use simply as a prison.

The next day, cheers announced that old Sweden had been sighted, but as we got closer, the men did not acknowledge the flat plains of Skåne as their homeland. Smålanders missed its hills, its pine forests, its heather moors, its goats; they considered Skåne too barren and treeless. They had seen well enough that the German could make a fire with peat, but that the Swede could submit to such penitence amazed them.[15] 'Damn to be in such a dog country! No, thank you, I want to be at home, where you can burn logs in the stove and be entertained with the occasional forest fire. There, the oats grow a quarter high.'[16] This is why the Samoyed, when treated to pineapples and turtle soup, longs for *trangryta*.[17]

Soon we sighted Copenhagen and were curious to see this remarkable city, but old Hauswolff must not have been Danish-minded, for when the pilot boat approached us in the Sound and wished us a safe journey, the old man mumbled something, which I interpreted as 'The Devil is most dangerous when he quotes the Bible.'[18]

We had such good weather that Ridderstråhle was rarely seasick, but when we got out into the Kattegat, we had such a strong wind in our sails that the sailors themselves considered it a storm. We had thought it impossible that a ship-of-the-line could pitch, roll or heave to such a degree, but now we discovered that the creations of men are small things to our Lord; for although this colossus was comparable to Uppsala Cathedral, it dived into the waves like a scoop and sometimes seemed to soar into the sky, sometimes threatening to sink our sinful regiment into the abyss. On deck the commander alone could be heard, shouting, 'Hoist, sheet, brace and haul!' We land-crabs, who have thoroughly mastered the art of standing upright, had to crawl and occasionally lick salt water. If you ventured below decks to attend to your men, you encountered stench, groaning and misery. Some groups of men were already singing hymns of death and thought they would soon be drinking a toast with the fish. They had often heard with indifference the whine of deadly flying lead, but water was an abomination to them. We comforted them as best we could and gave them hope to once again get drunk at Värnamo market. Unfortunately, we faced headwinds, so rode out the storm for a couple of days until it calmed down and the wind turned favourable, and then one evening the commander reckoned us to be close to the Bohuslän skerries, which we dare not approach at night.

---

15 Sweden is one of Europe's most peat-rich countries and lack of trees made peat a very common fuel in Skåne in the eighteenth and nineteenth centuries.
16 A quarter being an archaic unit of length, a quarter aln or about six inches, suggesting poor growing conditions. Småland is one of Sweden's most lake-rich and forested provinces, and has poor soil which was a key reason for mass emigration of about one in four of its population to the USA in the second half of the nineteenth century, when Hultin was writing his memoirs.
17 The Samoyed are an indigenous people from the northern Russian arctic. *Trangryta* is presumably what Hultin considers to be a Samoyed staple; *tran* meaning cod liver oil or similar liquid fat obtained by boiling seal blubber; *gryta* meaning either a stew or the pot in which it is cooked.
18 Being wished a safe journey would not appear to warrant Hauswolff's response, unless perhaps the Danish pilot was quoting more fully from the Bible, for example from Ezra 8:21 '… we might humble ourselves before our God and ask him for a safe journey for us and our children, with all our possessions'.

The next morning we sighted land, which was Swedish, with rocky hills that could laugh at the Armstrong cannon,[19] and then the old man took the pilot aboard who brought us as close to Gothenburg as the ship could go, whereupon our anchor was dropped onto the Swedish seabed. We invited our genial ship's commander and his officers to a jug of punch, in which he drank a toast with us one and all.

The following day I was ordered to go ashore to arrange accommodation and so set foot upon our dear fatherland, not much wiser than when I left it. The first thing that caught my attention was a boat, in the bottom of which live lobsters crawled, and for one riksdaler I packed five of them into one of the assistant-furrier's knapsacks, and, on arrival at our quarters on Hisingen,[20] I boiled and ate the two largest, without bread. Being born and raised in a place where the stranger believes that one must not stand a carriage near water lest crayfish crawl into it, and thus accustomed to and familiar with crustaceans, I thought myself quite able to consume a pair of lobsters, but paid for the feast with an indigestion which lasted several days, and have never since been able to eat lobster, nor can hardly tolerate the smell of it.

The customs-snoops[21] now found themselves nonplussed, for they had been ordered not to poke their noses into our knapsacks but to leave them untouched. Our older comrades, especially heads of households, were well supplied with souvenirs, but the youngsters, who had saved their money, had few such possessions. I had brought back a pair of double-barrelled shotguns, with which I could now cock a snook at the entire customs staff!

To behold proud and wealthy Gothenburg was not so impressive for us, who had come from Brussels; but on walkabout we found the ladies possessed of a degree of superiority. They had a sparkle in their eyes, a surety in their posture, a spring in their step, which the German women lacked. Perhaps their facial features were not so beautiful, but their complexion was healthier, their expression more positive. But women are the same the world over, they put into practice the verse, 'Do up your hair, pout your lips, and look like nothing in nature.'

It was natural for us to be stared at, for to our credit we appeared very different. Besides minor changes in our uniform, we had acquired shakos with gold braid and other vanities (these items cost us 80 riksdaler) but they caused such a stir that windows were opened and on the street we were surrounded by the city's rascals. We were accommodated partly in the city, partly on Hisingen, and now found that our domination was at an end, that we must live on peaceful terms and not invoke the right of the strong, for now we had to be content with a hovel to crawl into and not, as with our German hosts, enjoy a set dinner at table with wine bottle beside.

The troops were provisioned from the army's magazines, but we had to fend for ourselves in restaurants which plundered us without mercy. Fortunately, this did

---

19 In the mid-nineteenth century, Sir William Armstrong designed a range of rifled breech-loading heavy guns up to a seven inch/110-pounder, which were manufactured by the Elswick Ordnance Company and the Royal Arsenal. Ammunition was based on a Swedish design and Armstrong became a member of the Swedish Academy of Sciences in 1896.
20 Hisingen is a large river island on the north side of the Göta river opposite Gothenburg (Göteborg) which is on the south side.
21 *Tullsnokar*, an old derogatory term for customs officers.

Example of 1815 pattern shako and uniform coat. Although the shako only became standard Swedish army issue in 1815, individual units on their own commander's initiative acquired new uniforms and shakos during the 1813–1814 campaign. (Armémuseum)

not last long – otherwise we would have had to pawn our fine shakos – for after a few days we were removed to the countryside some 20 kilometres north of the city.

Old Zetterstedt once lamented the bad luck the people of Söderköping had with priests, 'First they had one who was not inclined to eat, then one who could not eat, then one who did not have anything to eat, and now they have got one who was eaten up.'[22] We came upon the same unfortunate situation now, for here there was nothing to eat but salt mackerel and *läfsa*, a kind of bread like Norrland's flatbread, but worse and impure. The menfolk were generally absent, either at sea or at other work, so that the houses were managed by the worst female dregs I ever saw. Poverty was perhaps just as great in Norrland, but neatness, order, and benevolence there hid to some extent what Tacitus calls '*foeda paupertas.*'[23] Here, if you

---

22 *Old Zetterstedt* is likely the botanist and entomologist Johan Wilhelm Zetterstedt (1785–1874), another of the Linköping high school alumni. The small town of Söderköping is about 40 kilometres east of Linköping, at the eastern end of the Göta Canal, which opened in 1832, connecting Gothenburg to the Baltic. The background and source of the quote concerning the Söderköping priests has eluded the translator.
23 Squalidly poor. Tacitus, Germania 46: *Fennis mira feritas, foeda paupertas: non arma, non equi, non penates; victui herba, vestitui pelles, cubile humus: solae in sagittis spes, quas inopia*

approached a house or cattle-shed, you encountered innumerable accumulations of fleas;[24] if you went into the splendid rooms, you got a friendly reception from equally hungry but quieter guests. As I had no forbearance for mortifying my body by sacrificing it to these insolent bloodsuckers, I kept my distance, settled myself down mostly outdoors, and slept more peacefully than comrades who lived beneath roofs, engaged in perpetual insect hunting.

During rest days, fowling piece and fishhook provided the occasional seabird and beautiful pike, but to prepare them you had to set up kitchen facilities in the field, let the stewards with knives and sharp stones scrape and scour the cooking pots and with twigs or needles remove flies and various other insects from a little bit of black butter which was worth its weight in gold.[25] Roasts could turn out reasonably well, but we never succeeded with fish. Neither we nor the stewards had read Miss Warg;[26] we took a large pot, often a field kettle, full of water, put the pike in it and let it cook for an hour. The fish became edible, but very unpalatable. I have since often regretted that I did not marry sooner, because although my good-natured 'nag' usually sniffs at me if I investigate the kitchen stove, I eventually mastered her art and can now cook fish as well as she and can serve delicious perch on the skerries in the *saltsjön*,[27] if the reader cares to visit me.

As I touch upon the noble art of cookery, I must mention another experiment, which may prove of benefit and enlightenment to young comrades who intend to go into the field. A group of us pooled our meagre funds and bought ourselves a sheep. When it was to be slaughtered, our stewards (who acted as priests for the sacrifice) thought it both a sin and shameful not to make use of the blood and proposed that we make *palt*.[28] Now *palt* is a plebeian dish, which is why one of us made the profound observation: if you can make *palt*, you can also make *palt* pudding, which sounds and should taste more distinguished. This was unanimously approved, and it was promised that, if successful, the inventor would be recommended to the Royal Order of Vasa or at least the Patriotic Society's medal. But where to obtain flour in the wilderness? The stewards reported that they still had some rye flour in their provisions, which they would hand over if they could partake of this magnificent

---

ferri ossibus asperant. The Finns are uncivilised and squalidly poor; they possess neither weapons nor homes; their food is herbs, their clothing skins, their bed the ground.

24 Hultin uses the term *svarta husarer* (lit. black hussars), at that time a slang term for fleas and lice.
25 Black butter (*svart smör*) is butter cooked on low heat until the milk solids turn dark brown. An acid such as white wine, lemon juice or vinegar is then added. It is typically served with fish.
26 Anna Christina Warg (1703–1769), also known as Cajsa, is perhaps the best-known cook in Swedish history. Her book on housekeeping was first published in 1755 and was reprinted in 14 editions until 1822. A Swedish equivalent to Mrs Beeton's *Book of Household Management* (which was first published in 1861).
27 *Saltsjön* today refers to the bay forming the main inlet to Stockholm from the Baltic but formerly meant all saltwater bays and inlets from the Baltic within the Stockholm archipelago.
28 *Palt* is a traditional Swedish dish which nowadays refers to meat-filled potato dumplings. Hultin is referring to what is now known as *blodpalt* which comprises a mixture of blood and flour formed into balls and boiled in water. It aimed to minimise wastage by using all parts of an animal.

Swedish soldiers around a campfire. Contemporary watercolour by Carl Johan Ljunggren (1790-1852). (Uppsala University Library collection via Alvin National Digital Cultural Heritage Platform)

dish. The blood was collected in a field kettle, stirred with flour to a porridge-like consistency, wrapped in an old cloth and squeezed into a field flask, which was then placed between a couple of stones to boil. Anyone who has seen a soldier's flask knows that it is spherical and wide at the bottom but narrow at the top. When we thought the mixture to be cooked, it was lifted from the fire and left to cool. The stakeholders stood around, their mouths watering in anticipation of the delicious dish, but when the time came, the unforeseen circumstance transpired, namely that it could not be extracted through the neck of the bottle. They pulled and pulled, until the cloth tore. The inventor demanded a knife, loosened a piece, tasted, spat, and shouted, 'Damn!'; the next man tasted, spat and exclaimed, 'Twice Damn!'; the third man, 'Thrice Damn!'[29] The stewards, who in the presence of their officers did not dare to swear, shouted, 'Bah! Boh! Buh!' And finally, the battalion's dogs, who were standing around, wagging their tails and licking their lips, were invited to feed but even they seemed to have reservations, for they grimaced and occasionally

---

29 Hultin escalates the profanities through *fy fan, fy sjutton* and *fy aderton*. *Fy fan* is a common and relatively mild profanity usually translated as 'damn' (*fy* being a simple interjection). However, *fy sjutton* (seventeen) and *fy aderton* (eighteen) do not readily translate; the latter term through rhyme is thought to be a euphemism invoking Odin or Satan, and the former used as a step back from this.

scratched at the cloth to find out if the fare might be tastier at the bottom. Thus, we put the business to rest; but to retain the memory in tradition, the inventor was sometimes called Pudding, and rightly so, for he was short and portly.

In short day marches and with little fanfare we progressed through this blessed land, which was similar everywhere, where Moses likely handed down the art of turning dust into insects, and approached Strömstad. Here we rested for a few days in a farm that turned out to be sufficiently good that the higher command could occupy the buildings and the subalterns a grain shed wherein we had to lie in stalls of such mean dimensions that the tall Henning and other giants had to lie on the diagonal to find room. The men camped in the open. Here I had the opportunity to experience how unusually rich in fish the region's lakes were. There was a small lake nearby and the men had barely stacked their weapons and put

Swedish military field-flask, green glass, mid nineteenth century, a type in use throughout the nineteenth and early twentieth century. (Sörmlands museum)

down their packs before the banks were full of anglers, because Smålanders like to bring their fishing gear with them. I went down to see how they were getting on and found with astonishment that despite their simple equipment many were already cooking their catch, mostly perch and roach, but even small eels, something which had never happened to me and which I would not have believed had I not seen it. I cadged some roaches for bait, grabbed a hop-pole,[30] asked a couple of friends to row a boat out and in a short while caught five beautiful pike. The rowers, happy with the catch, wanted to return, but as we were nine officers in the battalion, I wanted a pike for each. I managed to get two more, but the third one got away taking the hook with it, the only one I had. Of course, we were welcomed back with our bundle of fish, but the loss of the hook caused great sorrow, so we set about thinking how to replace it. We got hold of a nail, borrowed a file from the gunsmith, filed and ground in turn through half the night and ended up with a usable fishhook, and luckily our drum-major[31] had a spare bass-string with which the hook could be attached to the line, so that the next day we were back in business. On this hook, which I still keep, an unusually large number of pike were caught, especially in Norway, where the lakes were even richer in fish, the pike were fully-grown, and we were hungry.

---

30 Hop growing was widespread in Sweden and reached its peak in the seventeenth and eighteenth centuries; a hop-pole could easily be up to eight metres in length and thus serve as a makeshift fishing rod.
31 The Swedish term is *musikdirektör* (music director); the leader of a regiment's musicians.

17

The Norwegian Campaign (August 1814)

The invasion force was divided into two army corps, the first (approximately 14,000 men) under Karl Johan's direct command and the second (26,000) under Fältmarskalk *von Essen. Facing them were some 28,000 Norwegian troops. The declaration of war was delivered on 26 July. Essen's corps would advance north into Norway on the main route to the east of Iddefjord to capture Fredrikshald and Fredriksten fortress. Karl Johan would take a parallel route to the west, having to cross the Svinesund sound. The army was supported by the fleet under Generalamiral Puke which would also bypass the initial advance with an expeditionary force of 4,000 aiming for Fredrikstad. Meanwhile a smaller force of 1,500 men under Generalmajor Gahn would attack from further east towards Kongsvinger fortress 70 kilometres north east of Cristiana (Oslo) intended to divert Norwegian forces from the main focus of the invasion. The Jönköping Regiment was in Karl Johan's 1st Army Corps.*

When we passed through Strömstad, we heard one or two powerful cannon shots, by which we understood that Fredrikshald had saluted our advance-guard, which had crossed the Svinesund without much resistance.[1] The Västmanland Regiment under Brändström had forded the Tistedal river to the east of Fredrikshald, encountering serious resistance by a detachment under the notorious Captain Spork.[2]

This Captain Spork had been known since 1808 as the most renowned Norwegian partisan.[3] If you were in his vicinity, it was best to keep your wits about you. He tried

---

1 Scouts had reported the north bank clear of the enemy and a bridge of boats was put across the Svinesund on 2 August allowing the 1st Army Corps to cross unopposed. However, the crossing could not be directly observed from Fredrikshald and Fredriksten fortress eight kilometres away; more likely firing heard from that direction was directed against Essen's corps which had encircled the fortress the same day.
2 The aforementioned *Generalmajor* Pehr Brändström was the Västmanland Regiment's commanding officer and commanded the 3rd Brigade (six battalions, approximately 1,500 men) of *Generallöjtnant* Sandels' 2nd Division of von Essen's 2nd Army Corps. Johan Henrik Spork (Spørck) (1778–1849) commanded a force of circa 400 men. This action on 1 August 1814 resulted in three Swedes dead and 13 wounded; Spork's losses (killed, wounded, and captured) exceeded 70 men.
3 As previously noted, the term partisan means small detachments of regular troops to form raiding parties and the like rather than its present day meaning of insurgency or guerrilla warfare. Björlin (*Kriget i Norge*) notes that Spork had a bad reputation in the Swedish army.

The Svinesund pontoon bridge, still in place long after the war. (Engraving by I. Clarke in W.R. Wilson, *Travels in Norway, Sweden, Denmark, Hanover, Germany, Netherlands &c* (London: Rees, Orme, Brown and Green, 1826))

to trick Ensign Wästfelt of the Skaraborg Regiment into laying down his weapon. He approached to parley with Wästfelt's guard outpost and told him that the corps from which Wästfelt was detached had been surrounded and captured, and that its commander had ordered him to surrender. But little Wästfelt was not fooled and replied, 'If my commander is a prisoner, then you should understand that I no longer take orders from him. Therefore, keep your distance if you do not want to taste Swedish steel.' Spork's shameful lie aroused such resentment that he would likely have been killed if he had subsequently been encountered.

Thus, we had hopes of easily entering Norway, but at Svinesund unexpected difficulty was encountered on the treacherous slopes which made moving artillery with horses impossible, so that many soldiers were employed to manhandle the guns with block and tackle. Meanwhile, the sound of cannon fire from the nearby fortress had become livelier, from which we could conclude that our siege artillery, which had gone by sea and was deployed on islets in the strait, had now begun to bombard the garrison and test the strength of the fortress walls.[4]

As a partisan during the 1808–1809 campaign on the Swedish/Norwegian border he had acquired certain notoriety, but this was considered due to the Swedish army's ill-considered mode of operation rather any real skill on his part. During his defence of Enningdalen, he reportedly left his men to move belongings from a farm he owned on Ideslätten (Ystehede). In another incident in 1809 when he surprised a Swedish patrol in a cabin, Spork was accused of having let his men murder the Swedish officer commanding the patrol after he had surrendered and been taken prisoner; or at least of failing to prevent this from happening.

4 A squadron of gun sloops had arrived on 3 August and commenced an ineffectual bombardment; the heavy guns and mortars arrived on 4 August. Despite continuous

Having crested the steep northern bank, we saw smoke from the cannon and shortly afterwards the stronghold itself, with its walls, works and outbuildings on a high, conical mountain, spitting fire towards an islet, which responded with shells which made beautiful arcs in the air. We now approached very close and had an exposed passage of a few hundred paces where the heavier cannon could reach us; but as the gun crews either did not observe us or did not consider us to warrant an attempted shot, we quick-marched the battalion through the open valley and were soon completely protected behind a hill.[5] We then made a halt and rested for several hours, during which time we amused ourselves by crawling onto the ridge, where, barely a thousand paces away, we could discern the uniforms of the men serving the cannon. Eventually too many heads became visible to the enemy, so that a cannon was fired in our direction; however, we could see the whole thing, so that when the artilleryman put the linstock on the touchhole, everyone ducked down and laughed as the ball whizzed over our heads. This encouraged us to tempt them to fire more shots, so we now climbed to stand upon the crest, made rude remarks, and when the cannon fired, we dived down, but scarcely had the next ball overshot before the whole ridge was full of soldiers performing the same manoeuvre! Soon, however, these diversions were curtailed, for, following a shot, some men leapt up at the same moment as another cannon was fired at them from a separate battery, which they had failed to notice taking aim, and a swarm of bullets from a case shot buzzed about their ears, so that they dived for cover faster than they had stood up. Fortunately, no one was injured.

Our jägers now seemed to be in their element, for here, they could pluck the life from their neighbour whilst hidden behind bushes and rocks, and not, as on the plains of Germany, stand like targets at a shooting range. Nevertheless, they had heard of Staffeldt's jägers as unusually skilful shooters,[6] and had a certain respect for them, until later on, after we had engaged with them a couple of times, they would have remarked, had they understood Latin, *major e longinqvo reverentia*.[7]

We dared not leave our resting place before dark, for we had a couple of places to pass which could be swept by cannon-fire from the fortress. We remained for a while looking at the town, which lay just below us, barely a stones-throw away, and we saw merchants inspecting their timber and barrels of herring, calm and calculating, although we Philistines were above them; for our cannon and batteries built on the islets fired only upon the fortress (they had orders to spare the town), so that the garrison had no peace.

During the night we set off in silence, walked just a few thousand paces, camped without tents, instead erecting shelters from pine, juniper, and spruce branches, in

---

bombardment, Fredriksten did not fall until it surrendered to the Swedes on 16 August following the end of the war.

5   There were two battalions of the Jönköping Regiment in *Överste* Bergenstråhle's 5th brigade of *Generallöjtnant* Boije's 3rd Division but in common with most of the brigade formations, the jäger companies had been combined to form a separate jäger battalion.
6   *Generalløytnant* Bernhard Ditlef von Staffeldt (1753–1818) commanded the Norwegian brigade of around 4,000 men tasked with an active defence against the Swedish invaders south and east of the Glomma river.
7   Respect is greater at a distance (Tacitus, *Annals* 1.47).

Fredriksten Fortress, view from the Tista River bridge in Fredrikshald. From a print by Heinrich August Grosch (1763–1843) circa 1820. (Photo: Dag Andre Ivarsøy, Nasjonalmuseet, Norway)

which we slept well yet with due caution, for the enemy could easily make a sortie, which however, he did not dare to venture.

Here we now remained for nearly 14 days,[8] heard every shot, saw at night the projectiles being exchanged between our batteries and the fortress. We fared reasonably well, for we had permission to buy provisions from the magazines, consisting of herring, pork, and rye bread. Salted sea fish, lobster and oysters were also supplied to us for reasonable prices by both Swedes and the natives, with whom we lived on peaceful terms. Mutton and butter could be found in the villages albeit at extortionate prices, and sometimes you could sneak into the town and there, at an unholy price, obtain a bottle of rum and a bowl of sugar. Thereupon our delight knew no bounds and the commodity was *commune bonum*[9] which disappeared in the blink of an eye.

Sufficient troops were left to surround the fortress, and we went north, albeit with the utmost care, for it was not here as on the plains of Germany, where one could reconnoitre and detect the enemy from a distance. In these hills, forests, and marshes he could lie hidden, until he was stumbled on. Small detachments were sent well ahead and to the flanks, but since they could be easily cut off, they were not far removed from the main body, and we saw many positions where a mere company could hold off an entire regiment, if they had the sense to utilise them. At night

---

8   This cannot be correct since this would place Hultin here for the entire duration of the war! Hultin's jäger battalion was nearby for two days before moving north, although of course Swedish forces continued to besiege the fortress for the duration. However, the regiment would subsequently spend nearly two months in the vicinity from early September.

9   For the common good.

we had to surround ourselves with numerous and strong guard outposts, and, like outlaws, hide our fires in pits and crevices.

For five days we progressed without seeing or hearing any redcoat (the Norwegian uniform was red).[10] The land, filled with pine forests, was sparsely populated and even less cultivated. The inhabitants had not fled but received us as fellow countrymen; they swore better than we, gladly ate what we gave them, for they themselves had little in store, and comforted us with assurances that we would meet no resistance until we came to the Glomma river, where 'their boys' were gathered and would drive us back faster than we arrived.

Dwellings and surroundings were nicer than in Bohus County, and the womenfolk were more civilised, for they smoked tobacco as well as we did, though it smelled worse than ours. In general, the people were very poor and lived mainly on stockfish.[11]

At last, we came to a more cultivated and less hilly area, unexpectedly heard a couple of shots in front of us, and a report arrived that our advance guard had encountered an enemy picket. The jägers were ordered forward, formed a line and advanced, and after a while a rather lively fire was heard on the right flank. The infantry columns could not deploy but a battalion on each flank pushed through gaps in the forest to support the line, appearing so quickly that the Norwegians began to run, looking like boiled crayfish on the hills. We then came upon an old wooden church, in the centre of a village, where a larger enemy force was gathered. This was reported to the General, who gave a signal to halt the line, ordered forward the two cannons we had with us which then opened fire, so that smoke rose from the houses. Some shots from smaller guns answered our salute, but without much effect. The Norwegians became unsettled, withdrew, and our line continued to advance. We now saw a green-clad troop, and learnt from the inhabitants, who were not best pleased to be caught in the crossfire and had fled, that these were the so-feared Staffeldt jägers; but they were not so terrible, they did not shoot better than us, and their bullets were often heard in the treetops, so that our losses were insignificant. On our right flank were red-uniformed jägers, who immediately turned and fled. This was the battle at Askim church, if it can be called a battle, for in reality it was more like a hare-hunt.[12]

---

10 This description is consistent with the march north to the Askim area. Boije's 3rd Division had been reassigned to the 2nd Army on 5 August and was following a day behind Vegesack's corps; they missed the significant action at Rakkestad on 6 August.

11 Unsalted fish, typically cod, air-dried on wooden racks.

12 This engagement is usually known as the Battle of Langnes but is referred to in Vegesack (1850) as 'the Affair at Askim or Onstadsund'. It took place on 9 August at Langnes four kilometres northwest of Askim, where the Norwegian forces had a pontoon bridge across the Glomma and a redoubt on the south bank. However, Hultin's description and his subsequent reference to the wounding of *Löjtnant* Sparre suggests this may be the much earlier action at Ingedal Church. Baron Ulf Carlsson Sparre (1789–1864) was at that time a *löjtnant* in the Småland Dragoon Regiment's infantry battalion, part of *Generallöjtnant* Sandels' 2nd Division in Essen's 2nd Army. Björlin (1893), Vegesack (1850) and Götlin (1820) all record that he was wounded at the action at Ingedal Church on 3 August which was a reconnaissance in force comprising three battalions from Sandels' division plus some hussars against around 500 Norwegian jägers. Both army corps had united by 3 August, so it is conceivable that

Norwegian Troops in the 1814 campaign. Watercolour by Carl Johan Ljunggren (1790–1852). (Armémuseum)

Among our wounded was the then Lieutenant Baron Ulf Carlsson Sparre, later lieutenant colonel and for many years my battalion commander. When I mention this friend, this magnificent specimen of a Swedish warrior, who has already breathed his last, I become gloomy, teary-eyed and grimace more than usual, and thus render my audience ill-contented. He was shot through both knees, a wicked injury, from which he suffered discomfort for the rest of his life. But what was unusual was that the man who fired the shot was later welcomed with brandy and beer-money. At the camp in Skåne in 1819 we were at a bonfire in the company of some officers of Staffeldt's jägers, when Sparre enquired if they had been at Askim church, and when this was confirmed, he wondered if the man who had shot him was still serving. They said that it was impossible to know, but when Sparre said that he knew the man's number and company, their opinion changed, so he had a ramrod fetched from his tent, on which the man's number and initials were engraved; for when the Norwegian, who had been lying prone on a hill, fired the shot, the nearest of our jägers had rushed forward to seize him. He fled but left his ramrod behind and they picked it up. The man indeed still served, was located and he recalled very well that he had had a tall officer in his sights, but that his rifle had fired late and therefore hit too low. The chivalrous Sparre gave him a glass of punch, toasted him, thanked him, and invited him to his quarters, where he was properly regaled. We christened him *Sparre's bone-breaker* and he thereafter stood us many a dram.

We took some wretched prisoners who, when they were given some food and drink, thanked us and said, 'Damn! If our men had realised that they could get to eat so well, they would have come over to you en masse!' Their clothing was

---

Hultin's jäger company was involved at Ingedal. Sparre was appointed *major* in the Jönköping Regiment in 1821 and became its *överstelöjtnant* in 1836.

threadbare, their weapons rusty and unfit for service. A small and worn-out cape was not long enough to reach over the hips, their red uniforms were torn, patched with green and grey; a cloth bag instead of a knapsack and half a stockfish tied to the cover was all they had; bread they had not seen for a long time. Everything was reminiscent of our late militia. They nevertheless predicted a fine reception awaiting us when we reached the Glomma, 'for there stands our king, with an enormous number of men, who will thrash you.' Despite this terrible threat, our forces crossed the Glomma at Kölberg bridge, where the Norwegians indeed made the sharpest resistance of the whole war.[13]

Without being a fatalist and believing that every bullet has its billet, I must tell of an incident at this crossing that might strengthen a belief in fatalism. Our later famous and esteemed artist, Colonel Söderberg,[14] was then a lieutenant and, as a surveying officer, had reconnoitred and found a place where the troops could wade across. The First Life Grenadier Regiment had the lead and its commander, Baron Strömfelt,[15] was not usually overly polite with people. When the column reached the river in the morning, Söderberg pointed out the ford's location, but Strömfelt took him by the arm and said, 'Please go ahead, my good man' and thus he was forced to lead the way and face the worst hail of bullets.[16] Arriving on the opposite bank, he was dizzy, stumbled and fell several times, so that he was thought to be wounded, but he was completely unharmed, although three bullets had pierced his coat-tails and two his oil-cloth covered bicorne hat. The commander of the Second Life Grenadier Regiment, Skjöldebrand,[17] was severely wounded here, disabled for the remainder of his life.

Our brigade followed the east bank of the river for several days,[18] and on the opposite bank we passed several enemy outposts, who would, as soon as they saw

---

13 The Battle of Kölberg (Kjølberg) Bridge took place on 14 August, the same day the Convention of Moss was signed to end the war. The Swedes lost three dead and 15 wounded.
14 Gustaf (Gösta) Söderberg (1799–1875) combined a successful artistic career with his long military service. He became adjutant to Crown Prince Oskar in 1833 and transferred to his staff when he became king in 1844. He continued in service until 1858, retiring with the rank of *överste* to become President of the Academy of Arts.
15 Baron Carl Melker Strömfelt (1784–1857) was then *överstelöjtnant* of the *rotehåll* division of the Life Grenadier Regiment which only formally became the First Life Grenadier Regiment in 1816 (and the *rusthåll* division became the Second Life Grenadier Regiment). Two battalions from each division formed part of *Generalmajor* Mörner's 4th Division of Essen's 1st Army.
16 Kölberg bridge had been partially destroyed by the Norwegians; Mörner ordered a crossing to be attempted downstream to outflank the enemy. Hultin's account indicating that the river was forded conflicts with Gotlin (1820) and Bjorlin (1893) which state that the crossing was made in boats although Mankell (1887) does not mention how the river was crossed. However, the River Seut (Seutelva) is a small and slow flowing tributary of the Glomma, only about 10 metres wide, so is likely to have been fordable particularly in late summer.
17 Baron, Count and *Överste* Carl Eric Skjöldebrand (1780–1817) was the son of Count Anders Fredrik Skjöldebrand, Hultin's former commanding officer in the militia. He took personal command of the Life Regiment jägers leading the assault at Kölberg Bridge during which he was shot in the right leg, breaking both shin bone (tibia) and calf bone (fibula), and he died as a result of this injury less than three years later.
18 This and subsequent indications of elapsed time (about two weeks) and sequence of events through until the end of the war on 14 August do not tally with principal sources and must be

a Swede, even the smallest drummer boy, fire pathetic shots, sometimes at such a distance that they might just as well have fired at the moon. We hurled abuse at them, but it did not help – trying to instruct them in the customs of war was like pulling hair from a bald man. What a contrast to the chivalrous French, who never shot at an individual nor at a vedette and often greeted us with *'bonjour comrade'*.

Finally, we saw a fieldwork, manned in some strength, and lest the enemy should attempt to cross the river and make a diversionary attack, we halted and made camp to keep them under observation. A couple of jäger units were stationed beside the river, which was over a musket shot wide, but in the redoubt they had a pair of mountain guns, probably smaller than 3-pounders,[19] with which they were quick to fire on us, even a poor lone lad fetching water from the river, and as we were within shouting distance, we hurled insults at them, because they never hit anyone. The brigade commander, General Boije, one day visited us at the outposts, and we begged him to bring down a couple of guns to teach the Norwegians proper respect, and we promised that both officers and men would work night and day preparing ramparts; but either the General was Norwegian-minded, or he despised them, for he replied that they were not worthy of an honest Swedish shot.

In particular, they hindered our fishing, which was otherwise profitable. During my excursions I found in a croft an old fishing net which was in a poor state of repair, but in a regiment there are almost all kinds of craftsmen, including net menders who patched and made the net usable. The Glomma, which here comprised many bends, had beautiful bays in which we caught so many fish, that, since our own needs were satisfied, we were often able to send a considerable quantity back to the regiment. However, we only ventured out at night. Our guard post was situated behind a headland, completely protected from their pathetic guns, but when we wished to go fishing, we had to cross a couple of hundred paces to reach another bay. En route they could therefore shoot at us, but once we had rounded a headland, we were inaccessible. Therefore, we only risked going out at night, and then would despatch a non-commissioned officer with 20 to 30 men overland to guard this bay and to welcome them, should they launch boats to endeavour to hinder our legitimate occupation. One evening some comrades from the regiment arrived who perforce wanted to take part in a fishing expedition and immediately row out. I pointed out the route and the potential danger; they thought we could pass unnoticed, but I, who had been fired upon on two previous occasions, declared that I would positively not set off before dusk. When twilight arrived, we rowed out. However, it was still too light, because when we were halfway across, a shot was fired and the ball passed over our heads, whereupon I urged the oarsmen to row for their dear lives. We were very

---

considered due to unreliable memory. Hultin's jäger battalion had reached the Askim area on 8 August and only six days then elapsed before fighting ceased. The description that follows of shots being exchanged across the Glomma and fishing thereupon most likely took place after the action at Trögstad on 11 August which Hultin describes later, rather than before as implied in the narrative; in the final few days of conflict Vegesack's corps, including Boije's 3rd Division, remained in that area, securing the east bank of the Glomma against any possible Norwegian incursion.

19 The most widely used artillery piece in the Norwegian army at this period was the 1-pounder *amusette*.

near to the protective promontory when a second shot was fired, the ball falling so close that it splashed water upon us. By then we were almost safe, so I courageously stood up on the thwart, made the usual obscene gesture and shouted that they were shooting like wretches, when a genuine Danish voice, with porridge in his throat,[20] replied, 'Don't be so ill-mannered!'

Finally one day we saw the Norwegians pulling out their cannon and withdrawing from the redoubt, from which we concluded that our troops were approaching from the west side of the river to engage them, so we also broke camp and after a few days reached Onstadsund, where on the opposite shore we saw strong batteries, which were reconnoitred amidst heavy gun fire from both sides; but since we most often had protection from the hills and their fire was badly directed, our losses were small. Lieutenant Malmén of the Kalmar Regiment was wounded in an unusual manner: a large cannonball hit a rock beside the battalion, ricocheted towards him and tore away a large piece of his skull on the right side of his head but without damaging his brain or its membranes. He instantly lost his senses and consciousness but remained alive and retained muscle movement for several days, so that it was highly distressing to see him unconsciously flailing his arms, until he finally succumbed.

Two battalions were stationed to observe this position, and we continued to advance but now slightly away from the river, entering the wilderness, where we proceeded slowly with the usual precautionary measures, saw no human habitation for two days, and spent the nights in the pine forests where owls and nightjars sang their lullabies.

The troop carried five days' provisions in so-called dry rations,[21] and the officers likewise, for they had nothing but what their men kindly shared from their own scarce supply. It was not advisable to try one's luck with a gun or fishing tackle, for one could easily be caught, and to allow oneself to be caught by the Norwegians was considered inglorious; but to capture them was easy. For example, an enemy patrol was taken by a brigade adjutant with his hussar orderly, who was due to ride away with orders. When we embarrassed the prisoners by enquiring how they, a corporal and four men, could be captured by two unarmed men, they replied, 'Just so, sirs – if we had run, those mad devils would have ridden us down!'

For a couple of days, we walked undisturbed through the wilderness, until we came to an inhabited area, when we heard a few shots fired ahead of us. The jägers immediately formed a line and moved forward without seeing or hearing any enemy, until in the distance we saw a small redoubt thrown up across the road. A report was sent to the brigade commander who ordered up a cannon which fired a couple of shots without receiving a reply whereby it was considered probable that they had no artillery. He decided to attack, and the line was signalled to advance. A well-built homestead, probably a rectory, was situated on the side of a valley, and as redcoats were seen there, they were also greeted with a cannon shot, which must not have been welcome, for the Norwegians ran out of the building and behind a

---

20 The Swedish phrase *med gröt i halsen*, literally 'with porridge in the throat,' is a reference to the Danish language sounding to a Swede as if the speaker is continually clearing his throat.
21 *Torrföda*, literally 'dry food,' rations that do not require to be cooked. Equivalent to modern-day field or combat ration.

hill, where they probably had their camp. Our infantry columns were able to deploy here, and the regiment formed a line facing some wetland, which looked marshy and difficult to cross. The regiment was commanded by the jovial and pleasant Colonel von Hartmansdorff, generally known for his cheerful temperament and quick wit. He was then our lieutenant colonel, but because our regimental commander commanded the brigade, the old man led the regiment during the campaign. He was widely beloved, and his ability was demonstrated by the fact that he subsequently became our commanding officer. All military pedantry was subject to his witticisms and derisive remarks.

By nature and inclination, he was sober and honest, but he must be counted among those unfortunates who are never allowed to be left in peace, for whenever and wherever the gentry drank and socialised, old Hartmansdorff had always to be present to bring life and soul to the party. Through such revelry the old man had become afflicted with a touch of gout and was delicate, especially with his feet.

As acting regimental quartermaster, I was his adjutant throughout the war in Germany, and thus understood his habits and his health. When he now dismounted from his familiar grey horse, which was as lively as its master, and prepared to foot-slog through the marsh, I, who loved him like a father, could not hold back but exclaimed, 'How in the name of God will it go with the Colonel's feet?' He replied in his usual humorous manner, 'In this ballet my feet will probably fare better than my arms and legs, being burdened with limbs somewhat weightier than my high-living adjutant.' And then the short and portly old man sprang though the tussocks like a Lapp and crawled over the hills like a hunter, and when we met in the evening, he lifted one foot and asked me to scientifically opine whether he was suffering from stringhalt.[22]

Our line had slowly advanced a few hundred paces, whereupon the Norwegian jägers commenced shooting, but at such a distance that the balls could scarcely reach, so we proceeded in silence without responding, until heavy firing was encountered from the redoubt, where a considerable body of men appeared to be ensconced. They could easily have been dislodged using our cannon, but they could not be employed without hitting our own line, which was in the way. Their skirmishers on the flanks eventually withdrew and gathered behind the redoubt, from where a lively but not very dangerous fire was being maintained. We were about 300 paces away when the signal to assault was sounded, which, as usual, was answered with cheers. The 1st Battalion, led by old Hartmansdorff, was close behind us to support the attack, which the enemy did not wait to receive but bade us a farewell salvo and withdrew.

When the redoubt was abandoned as we approached at a rapid pace, one grey-coated soldier remained beside the earthwork, completely exposed. Our jägers fired shot after shot at him, and I expected at any moment to observe his death-wish granted. When we were 20 or 30 paces away, he coolly turned around and was about to move off, when one of my non-commissioned officers dashed forward and

---

22 Hultin, presumably recalling his commanding officer's words, uses the word *tuppspatt* which is an equine neurologic disease causing a horse to involuntarily yank a leg up and hold it there before taking another step; the condition is known as stringhalt in English, and clearly is applied figuratively here!

grabbed him by the collar. He slashed behind him with his sword a couple of times until I reached him, made him aware that he was a prisoner of war and told him to beware of being cut down, as he stared at me with glazed eyes, so that I understood that he was intoxicated. Although he was a captain, named Schultz, of German nationality, we had no respect for this prisoner, and, from what we later heard from Norwegian officers, they were glad to be rid of him. You rarely see drunkards injuring themselves and they will often escape danger unscathed, but the proposition that the bullet also has respect for intoxication should be tested further before claiming *probatum est*.[23]

Later a sport began between the jägers, when, from behind rocks and tree stumps, they fired at each other largely for the sake of it, and more sweat flowed than blood; for in hilly ground a couple of skirmish lines can engage for long periods with little loss. Like hunting dogs, the men are encouraged by the loud bangs, however, the commander is most at risk, because he has to observe and cannot hide behind rocks.

Darkness dictated a ceasefire and determined that we bivouac where we stood. During the night our weapons were cleaned, ammunition was distributed, and we rested on our laurels, ready to resume the dance the next day.

Our surgeons worked fast to tend our few wounded, swearing because most balls remained lodged within the wounds and had to be removed under torchlight. But this also confirmed our presumption that the enemy had poor ammunition.

Apart from the above-mentioned Captain Schultz, our unit did not take any prisoners, which was just as well, for we had little to eat ourselves.

After our reconnaissance patrols reported back next morning that the enemy was nowhere to be seen and that peasants had advised that during the night the Norwegians had retreated and intended to cross the Glomma, we broke camp to pursue and harass them. At noon shots were heard from our left flank patrol, a company was despatched thereto, and it was later reported that a small enemy force had been sighted on a hillside, that they had been fired upon, but neither seen nor heard thereafter.

Our vanguard reported sighting a sizeable plain, where, according to the peasants, a Norwegian regiment had its training ground. We camped there, and at the same time provision wagons arrived together with orders that the brigade would halt for the time being, as truce negotiations were taking place with good prospects of success.

The aforementioned battle was called the affair at Trögstad and Holmtvet.[24] It was the most serious and the last that we had, and well that was, for now it began to rain day and night, so that we had not a dry thread to our name and our firearms became unusable.

---

23 It is proven.
24 The action at Trögstad (Trygstad/Trøgstad) took place on the afternoon of 11 August (some sources state 10 August). The attack was carried out by the 5th Brigade's jäger battalion from *Överstelöjtnant* Boije's 3rd Division, supported by the Jönköping Regiment. The Norwegian force was a rearguard of 2,000 infantry and four guns; however, the guns had already been silenced by Boije's own artillery before he ordered the assault. The 3rd Division lost four dead and eight wounded. Norwegian casualties are not recorded, but in addition to *Kapten* Schultz, some 200 prisoners were taken.

Instead of camping on the plain, called Momarken, according to standing orders, we crept into the surrounding fir groves, where we would be more sheltered, and built birch huts, which kept the rain at bay for a few minutes, but then refreshed us with a rich supply of drips from the roof.

As I often enjoyed hospitality at charcoal huts and tar pits during my hunting and fishing trips in Småland, I had learned the trick of stripping large pieces of bark from fir trees, binding them together with juniper roots and erecting a Lapp hut where I could lie in the dry,[25] my legs excepted since they reached beyond the entrance. My comrades wanted to crawl in with me, but since 'there was no room at the inn', they avenged themselves by hanging spruce wreaths to suggest that this hut was a tavern, as well as with less favourable words. Old man Hartmansdorff and the other gentlemen squeezed themselves into a small timber barracks, where most likely the Norwegian regimental officers had gathered, because there was no other building on the Momarken plain.

We remained here for four days subjected to almost constant rain. Fortunately, there was wood for large log fires, so that when the rain stopped the men could gather around and dry themselves, until the next shower arrived, whereupon, as when a hawk strikes a chicken run, they dashed to find shelter; and when soaked through and beginning to drip, they went back to the fires, swearing at the sky and clucking like turkeys.

On the fourth day, orders arrived to return to Onstadsund, where we received notification of the cessation of hostilities and an order to remain there until further notice. The staff were accommodated in houses and barns, and we built shelters as usual.

---

25 A Lapp hut (*Lappkåta*), was a conical shaped temporary shelter used by the Sami people, similar to the Native American teepee.

18

After the War in Norway (August–October 1814)

> *The Convention of Moss ending the war was signed on the evening of 14 August. It would result in the Union of Norway and Sweden which lasted until 1905. However, Karl Johan kept his army in Norway for several months thereafter to strengthen his hand in negotiations regarding its implementation and to counter any threat of resumption of hostilities.*

Foraging could now be undertaken without danger of being attacked, but unfortunately there were no lakes in the vicinity, and the Glomma was a torrent not suitable for fishing.[1] Neither would hunting in the wilderness succeed without dogs. A Norwegian artillery lieutenant, with whom the brigade commander had been quartered, lived on a property nearby. The man was with the army, leaving his kind and energetic wife in charge of the house. I saw there a couple of beautiful black dogs, which folk told me were excellent hunting dogs, so I approached her with a request to borrow them; but because her husband was very protective of them, she was unwilling to agree. The brigade commander then assured me that I might employ a little deceit, but not take without consent, so I promised to be responsible for their care and safe return, whereat she gave her approval. I then took them to the camp, where our jägers set about preparing their hunting guns or, for lack of them, their army-issue firearms, now hoping to be able to supplement our diet with game.

The next morning, we went out, 10 people I think, but 'that night they caught nothing'.[2] They quarrelled with each other, blamed failure on a repulsive hat, on a big nose, on Henning's terrible eyesight and clumsy hands, on the smell of brandy and snuff – and so we returned to be duly shamed. On the following day, the hunting party was reduced to three. Then the dogs took a young hare, and we came home triumphant. Later we fared better, for the dogs were good, and we often got a brace of hares and sometimes a bird, although we did not always reap the benefit, for often one of the staff officers got wind of our success and purloined our prize. In general,

---

1 In contrast to Hultin's earlier description of abundance of fish in pleasant bays on the same river! The rain which Hultin remarked upon may have been responsible, but the character of the river was in any case varied, with sections of rapids and others of a more quiescent nature.
2 John 21:3: "'I'm going out to fish," Simon Peter told them, and they said, "We'll go with you." So, they went out and got into the boat, but that night they caught nothing.'

there was a shortage of hares in the large forests. Capercaillie were often seen, but the dogs never enabled us to bag one. We never came across any bears although evidence of their presence in the area could be seen in the broken and shredded rowan trees (which were quite common) because bears ate the berries.

After eight days the Norwegian lieutenant returned home, reclaimed his dogs, and received them back in good health. Those who so wished were invited to join him on his hunts, which did not bring in much more than ours, but often a grand breakfast, which provided us ample reward.

Norwegian officers sometimes came across the river to visit us. Among them were many decent and educated men but also the occasional chump. Luckily, our good prince had given us a few bottles of brandy per man, so that we could offer them a dram.

As two brigades set up camp here, speculators began to line up to offer luxury items and groceries. Of course, they were unchristianly expensive, but you considered yourself lucky if you could get what you needed for money, if you had any.

One heard rumours that the Norwegians intended to dishonourably discharge their king or that he intended to thank them for their good service; but that they still had reservations about joining Sweden, which, however, could not be avoided.

No one would have believed that Norway would become anything other than a Swedish province, but the twists and turns of diplomacy are like 'the way of a snake on a rock'.[3] It was claimed that England had agreed to the union on condition that Norway should become self-governing. It was believed that Jarlsberg and Anker had told our Crown Prince that this was necessary for his own safety,[4] since he was now the only Napoleonic on a European throne and Tsar Alexander had taken guardianship of the Vasas which still had followers in Sweden and the aristocracy of the kingdom would readily fish in murky waters. A misunderstanding could easily persuade our eastern neighbour to take advantage of circumstances and invoke the principle of legitimacy which had recently been applied in restoring the cowardly Bourbons. 'Therefore make Norway independent. We are grateful. With your ability to organise, with your great military talent, you can defend yourselves against the whole of Europe in our mountains. But if you make us a Swedish province, we will be overwhelmed by Swedish nobility, which would be incompatible with our innocence, which would skim the fat from our stew, make the nation dissatisfied and fractious and create troubles for the future.' Most likely, however, was that the Prince's own inclination and feelings for social justice and human dignity enabled him to give a nation, which for centuries had been a Danish slave, more freedom

---

3   Proverbs 30:18–19: '... four things that I do not understand: the way of an eagle in the sky, the way of a snake on a rock, the way of a ship on the high seas, and the way of a man with a young woman.' i.e., a metaphor for something incomprehensible.

4   French-born Herman Wedel-Jarlsberg (1779–1840) was a Norwegian statesman, state governor and leader of the pro-Swedish party in Norway; his father-in-law Peder Anker (1749–1824) was also a unionist and was appointed Norwegian Prime Minister in November 1814.

View from Veden Manor over Tistedalen to Fredriksten and Fredrikshald. From a print by Heinrich August Grosch (1763–1843) circa 1820. (Photo: Dag Andre Ivarsøy, Nasjonalmuseet, Norway)

and greater constitutional benefits and rights than Sweden itself. History shows how they thanked him thereafter.[5]

After 14 long days of rain and inactivity, we left for Fredrikshald where we were accommodated for a few days in a barracks located in the town, and now got to view from both outside and inside the famous mountain fortress which had cost so much Swedish blood. We saw the blue and yellow flag flying at the spot where our fairy-tale king ended his eccentric path.[6]

The commander, a stubborn old general, had vowed to be buried under the ruins of the fortress, but as a result of repeated orders from the proper authorities he was forced to surrender. A continued bombardment would probably have met his wish, because both the defences and barracks had been badly damaged by our batteries. A storming of the fortress would only have befitted Charles XII, and with its present level of defence not even *Iron Head* would have succeeded.[7]

The Kalmar Regiment was placed in garrison here, and the rest of the brigade left for Veden manor, two and half kilometres away, at Tistedalen's great and beautiful

---

5   Despite various attempts by the Swedish monarchy to bring the two countries constitutionally closer and increase the monarch's power over Norway over the course of the nineteenth century, the Norwegians consistently blocked such attempts and indeed chipped away at the arrangements to steadily increase their independence, until finally becoming fully independent in 1905.
6   Charles XII, who was killed at the siege of Frediksten in 1718.
7   The Ottoman Turks gave Charles XII the nickname *Demirbaş* meaning 'Iron Head'.

waterfall, where we built a camp so comfortable and durable that we could happily have stayed there for the winter.⁸

For each company, four barracks were erected from vertical timbers, roofed with spruce branches then covered with turf. Inside, racks for firearms and equipment were erected, as well as bunks, where the men could sleep on straw and heather beds. The doors were made of planks, and the huts were so warm to begin with that the physicians insisted we provide ventilation.

A smaller hut for the non-commissioned officers and the company office was erected behind the barracks. The officers' quarters were situated in front and deserve close attention, for they comprised the neatest and most comfortable dwellings one could wish for, built of planks and boarded-out, and divided into two rooms, of which the company commander inhabited one and the subalterns the other. As I was the sole officer with the jägers, I had my own hotel room, four paces square, duly furnished with three four-legged assemblages that had the name, honour and dignity of chairs, a bed attached to the wall with its eiderdown mattress consisting of a provisions sack stuffed with heather, two soldier's knapsacks with the same delicate stuffing to serve as a long pillow and pillowcase, and a table with four thick wooden legs intended mainly for the serving of peas and porridge but which had the immense luxury of being planed smooth, since problems and theorems in contract bridge and *Vira*⁹ were often to be demonstrated thereon.

Pegs were drilled into one wall on which to hang uniform and weapons; on another a board was fixed as a shelf, on which was placed a smooth-planed piece of wood which served as a plate for dry food, a copper container with its lid as a tureen for the peas, an empty bottle with a piece of candle in the neck and next to that some rye bread and a saved piece of salted pork or herring. On the third wall was a square opening with a shutter forming a window. This was improved, however, after I managed to negotiate for some panes of glass from an outbuilding window, which were then inserted together with a larger paper pane. But envy, much apparent, soon rendered the paper window useless, for it happened too often that a grinning head would poke through it, asking if I was at home and how I was feeling, so that I had to put wood in its place. But best of all was a delightful brick fireplace in one of the corners, which in the evenings provided heat, light, embers for lighting tobacco and a smoky and homely atmosphere.

Of course, my friend Henning had difficulty standing upright without creating a hollow echo against the ceiling, but as I was just five foot 10 inches I had ample head-room.¹⁰ Such was my pleasant abode, where I calmly heard the wind howling and the rain splattering, ate well, slept even better, and received by turns either compliments or stones thrown at the wall or down the chimney. Others' quarters were not dissimilar, although many had poorer furnishings and beds on the floor. One might wonder where the wood was obtained for this Roman camp; but a large pine forest

---

8   Veden was a large estate with numerous farms and sawmills situated on the north side of the Tista river between the Tistadel falls and Femsjøen lake. Karl Johan took quarters here during the campaign and offered to buy it from the former owner's widow, but the price was too high.
9   A traditional Swedish card game for three players popular in the nineteenth century.
10 Hultin quotes his height as a precise three aln = 1.77 metres or five foot 10 inches.

A typical hut of the form described by Hultin, this example from Dalaborg. (Vänersborg museum)

surrounded us on all sides, and by the river there were innumerable piles of planks and boards, which went into the construction. To whom they belonged, and from whom they were bought, I know not. Our otherwise efficient commissariat has not thus far honoured me with any information, and I hope the matter is now *extra fatalia*.[11]

When we had the camp ready and all the streets were swept, tidied, and gritted, the brigade commander, General Boije, arranged a grand reception for the Crown Prince and Prince Oskar,[12] the most amiable young man one might see, to be greeted by 'a crowd no one could count.' However, neither parade nor formal ceremonials were the order of the day, only a choir which recited some laudatory verses composed for the occasion, in which it was proposed that the camp at Veden should be renamed Oskarsberg; and when this was graciously acknowledged, the baptism was solemnly celebrated, though not according to formal doctrine with holy water, for instead all the field kettles were filled with a hearty punch, and the soldiers received their share of schnapps.

The paternal benevolence of the great army commander for 'his children' was expressed even now. He went into the soldiers' barracks, sat down on their bunks, and nodded most kindly. It was clear that he wanted to chat, but he only knew the words, 'good, my children, very good'. He peered into the officers' huts, nodding and laughing. He watched races, wrestling and other sports with a look as if he wanted to

---

11 Beyond the legal time limit.
12 When *Maréchal* Bernadotte was elected as Crown Prince in 1810, his son Oskar (1799–1859) was also made a Prince of Sweden. Oskar moved from Paris to Stockholm with his mother in 1811 and would succeed his father as King Oskar I of Sweden and Norway in 1844.

Prince Oskar (1799–1859) in Hussar uniform. Painting by Fredric Westin (1782–1862). (Nationalmuseum)

participate, and when someone took a tumble, he laughed heartily. If he saw a grey-haired soldier, especially if he had a medal, General Boije, acting as interpreter, had to ask how long he had served and where and why he had received his decoration, after which the Crown Prince would pat him on the shoulder, saying, 'Very good, fine soldier,' and there was always some reward, often a lifetime pension from his own coffers.

Such was the man who received Sweden in poverty and a state of dissolution and left it debt-free and independent. Yet still people criticise him.

In our now distinguished Oskarsberg, we became the laziest dogs the crown ever employed. Drill was not needed and seldom considered, only those on guard duty were on call and work parties to Fredrikshald were rarely required. However, when the weather was suitable, the troop had to exercise, wherein the subalterns led their companies without firearms, showing their tactical skills in mock battles where the projectiles were spruce cones, which were found in abundance. These battles were murderous, for it was the rule that those hit in life-threatening places would fall stone-dead to the ground, whilst those hit in the legs and arms would limp and not use the affected arm. Of course, the commanding officer stood behind the lines and was thus initially protected from the salvos, but when the ranks were depleted, he might also be forced to bite the dust, until the trumpet sounded and the dead would rise, pick up fresh ammunition and recommence jäger-fire in skirmish lines, and it could easily happen that the men would resort to blows. This amused both the subalterns and their men; even the regimental officers were spectators and gave advice on the manoeuvres. It was once alleged that the great Henning lay stone-dead in a very comfortable place without having been hit, in consequence of which a drum-head court-martial sentenced him to be shot in the back as a traitor. But there being no henchmen capable of detaining him to face such punishment, he then received such heavy salvos that he was forced to flee.

In the evenings, games were played, or stories told, often so far-fetched and wonderful that Alexander Dumas himself could have used them, and I have since many times regretted that I did not collect and record these echoes of Swedish folklore which I knew in my childhood but are now faded from memory.

Now I was in my element, for to the east, a hundred paces from the camp, lay a large fish-rich lake, and to the west, almost equidistant, the majestic Tistedal Falls with its large salmon trout. I purloined suitable fishing-tackle in Fredrikshald, but the fish were unreasonable, for they broke my fishing line, and I never managed to catch any larger than eight pounds, although the locals assured that there were many twice as big; but I needed to learn from Lloyd and the English.[13] I was much more successful with pike and perch, with regard to which the experienced English fisherman could learn a lesson from me.

---

13 Presumably a reference to the Welsh naturalist E. H. Llewelyn Lloyd (1792–1876) who spent more than 20 years in Sweden. His first book *Field Sports of the North of Europe: Comprised in a Personal Narrative of a Residence in Sweden and Norway, in the Years 1827–28* was translated and published (with great success) in Sweden in 1830 and includes sections on salmon and trout fishing.

As the jägers were now back with their units, I had spare time but unfortunately lacked hunting dogs. However, the Lord provides for the victim. The commander of the army, His Excellency von Essen,[14] was a great hunter and he always had German hunters and hunting dogs in his retinue. But as he was residing in the town, where the dogs would not feel at home and could not be exercised, he enquired if there was not some half-wit in the camp, probably an experienced hunter, who would both desire and be able to look after his fine animals. He got to hear of me, and I received an order to present myself. Unsure whether I was accused of some misdemeanour or whether I was destined to be promoted to captain in the General Staff, I appeared in full parade uniform and found to my satisfaction that I was to be made 'governor' of these noble hounds, albeit with no increase in rank and allowance. Nevertheless, funds granted for the care of my 'pupils' were so generous that I was able to feed a couple of pigs with the surplus.

Baron Hans Henrik von Essen (1755–1824). Watercolour dated 1802 by Johan Erik Bolinder (1768–1808). (Nationalmuseum)

Thus, I returned to the camp accompanied by a high-born German flunky in green livery with silver braid leading a pack of six red-brown Waldmann hounds,[15] which aroused such a commotion that the guards were about to grab their guns. A kennel was erected wall-to-wall with my cabin with an appropriate level of comfort, wherein these aristocratic beasts were accommodated.

The instructions I received included that the dogs should be treated as befitted hunting animals; not used more than twice a week; that a German hunter should accompany them at first until the dogs and I were acquainted; and that not more than three or four people should take part in any hunt.

A couple of days later, the hunter arrived so early one morning that no one was awake. Once we had set off and released the dogs in a pasture some distance from

---

14 Baron Hans Henrik von Essen (1755–1824) commenced his military service as a *kornett* at the age of 18, reaching the rank of *fältmarskalk* in 1811. He was also Governor-General of Pomerania from 1800 to 1809 and was appointed Governor-General of Norway on 13 February 1814, taking up the post on 11 November.
15 The Waldmann was German breed of hunting dog used in forests, larger and more hound-like than the present-day Dachshund which is descended from it.

the camp, the sporting chase began immediately and soon a flock of sheep appeared being pursued by the six dogs with wicked and selfish intent. Luckily, we were able to 'nip it in the bud' and recall them before they could do any harm. The hunter could not understand why they had behaved so badly, since in Pomerania, where His Excellency had been governor for several years, they frequently saw sheep and paid them no attention; but I explained to him that the situation was different on those flat plains where flocks of sheep were guarded by a shepherd with his trained dogs, and that German dogs usually exhibited this failing in Sweden.

Thus, from then on, I had to keep my distance from inhabited areas, so in the mornings I exercised the dogs out in the wilds. Although there were more birds than hares, I would still catch one or two. In my opinion, however, hunting here was not the German's forte, for although their dogs were much larger than our Småland hounds, they did not run faster than one could follow, and in the hills they got sore feet, so that when they hunted for one day, they were lame for two. Nevertheless, once they got a hare's scent, they never lost it, so that unless darkness intervened, you could be sure to end up with one in the bag.

One evening the hunter came with a message that on the following day I should report with the dogs to an appointed place, because His Excellency himself was coming out, and, after waiting there for a while in the morning, what seemed like a whole cavalry squadron turned up. Of course, I had been on high-ranking hunting parties before, but nothing like this. His Excellency, fine and handsome, three more and less presentable generals, four or five colonels and a swarm of adjutants and orderlies, all on horseback. A couple more German hunters followed on foot with partridge-hounds and dachshunds as well as a couple of two-legged pack-animals bearing food and drink. When the horses could not traverse the hillsides and marshes, they were handed to the orderlies, and both higher and lower classes resorted to Shanks' pony.

I humbly warned them that the dogs would hunt sheep, but they did not want to believe it, and the German hunter did not dare to confirm our experience, lest he be accused of poor training; but they had not long been loose when they found a flock of sheep, two of which in their innocence were savaged to death, and five in fright fell into a lake where they unfortunately perished; but all were paid for. Thus, His Excellency's hunt yielded no other treasure than the scorn of an ugly, lame old woman and the common and bog bilberries that he picked in the marshes. The latter activity I drew to the attention of an adjutant, of similar age to myself, and His Excellency must have overheard, for he asked what I had said, and when the adjutant recounted that I had never seen any such noble eat bilberries, His Excellency turned to me, saying, 'Oh, my dear Smålander, do not be so insolent, for in my days I have picked more bilberries than you.'

Amongst this worldly company was the most well-known and excellent Swedish huntsman, the Court Huntmaster and now Colonel J.L. von Greiff, also famed for his ability to seize fleeing kings.[16] That he became my exemplar is understandable

---

16 The Court Huntmaster (*hovjägmästare*) was an official who arranged hunting parties and had oversight of the hunting staff at court and the royal hunting grounds, a position von Greiff had held since 1803 after retiring from the army. He had however also been re-engaged

and I have every reason to believe that I found favour with him, for oftentimes since I was asked to go with him. I have never met a finer marksman and hunter. He was always accompanied in the forests by a small white partridge-hound called Caresse, who seemed to have more understanding than many people, and whose training often amazed me.

When I had run to fetch the dogs during the sheep hunt, I had startled a capercaillie with her chicks and so informed the hunting party, which was sat around with their canteens and bottles. Von Greiff immediately arose and asked me to show him. When we approached the place, he released Caresse, who had so far, like an orderly, been following close behind, and she immediately disappeared into the woods, returning a few minutes later with a look of cunning, scratched at him with her front paw, then led us on, glancing back from time to time to make sure we were there, and finally placed her front paws carefully upon the trunk of a spruce and raised her head upwards. Von Greiff then whispered to me, 'There sits the bird.' We walked slowly in opposite directions around the tree, straining our eyes. Then he fired a shot and a young capercaillie dropped from the branches and was retrieved by the dog, who carried it to her master. I bagged the bird, and Caresse was sent off again. She did not appear for a long time, so that von Greiff blew on his whistle, whereupon she returned and once again beckoned with her paw. We followed her for several hundred paces, when she finally began to creep forward very slowly. He then whispered, 'Now she has the bird on the ground, and I believe it is the old hen.' She stopped in front of a couple of spruce saplings motionless as a painting. He nudged her slowly forward with his knee until a bird flew up and fell to his shot. And it really was the old hen. Her other chicks were on the ground within a dense stand of trees so that they could not be shot at, nor did we have time, for the company, which had now eaten and drunk their fill, signalled for us to return. We were praised, and our birds were examined so closely and with such expertise that many finely dressed hunters marvelled that capercaillies had beaks and claws!

Then the horses were fetched, the gentlemen mounted up, and I returned to the camp, overwhelmed with exhortations to take care of the hounds, and not have them attack sheep.

Some time afterwards a hunt took place at which His Excellency shot nothing but a poor hare, which must have cost him 50 riksdaler in food, wine, and sundry expenses.

I have seen all kinds of dogs from the great German bulldog, who could take a bear by the neck, to the noble, impudent lapdog, fed by her ladyship with sweet biscuits and cream, but I have never seen the likes of His Excellency's dachshunds. They were no bigger than a small lap dog and were usually carried in the hunter's shooting bag. If they were released into the forest, they would not get through heather quickly with their short legs but would have to be picked up and set down.

---

into military service as chief adjutant for the campaign of 1814 with the rank of *överste*. As noted earlier, it was von Greiff who seized the king as he tried to flee through the palace courtyard during the 1809 coup. As well as publishing several accounts of the coup, his 1821 book *Anteckningar angående jagt och djurfångst i Sverige* (Notes on hunting and trapping in Sweden) was the first significant Swedish work on this subject.

But no one in our entire army has more deserved a medal for bravery, for they could show their battle scars with as much pride as a French Imperial Guard Grenadier. One had lost an eye, the other had lost half his ear and his whole head was scarred with injuries. I asked the hunter why they were brought and what they were to be used for, since it seemed so much more likely that a fox or badger would crush these little things in a single bite, given that I had seen four strong, fierce dogs turned back by a badger which they had cornered against a rock; but the hunter assured me that these small dogs could drive both foxes and badgers out of their burrows, because their size allowed them to get around and behind their quarry and they assisted one another. However, I never got to see this in practice.

Camp life went on as usual. If you had something to eat, you ate, otherwise you went into the town and used your daily wage for a slap-up meal in an expensive restaurant which had recently opened. Afterwards you retired to the Kalmar Regiment barracks and slept off dinner, if you could be left alone. One of our friends there, Lieutenant Aminoff, was a snake-charmer. He usually carried a couple of such reptiles in his trouser pockets and thus had an assured means of remaining undisturbed, when he so wished; for if any unwanted visitor entered, he directed one of these silky ribbons at the intruder's face, thereby ensuring that he would leave, spitting and swearing. You therefore had a special respect for his room, first pushing the door ajar to see if you were welcome. But if Aminoff put his hand in his trouser pocket, it was best to leave in a hurry, if you did not want to be kissed by his foster children! It was said, and he said so himself, that he could handle poisonous snakes, but I never succeeded in finding out, for he drowned shortly after our return home. However, it is most likely that they were grass snakes or had had their fangs removed.

We renewed our acquaintance with little 'Kniggan' who was still dressed in men's clothes and looked just the same. She sometimes visited her friends in the camp and could drink half a glass of punch in our huts, if we had any to offer, and leave without risking her reputation. She had now been rejected for Swedish military service and intended to return to Germany without having been back at all since coming to Sweden.

Negotiations between the Prince and the Norwegians continued with new ultimatums every day; they twisted and turned like a fox around a rowan tree. People admired his boundless patience and might sing with Bellman, 'Oh, had I been in Joseph's place, I know what I'd have done.'[17]

We took care of our entertainment, and our hunting became more successful because a friend had sent from home a couple of Småland dogs, which put some spirit into our sport. They could be released anywhere without having to take out life insurance for the sheep, and we could now get as much game as we wished without putting too much effort into using His Excellency's unhurried, tender-footed

---

17 Song No. 38 from the aforementioned *Fredman's Epistles*. The story is from Genesis 39:1–20. Joseph was bought as a slave by Potiphar, one of Pharaoh's officials, and so gained his master's trust that he was placed in charge of the household. Potiphar's wife tried to seduce him, but Joseph refused her advances. But she then falsely accused Joseph of assault for which he was imprisoned.

hounds. Once a week, however, I had to report on their well-being, describing in detail their hunting feats and actions right up to the hare's blissful demise, since I could plainly see that His Excellency would take delight in the account.

One evening His Excellency's hunter came with instructions to assemble and prepare as many boats as possible for the following day for His Excellency and his retinue to venture out. I managed to have six craft available by the time they arrived. It was now announced that this was to be serious sport, for their intended quarry was no less than a bear. A couple of farmers were present and had informed us that on an isthmus between two lakes, *Nalle* had his favourite haunt.[18] As many as could find room went in the boats, the rest by land with one farmer as a guide. We rowed to the end of the lake, went over a neck of land to another lake, where the farmers had three boats ready, which the most distinguished members of the party boarded, then came to a smaller lake, where only two boats were available, and at the end of this lake was the hunting ground.

When the party had assembled and the farmers had given a description of the locality, a council of war was held. Shooters were deployed in a line that would prevent the bear from escaping, if he was within the isthmus, and hunters and farmers set off with the dogs to find the bear. I, who (by the way) was considered to be a sure shot, was positioned in a bog. I was full of confidence and thought it would be fine sport to bag this four-legged beast and so avenge all the quarrels I'd had with the two-legged variety, although I was feebly armed with a small Liege double-barrelled shotgun, loaded with pistol bullets, which I had got from a hussar.

Having stood for a while and heard nothing, I went a few steps forward to orient myself and came to a spot which was entirely devoid of vegetation and consisted only of pure mud. There I saw some tracks, as big as if I had pressed down both hands together. Standing off to my right was the Norwegian Colonel Holst, who had been commander in Lübeck,[19] and I shouted to him, 'Come here, the Colonel should see this, this must be an antediluvian beast, for such a large bear cannot exist today!' He looked at the tracks and said calmly, 'This is not such a large bear.' 'Well,' I said, 'then I must solemnly explain to Herr Colonel that if the bear should come at me, I will not shoot with the feeble weapon I possess but would rather stand still like a pine tree and with great respect doff my hat as he passes.' But the Colonel replied, 'The Lieutenant shall shoot, for otherwise I shall report his cowardly behaviour to His Excellency and von Greiff, and he will then be rewarded with something other than a medal for bravery.'

Fortunately, the bear was not on the headland. Only a few poor hares came dashing out, at which several shots were fired but missed their mark, which was not unexpected because most were armed only with hunting rifles. A capercaillie hen came

---

18 At the time, *Nalle* was used as a proper name for a bear; today it is taken to mean a teddy bear.
19 *Överste* Johan Hübner von Holst (1774–1836) was born in Fredrikshald and joined the Norwegian army in 1782; but he resigned the service in 1810 to accompany Prince Christian August to Sweden and subsequently served as adjutant to Karl Johan, including during the 1813 campaign. He was commander in Lübeck from December 1813 to February 1814. He helped plan the invasion of Norway and briefly served as commandant at Fredriksten after the war; however, he was considered a traitor in his native land, so settled in Sweden where he was ennobled in 1817 and promoted to *generalmajor* in 1821.

flying towards His Excellency, who snatched a shotgun from the hunter standing behind him and brought the bird to the ground, which aroused such delight and appetite that canteens and bottles were produced, whereby 'I too got to eat at His Lordship's table.'[20]

After everyone had eaten and drunk their fill, His Excellency ordered that our guns be cleared as a precaution against accidents in the boats, so a target shooting exercise was decided upon and a 12-shilling note (at that time made of paper bearing the motto *hinc robur et securitas*)[21] was pinned onto the wall of a barn at the customary distance. Some hit the wall, some did not, until von Greiff stepped forward to show what he was capable of. He had a short double-barrelled fowling-piece, made in Norrtälje, and fired both barrels. Everyone rushed to the target to discover that he had not hit the 12-shilling note, although one ball had missed by one inch and the other by just half an inch. I heard several opine that it was unusual for him to miss; he himself said that the foggy weather had caused a delayed powder ignition (percussion locks and percussion caps were unknown at the time).[22]

When I mention percussion caps, may I be forgiven if I make a digression that can only interest hunters. Born and raised in a place which could be called Småland's college for hunters, I have certainly shot more game with flintlocks than with percussion lock pieces. Everything then depended on good gunpowder, and if one managed to get a flask of fine English gunpowder, it would be used with the greatest thrift on the priming pan together with a few grains in the bottom of the barrel; if in addition the main charge utilised Fliseryd gunpowder or, even better, Dalabond powder, one might then even make the occasional successful shot at a bird in flight. It was quite different for the common folk, of whom almost every man in that province was a hunter: he would struggle with an inferior lock, poor quality gunpowder, bad flint (often just a pebble) and frizzen-steel, so his weapon often misfired or fired late. This preserved a lot of game, since he would barely hit a quarter of what he aimed at. At that time numbers were plentiful, so that bagging a hundred hares a year was not unusual, and bird-shooting in the spring yielded capercaillie and grouse in proportion. One could shoot six to eight capercaillies in a single session without destroying the population. Black Grouse wandered about en masse on marshland and into traps.

I first saw a box of percussion caps in 1816, which then cost three riksdaler. The invention was excellent; they were unaffected by wind and weather, ignited instantly and seldom misfired. But within a year, the peasantry had acquired percussion locks; now they could shoot as effectively as me, so that after a few years our wild game was almost extinct. If the current hunting statutes are complied with, the former golden

---

20 A line from the poem 'The Christmas Party' by Swedish poet and writer Erik Sjöberg (1794–1828) who used the pseudonym Vitalis.
21 Here is strength and security. This motto became standard on all Swedish Riksbank banknotes from the 1890s to the 1960s.
22 The precursor to the conventional percussion cap was in fact available on some fowling pieces of this period, known as the scent-bottle lock, invented by a Scotsman, Reverend A.J. Forsyth and patented in 1807.

times may return, but then I, like the Mohican, will have passed on to the happy hunting-grounds.[23]

Now back to our bear. On the way home, one of the farmers said that if he had an old horse, he would soon shoot the bear. The commanding officer of the Horse Guards, Colonel Arfvidsson, who was in the boat, replied, 'Come down to Fredrikshald, where you can take a guard horse which has glanders and is destined to be shot.'[24] The farmer took advantage of the offer, and a few days later he appeared at the camp and asked for help to carry the bear from the boat. We then saw a true fighting-bear or, as the Norwegians called them, a *horse-bear*.[25] For sure, I had seen dancing-bears with their handlers, but they were in relation to him like an Ölander to a warhorse. With a cord I measured its front leg: I was then a slender youth, but its leg was almost as thick as I was about the waist. The Norwegians themselves said that it was one of the biggest they had seen, and I vowed that I would sooner eat than quarrel with such animals! Now the farmer was subjected to a detailed interrogation. He recounted that he had got the horse in Fredrikshald, took it to the isthmus and then slaughtered and skinned it. When he went to check it the next day, he found that it had been dragged away, so he warily followed the trail and encountered the bear hungrily gorging on this delicious breakfast. The farmer was armed with an old, discarded soldier's musket loaded with two home-made bullets, with which he shot the bear, whereupon it roared so terribly that the farmer immediately ran home, barred the door, and made ready with axes and picks in case his sanctuary would be disturbed. But after several hours had passed without incident, he crept out to investigate and found the horse still there. A trail of blood then led him to the bear, which lay stone dead. Both bullets had entered its hindquarters and exited through its chest, and yet the mighty animal had walked a hundred paces before falling. The Prince bought the beast for 50 riksdaler,[26] and it remained on display in the camp for several days, until the smell indicated that it was fit for a French ragout. I do not know where it subsequently ended up.

In Fredrikshald there flourished a highly enlightened, open-minded fraternal society, known as *The Unnamed Brothers*, who were founded during the German campaign, or more correctly revived in accordance with old traditions and legends, by the army's field surgeon, Professor Weltzin,[27] and several other merry-makers

---

23 The phrase 'happy hunting-grounds' as a term for some American Indian tribes' concept of paradise had first appeared in James Fenimore Cooper's *The Pioneers* published in 1823, a few years before *The Last of the Mohicans* in 1826.
24 Glanders *(Rots)* is an infectious, chronic bacterial disease that was historically a common and significant killer of horses in military service.
25 *Slagbjörn* (lit. fighting-bear) or *hästebjörn* (lit. horse-bear), a carnivorous brown bear that will attack and maul to death horses and large cattle.
26 Government policy in Sweden and Norway during the nineteenth century paid a bounty for every bear killed. At a rate of up to 300 per year, populations came close to extinction. Protective measures in the twentieth century have allowed numbers to recover significantly (around 3,000 today) but about 300 bears are still being legally hunted and killed annually.
27 Carl Fredrik Weltzin (1778–1828) was a professor at the Karolinska Institute in Stockholm, a medical facility founded in 1810 in part to improve the training of military surgeons. He was chief physician to the Swedish army during the 1813–1814 campaign and at the Stockholm garrison (1811–1815).

including the poet Wadman, who had been entrusted with management of stores, which appointment he lost, however, when he answered a question concerning unaccounted-for brandy with the simple truth, 'Drunk.'[28] As a brother of the highest degree, I can, of course, not tell the profane of this Order's greatest secrets, but merely hint that it bears much resemblance to the venerable Order of Drabbis, whose records were considered lost until, through the power of clairvoyance, they were discovered and rescued by the highly-renowned Drabbis master, brother Fredrik Behm, who resurrected the Order in accordance with both the spirit of the times and the existing liquor legislation.[29]

Certainly there is some jealousy concerning the age and origin of these Orders, for brother Behm claims that his documents go all the way back to the Creation, which, however, with due respect for his arduous research, cannot be fully proven; but The Unnamed Brothers possessed an authentic Syro-Chaldaic text on official paper certifying that Noah, after planting a vineyard in Ararat and considering his sons lazy, stupid and sober, disinherited them, placed the winemaking procedures into an empty wine barrel which he entrusted into the still prevailing Flood, which brought it to Sodom, where it was retrieved by Lot's daughters, who, according to custom, dubbed their aged father a master of the third degree.[30]

Many happy evenings were spent here with music, song, and joviality; and as the members were numerous, the Order's coffers were in such a healthy position that one did not have to sing in a sober state. For further convenience, a dedicated saloon was constructed in the camp, where a branch lodge was inaugurated with due ceremony, thereby avoiding the trouble of taking the long and bumpy road back from the town at night, which on occasion caused much suffering.

The Order is still prevalent in southern Sweden, and those who know how to value cheerful and pleasant company can join, as long as they are not too prejudiced. Known 'Bible-bashers' are however, admitted only under a personal guarantee.

---

28 Johan Anders Wadman (1777–1837) was a poet and comrade of Weltzin. In 1811 he was a hospital clerk at the General Garrison Hospital in Stockholm and Weltzin engaged Wadman to support him as hospital commissioner in the campaigns in Germany, Belgium, and Norway. The brandy in the medical stores was intended for anaesthetic purposes and Wadman is better known today for the single expression explaining its disappearance '*Utsupet, sa' Wadman*' ('Drunk' said Wadman) than for his poetry!

29 Fredrik Behm (1797–1876) was born and raised in Linköping. He studied law at Uppsala and was inspired by a similar tradition there to create the Great Order of Drabbis in the 1820s after he had returned to Linköping and had become its honorary mayor. It was entirely his own invention and was named after Drabbisdal a few kilometres northwest of the city where he had his summer house. As well as creating various games and festivities, his order also parodied the many rituals and degrees found in other similar societies. It grew rapidly in popularity; the future King Oscar II was granted the title 'Admiral of the World's Oceans' when he visited! Regarding liquor legislation, relaxed laws had resulted in a flourishing of domestic stills reaching over 170,000 by the 1830s, alongside commercial distilleries. Laws were tightened mid-century and domestic distillation became illegal after 1860.

30 A fanciful tale for the origins of this Order! In Genesis 9:20-27, Noah plants a vineyard in order to make wine, the first reference to wine in the Bible. His sons were later embarrassed at finding Noah naked and drunk in his tent. Genesis 19:30-38 tells the story of Lot's daughters making their father drunk before they 'lay' with him.

19

Home (November–December 1814)

Negotiations following the Convention of Moss continued until 4 November 1814 when the Constitution was finally settled and the Storting (the Norwegian Parliament) formally elected Charles XIII of Sweden as King of Norway. This allowed the bulk of the Swedish forces, some 30,000 men in all, to return to Sweden during the next few weeks.

The business with Norway now seemingly concluded, people began to talk about going home, and the cavalry trooped off. It being the start of November, we were greatly concerned for the state of the sunken roads, but fortunately we did not break camp until the beginning of December, when frost rendered them solid underfoot, although hard going for the baggage cart which had to be repacked and repaired several times a day.

I had now to take leave of my pleasant hut wherein I had resided warm and dry for so long, where so many happy moments had been spent in the company of comrades and friends, where so much had happened. Of course, my hometown was dear to me, but I could not leave the hovel without some regret, and this I expressed in a long melancholy poem written with chalk on the wall, which principally recorded 'that here dwelt a soldier of Karl Johan, who often wanted for food.' The signal to march was sounded and our pleasant camp with all its facilities and amenities now became 'the city of the dead' like the catacombs of the Orient. I dashed back to my hut once more to bid a final farewell to its Lares and Penates,[1] and there met a boy busy pulling out nails and rifling through old despatches and papers for something useful. I wished him luck and good hunting, and then came the word of command, 'Forward march!'

For the final time we passed through Fredrikshald and we barely had time to take a light breakfast at Harald Hårfager's club. Then it was off to Svinesund, and soon we were wrapped in the arms of old Mother Svea;[2] but her embrace was not overwhelming, for she first showed us Bohuslän, through which we must pass, and whose acquaintance we had had the honour of making on our way north. Outdoors, however, the atmosphere was calmer, for the insects which had then so tormented us, had now taken their leave; but the domestic situation was much the same, the madams were still unwashed, and, apart from herring, salt mackerel and *läfsa*

---

1 Lares and Penates were Roman deities commonly worshiped in domestic shrines as family guardians.
2 The Swedish equivalent of Britannia, the personification of the nation as female warrior.

flatbread, there was not the smallest crumb to be had. The men were provisioned from our magazines. We bought pork and ryebread to vary the diet of fish and stave off the Radesyge, which is very common in coastal residents, and is believed to arise from salted fish taken without brandy.[3]

An incident occurred at Tanum. I was there ordered to a village five kilometres from the road, where my jäger company would take quarters overnight. The local constable,[4] who accompanied us as a guide, suggested that the villagers were well-disposed, that we would have decent accommodation and that, in accordance with my status, I would lodge with an old sea captain. When we arrived, we were split up and I, together with my steward and the constable, went to the captain's house, which looked pleasant enough. We were met in the hall by an elderly man who was somewhat taken aback and asked what we wanted. I stated that I had the honour of being quartered here and wished to cause as little inconvenience as possible; but he replied in a harsh nautical voice, 'I do not take in any lodgers.' I therefore turned to the constable, begging him to find an alternative, but he took out the sheriff's accommodation list and pointed out to the captain that he was *required* to take in an officer, at which the old man retorted with a bold oath that if 10,000 sheriffs had written in all the languages of the world, his house was his own and he would receive neither officer nor common soldier. Now this was an embarrassing situation; but the constable firmly insisted that I was to be billeted there, so, to progress the matter, I had him show me what room I should occupy, at which he opened the door to a chamber, which I entered, accompanied by the landlord and his protests.

I then turned to my host, saying, 'This room is now assigned to me by the sheriff and is therefore mine. If Herr Captain now wishes to evict me, then it would be both wise and most necessary to gather support, since, if I cannot defend myself, I have 50 jägers in the village who will surely come to my aid.'

He replied, 'Well, I have never encountered the like. Pure imposition; violation of my home – I shall complain to the king's commander, to the justice ombudsman …' and then turned about and went out.

I reclined on a sofa, philosophizing about nothing. My steward unpacked the toiletries, prepared water for washing and mumbled, 'These are not such fine quarters, we will get nothing here but what we have brought with us.'

Barely half an hour had passed, when the door opened and the landlord came in with a large bowl full of steaming punch, put it on the table and said, 'since the situation cannot be changed, it is probably as well that we make friends.' Behind him came the maid with butter, cheese, smoked salmon, fowl, brandy and porter. When the old man had taken a drink and some sandwiches and other sundry dishes, he settled down and we learned that as a young man he had served at the Admiralty, retiring

---

3   From the mid-eighteenth to the mid-nineteenth century, Radesyge (also known as Norwegian Leprosy) was a terrifying endemic disease in Western Norway and Bohuslän that produced malignant skin ulcers and disfigurement similar to the tertiary stage of syphilis. The cause remains unknown.

4   A simplistic translation of the role of the *fjärdingsman*, a part-time local government official who assisted the county sheriff with debt collection, police operations, road inspections and the like. The name derives from division of districts into quarters, similar to the English term 'farthing'.

with the rank of captain, and then for many years he commanded merchant ships, earning enough to buy the property where he now resided. When the supper, which after a long march tasted good, had been eaten, we partook of the punch, which was so powerful that before it was finished, we had drunk a toast as 'drinking brothers' that I was a fair landlubber and might call him 'uncle' if I felt embarrassed to be considered as a brother. An evening meal was offered, but the supper and the punch sufficed. Breakfast the next morning featured oysters, caviar and much more besides, and when I returned to my room, his kindly old wife was busy packing groceries in the steward's haversack, begged me not to castigate the old man and added with tears in her eyes, 'He has become so strange since our eldest son, who was in English service, was shot.' The old man and I tenderly said goodbye to each other with the desire to drink each other's health once again, which, however, did not come to pass. When we were alone again, my steward made a profound reflection that it might be best to take quarters by force, since we had fared well by so doing.

In Uddevalla we had three rest days including dances, entrance to which was worth every penny, for I have never seen such a gathering of beautiful ladies in one place, so that our few married friends were warned to carefully consider their wedding vows before attending.

We were now in a civilised place, often found quarters with demanding patrons, belligerent rectors, law-quoting magistrates, etc., but felt good and rewarded our delighted hosts with tales from recent world history, particularly our own great deeds: how we sent Bonaparte to a small island to there forge thunderbolts with which to rouse his warriors from their sleep; showing how we bathed in blood, our boots worn out, exposed in storms and tempests which could blow the horns off animals and rendered our coats thread-bare; how we ate horses, dogs and cats, seasoned with gunpowder, which is why we were now so thin and swarthy of appearance, etc., which brought honour upon us and enlightenment upon them.

At the Jönköping county border, the men began meeting their wives and relatives. Those who had their homes on the way were allowed to return, and many were seen with tears in their eyes saying farewell to officers and comrades with whom they had shared everything for almost two years. It is a joy for the commander to know that his flock, which has been herded for so long and with so much care, have their own peaceful cottages, where relatives will greet them, where they will hang up their weapons over their beds, and will tend their own cattle and pigs, but will reunite trained and ready to fight when the drum is sounded.

The changes that are imminent and are so much needed in our defences, I neither can nor wish to judge, but during the three wars in which I partook in fraternal union with our provincial soldiers, I have gained complete conviction that a better and safer foundation for our national defence cannot be conceived and almost certainly not at a lower cost. I have seen and experienced the difference between provincial and enlisted soldiers: the latter's home is the barracks, where our raw conscripts should only exceptionally be stationed. The provincial soldier provides the starting point for the people he is to defend. There he has house and home, his wife, children, and relatives. The conscripts from the parish know him, treat him like an older brother with whom they can converse in the local dialect, who can instruct them on discipline, about life on campaign. They may have quarrelled at playhouses, auctions, and markets, but reconciled with drink and entered into foster brotherhood. When he is no longer fit for service, he returns to his folk and may typically build a cottage, cultivate a potato field, and become the *rote* holder. His eldest son often takes his number and position in the ranks. But a recruited soldier becomes alien and mistrusted; at least in Småland, I have never seen a good peasant-boy take recruitment, or, as they put it, 'enter the unknown,' whilst on the other hand every vacant position in a provincial company would be heavily over-subscribed. Only those whom we have rejected for moral deficiency are sometimes intercepted by itinerant recruiters, enlist, and serve their term, return home even worse than when they left and usually end up in their rightful place – the penitentiary.[5]

May this old soldier be forgiven for touching on subjects that should only be dealt with by our government, which surely understands them better than the loudmouths that sound off at popular meetings, and instead re-join him on the march to the Dunkehalla hills, where we first get see our dear Jönköping, a Småland Venice by dint of its lagoons, the clear Lake Vättern with its pearl, the island of Visingsö, and the fertile Gränna region, where many of us had our homes. All this was greeted by us with cheers, so that the whole city erupted into activity; the people came out to meet us and followed us, dancing, jumping, and nodding to the beat of the music, to the square, where a service was held with thanksgiving to God that we had survived this far. At our quarters we were dismissed, and invitations to morning, noon and evening celebrations came thick and fast. One limb was severed from our body: the regiment's life company was discharged and made their way well inebriated to their nearby homes; the remaining companies were given two days off and were warned not to over-indulge.

On the second day, a wealthy merchant treated the officers to a breakfast, which began at 10:00 a.m. and ended at 10:00 p.m., but which was attended intermittently as the officers came and went, for they had much to take care of with returns into store, wages, and accounts. The following day a service was held in the square, the men bade their sad farewells, and the companies went their separate ways.

I rode off to my hometown on a 'partridge'[6] and arrived safely at my parental home,[7] where the entire proceeds of such a glorious campaign consisted of a little money, two double barrelled fowling pieces and a gold watch, together with the tattered clothing in my knapsack.

Naturally I was interrogated, but now I could not tell such blatant lies as I had on my travels. They considered it unforgivable that I had not seen and formed an acquaintance with Napoleon himself and they did not think it sufficient that I had twice paraded for Tsar Alexander and Fredrik Wilhelm and seen many other notables!

---

5   Hultin's defence of the provincial *indelta* system was in vain; the government voted for its abolition in 1873, the year after Hultin's book was published, and it was phased out gradually through to 1901, being replaced by conscription.
6   A simple two-wheeled cart without springs.
7   Hultin was born in Vimmerby but his father had died shortly before his birth from wounds received at the Battle of Hogland in 1788. His mother, Christina, subsequently remarried Sven Hultin, a wealthy councillor in the same town, and it was thus his stepfather from whom he took the name Hultin. In 1806, his stepfather had purchased Rumskulla manor, about 15 kilometres west of Vimmerby, which was thus Hultin's parental home in 1814.

20

Epilogue

In 1822 Hultin married Constance Wänman who he had met on Åland in 1808 with her father Israel Gustaf Wänman who had subsequently been appointed as Vimmerby parish priest in 1811. Hultin continued in service with the Jönköping Regiment, promoted to staff captain in 1826 and company commander in 1828, which rank he held until retiring from military service in 1842 aged 53. The family eventually settled at Kallernäs farm, part of the Sundsholm estate owned by Emil Key. It was Emil Key who, as a result of a bet, persuaded Hultin to publish his memoirs.

Fifty-six years have passed since then. In the veins of the happy, agile, and lively boy, the blood has cooled for 82 years. It has been a long time since he drew his sword for his company, which next to his wife and children was his hobby-horse. The hunter is now lame, for his joints are beginning to stiffen, but should hare or woodcock come within range, he can still show that he learned the craft. Nevertheless, pike and perch provide a better livelihood.

My old comrades have, one after another, trooped off to the great muster, and while I wait for the call, it has been a pleasure for me to recall them and the events in which we acted together, and to thereby relive those happy days of my youth. Admittedly, I miss these old comrades with whom, during 34 years of service, I 'shared the young game of life'[1] – but if every day brings its torment, it also brings its blessings in my happy domestic situation.

Although friendships are mostly formed in youth, I have, however, in this corner of Småland where I have found peace and quiet for over 20 years, even in old age experienced the blessing of unfailing and faithful friendship. This, dear reader, may be indifferent to you, but for me it is a necessity to express my gratitude to a warm and selfless friend.

And now, dear readers, my task as a historiographer has been completed – I am well aware of its antics and deficiencies but console myself with the fact that I did not write for praise.

Now it is up to you to applaud or dismiss *An Old Soldier's Memoirs*.

---

1 A line from the poem 'The new Blondel' by one of Hultin's Linköping alumni, Per Daniel Amadeus Atterbom. It concerns the poet's childhood and was published in 1815.

EPILOGUE 195

Hultin's final home, Kallernäs farm, circa 1890. (Reproduced from Louise Nyström-Hamilton, *Ellen Key En Lifsbild* (Uppsala: Almqvist & Väiskels, 1904))

Sundsholm, after a painting by the Bavarian painter Meixner in the mid-1850s. Kallernäs lay on the long headland to the right a little above the field with the haystacks. Captain Hultin is in the punt. (Reproduced from Ellen Key, *Minnen av och om Emil Key* (Stockholm: Albert Bonniers, 1915))

Bibliography

The following principal references were used for checking on military aspects of Hultin's memoirs.

Printed Works

Anderson, R.C., *Naval Wars in the Baltic, 1522–1850* (London: Francis Edwards Ltd, 1969)

Barton, H. Arnold, *Scandinavia in the Revolutionary Era, 1760–1815* (Minneapolis: University of Minnesota Press, 1986)

Björlin, Gustaf, *Kriget I Norge, 1814, efter samtidas vittnesbörd framställdt* (The War in Norway, 1814, based on contemporary testimony) (Stockholm: P.A. Norstedt, 1893)

Brasch, Friedrich, 'Der Feldzug des Marschalls Davoust in Mecklenburg, im August 1813, In Hinsicht der strategischen Gesichtspunkte dargestellt' (*Maréchal Davout's campaign in Mecklenburg, August 1813, Presented from a strategic point of view*), in Anon. (ed.), *Archiv für Landeskunde in den Großherzogthümern Mecklenburg* (Schwerin: A.W. Sandmeyer, 1862), vol.12

Cassin-Scott, Jack, *Scandinavian Armies in the Napoleonic Wars* (Oxford: Osprey Publishing Ltd, 2001)

Götlin, L.E., *Anteckningar under Svenska Arméens Fälttåg 1813 och 1814* (Notes on the Swedish army's campaign 1813 and 1814), vol.1 & 2 (Örebro: N.M. Lindh, 1816), vol.3 (Uppsala: Palmblad, 1820)

Ljunggren, Carl Johan, *Minnes-Anteckningar under 1813 och 1814 Årens Kampagner, uti Tyskland och Norge* (Memories and Notes of the 1813 and 1814 Campaigns in Germany and Norway) (Stockholm: Adolf Bonnier, 1855)

Mankell, Julius, *Anteckningar rörande svenska regementernas historia* (Notes on the history of Swedish regiments) (Örebro: N.M. Lindh, 2nd edition, 1866)

Mankell, Julius, *Fälttåget I Norge år 1814* (The Campaign in Norway, 1814) (Stockholm: Carl Suneson, 1887)

Mankell, Julius, *Uppgifter rörande Svenska Krigsmagtens styrka, sammansättning och fördelning sedan slutet af femtonhundratalet, jemte öfversigt af Svenska krigshistoriens vigtigaste händelser under sammatid* (Data concerning the strength, composition and distribution of the Swedish Armed Forces since the end of the fifteenth century, together with an overview of the most important events in Swedish military history during the same period) (Stockholm: C.M. Thimgren, 1865)

Sandstedt, Fred (ed.), *Between the Imperial Eagles: Sweden's Armed Forces during the Revolutionary and the Napoleonic Wars 1780–1820* (Stockholm: Armémuseum, 2000)

Online Sources

Hans Högman, *Swedish Military History*, <http://www.hhogman.se/military.htm>
Magnus Olofsson, 'The Swedish Army in the Napoleonic Wars', *The Napoleon Series*, <https://www.napoleon-series.org/military-info/organization/Sweden/Army/Organization/c_swedisharmy.html>
Swedish Nobility, *Adelsvapens genealogi Wiki*, <https://www.adelsvapen.com/genealogi/Huvudsida>
The Swedish Biographical Lexicon, *Svenskt biografiskt lexicon*, <https://sok.riksarkivet.se/sbl/Start.aspx>

From Reason to Revolution – Warfare 1721-1815

http://www.helion.co.uk/series/from-reason-to-revolution-1721-1815.php

The 'From Reason to Revolution' series covers the period of military history 1721–1815, an era in which fortress-based strategy and linear battles gave way to the nation-in-arms and the beginnings of total war.

This era saw the evolution and growth of light troops of all arms, and of increasingly flexible command systems to cope with the growing armies fielded by nations able to mobilise far greater proportions of their manpower than ever before. Many of these developments were fired by the great political upheavals of the era, with revolutions in America and France bringing about social change which in turn fed back into the military sphere as whole nations readied themselves for war. Only in the closing years of the period, as the reactionary powers began to regain the upper hand, did a military synthesis of the best of the old and the new become possible.

The series will examine the military and naval history of the period in a greater degree of detail than has hitherto been attempted, and has a very wide brief, with the intention of covering all aspects from the battles, campaigns, logistics, and tactics, to the personalities, armies, uniforms, and equipment.

Submissions

The publishers would be pleased to receive submissions for this series. Please email reasontorevolution@helion.co.uk, or write to Helion & Company Limited, Unit 8 Amherst Business Centre, Budbrooke Road, Warwick, CV34 5WE.

Titles

1. *Lobositz to Leuthen: Horace St Paul and the Campaigns of the Austrian Army in the Seven Years War 1756-57* (Neil Cogswell)
2. *Glories to Useless Heroism: The Seven Years War in North America from the French journals of Comte Maurés de Malartic, 1755-1760* (William Raffle (ed.))
3. *Reminiscences 1808-1815 Under Wellington: The Peninsular and Waterloo Memoirs of William Hay* (Andrew Bamford (ed.))
4. *Far Distant Ships: The Royal Navy and the Blockade of Brest 1793-1815* (Quintin Barry)
5. *Godoy's Army: Spanish Regiments and Uniforms from the Estado Militar of 1800* (Charles Esdaile and Alan Perry)
6. *On Gladsmuir Shall the Battle Be! The Battle of Prestonpans 1745* (Arran Johnston)
7. *The French Army of the Orient 1798-1801: Napoleon's Beloved 'Egyptians'* (Yves Martin)
8. *The Autobiography, or Narrative of a Soldier: The Peninsular War Memoirs of William Brown of the 45th Foot* (Steve Brown (ed.))
9. *Recollections from the Ranks: Three Russian Soldiers' Autobiographies from the Napoleonic Wars* (Darrin Boland)
10. *By Fire and Bayonet: Grey's West Indies Campaign of 1794* (Steve Brown)
11. *Olmütz to Torgau: Horace St Paul and the Campaigns of the Austrian Army in the Seven Years War 1758-60* (Neil Cogswell)
12. *Murat's Army: The Army of the Kingdom of Naples 1806-1815* (Digby Smith)
13. *The Veteran or 40 Years' Service in the British Army: The Scurrilous Recollections of Paymaster John Harley 47th Foot – 1798-1838* (Gareth Glover (ed.))
14. *Narrative of the Eventful Life of Thomas Jackson: Militiaman and Coldstream Sergeant, 1803-15* (Eamonn O'Keeffe (ed.))
15. *For Orange and the States: The Army of the Dutch Republic 1713-1772 Part I: Infantry* (Marc Geerdinck-Schaftenaar)
16. *Men Who Are Determined to be Free: The American Assault on Stony Point, 15 July 1779* (David C. Bonk)
17. *Next to Wellington: General Sir George Murray: The Story of a Scottish Soldier and Statesman, Wellington's Quartermaster General* (John Harding-Edgar)
18. *Between Scylla and Charybdis: The Army of Elector Friedrich August of Saxony 1733-1763 Part I: Staff and Cavalry* (Marco Pagan)
19. *The Secret Expedition: The Anglo-Russian Invasion of Holland 1799* (Geert van Uythoven)

20 'We Are Accustomed to do our Duty': German Auxiliaries with the British Army 1793-95 (Paul Demet)

21 With the Guards in Flanders: The Diary of Captain Roger Morris 1793-95 (Peter Harington (ed.))

22 The British Army in Egypt 1801: An Underrated Army Comes of Age (Carole Divall)

23 Better is the Proud Plaid: The Clothing, Weapons, and Accoutrements of the Jacobites in the '45 (Jenn Scott)

24 The Lilies and the Thistle: French Troops in the Jacobite '45 (Andrew Bamford)

25 A Light Infantryman With Wellington: The Letters of Captain George Ulrich Barlow 52nd and 69th Foot 1808-15 (Gareth Glover (ed.))

26 Swiss Regiments in the Service of France 1798-1815: Uniforms, Organisation, Campaigns (Stephen Ede-Borrett)

27 For Orange and the States! The Army of the Dutch Republic 1713-1772: Part II: Cavalry and Specialist Troops (Marc Geerdinck-Schaftenaar)

28 Fashioning Regulation, Regulating Fashion: Uniforms and Dress of the British Army 1800-1815 Volume I (Ben Townsend)

29 Riflemen: The History of the 5th Battalion 60th (Royal American) Regiment, 1797-1818 (Robert Griffith)

30 The Key to Lisbon: The Third French Invasion of Portugal, 1810-11 (Kenton White)

31 Command and Leadership: Proceedings of the 2018 Helion & Company 'From Reason to Revolution' Conference (Andrew Bamford (ed.))

32 Waterloo After the Glory: Hospital Sketches and Reports on the Wounded After the Battle (Michael Crumplin and Gareth Glover)

33 Fluxes, Fevers, and Fighting Men: War and Disease in Ancien Regime Europe 1648-1789 (Pádraig Lenihan)

34 'They Were Good Soldiers': African-Americans Serving in the Continental Army, 1775-1783 (John U. Rees)

35 A Redcoat in America: The Diaries of Lieutenant William Bamford, 1757-1765 and 1776 (John B. Hattendorf (ed.))

36 Between Scylla and Charybdis: The Army of Friedrich August II of Saxony, 1733-1763: Part II: Infantry and Artillery (Marco Pagan)

37 Québec Under Siege: French Eye-Witness Accounts from the Campaign of 1759 (Charles A. Mayhood (ed.))

38 King George's Hangman: Henry Hawley and the Battle of Falkirk 1746 (Jonathan D. Oates)

39 Zweybrücken in Command: The Reichsarmee in the Campaign of 1758 (Neil Cogswell)

40 So Bloody a Day: The 16th Light Dragoons in the Waterloo Campaign (David J. Blackmore)

41 Northern Tars in Southern Waters: The Russian Fleet in the Mediterranean 1806-1810 (Vladimir Bogdanovich Bronevskiy / Darrin Boland)

42 Royal Navy Officers of the Seven Years War: A Biographical Dictionary of Commissioned Officers 1748-1763 (Cy Harrison)

43 All at Sea: Naval Support for the British Army During the American Revolutionary War (John Dillon)

44 Glory is Fleeting: New Scholarship on the Napoleonic Wars (Andrew Bamford (ed.))

45 Fashioning Regulation, Regulating Fashion: Uniforms and Dress of the British Army 1800-1815 Vol. II (Ben Townsend)

46 Revenge in the Name of Honour: The Royal Navy's Quest for Vengeance in the Single Ship Actions of the War of 1812 (Nicholas James Kaizer)

47 They Fought With Extraordinary Bravery: The III German (Saxon) Army Corps in the Southern Netherlands 1814 (Geert van Uythoven)

48 The Danish Army of the Napoleonic Wars 1801-1814, Organisation, Uniforms & Equipment: Volume 1: High Command, Line and Light Infantry (David Wilson)

49 Neither Up Nor Down: The British Army and the Flanders Campaign 1793-1895 (Phillip Ball)

50 Guerra Fantástica: The Portuguese Army and the Seven Years War (António Barrento)

51 From Across the Sea: North Americans in Nelson's Navy (Sean M. Heuvel and John A. Rodgaard)

52 Rebellious Scots to Crush: The Military Response to the Jacobite '45 (Andrew Bamford (ed.))

53 The Army of George II 1727-1760: The Soldiers who Forged an Empire (Peter Brown)

54 Wellington at Bay: The Battle of Villamuriel, 25 October 1812 (Garry David Wills)

55 Life in the Red Coat: The British Soldier 1721-1815 (Andrew Bamford (ed.))

56 Wellington's Favourite Engineer. John Burgoyne: Operations, Engineering, and the Making of a Field Marshal (Mark S. Thompson)

57 Scharnhorst: The Formative Years, 1755-1801 (Charles Edward White)

58 At the Point of the Bayonet: The Peninsular War Battles of Arroyomolinos and Almaraz 1811-1812 (Robert Griffith)

59 *Sieges of the '45: Siege Warfare during the Jacobite Rebellion of 1745-1746* (Jonathan D. Oates)

60 *Austrian Cavalry of the Revolutionary and Napoleonic Wars, 1792–1815* (Enrico Acerbi, András K. Molnár)

61 *The Danish Army of the Napoleonic Wars 1801-1814, Organisation, Uniforms & Equipment: Volume 2: Cavalry and Artillery* (David Wilson)

62 *Napoleon's Stolen Army: How the Royal Navy Rescued a Spanish Army in the Baltic* (John Marsden)

63 *Crisis at the Chesapeake: The Royal Navy and the Struggle for America 1775-1783* (Quintin Barry)

64 *Bullocks, Grain, and Good Madeira: The Maratha and Jat Campaigns 1803-1806 and the emergence of the Indian Army* (Joshua Provan)

65 *Sir James McGrigor: The Adventurous Life of Wellington's Chief Medical Officer* (Tom Scotland)

66 *Fashioning Regulation, Regulating Fashion: Uniforms and Dress of the British Army 1800-1815 Volume I* (Ben Townsend) (paperback edition)

67 *Fashioning Regulation, Regulating Fashion: Uniforms and Dress of the British Army 1800-1815 Volume II* (Ben Townsend) (paperback edition)

68 *The Secret Expedition: The Anglo-Russian Invasion of Holland 1799* (Geert van Uythoven) (paperback edition)

69 *The Sea is My Element: The Eventful Life of Admiral Sir Pulteney Malcolm 1768-1838* (Paul Martinovich)

70 *The Sword and the Spirit: Proceedings of the first 'War & Peace in the Age of Napoleon' Conference* (Zack White (ed.))

71 *Lobositz to Leuthen: Horace St Paul and the Campaigns of the Austrian Army in the Seven Years War 1756-57* (Neil Cogswell) (paperback edition)

72 *For God and King. A History of the Damas Legion 1793-1798: A Case Study of the Military Emigration during the French Revolution* (Hughes de Bazouges and Alistair Nichols)

73 *'Their Infantry and Guns Will Astonish You': The Army of Hindustan and European Mercenaries in Maratha service 1780-1803* (Andy Copestake)

74 *Like A Brazen Wall: The Battle of Minden, 1759, and its Place in the Seven Years War* (Ewan Carmichael)

75 *Wellington and the Lines of Torres Vedras: The Defence of Lisbon during the Peninsular War* (Mark Thompson)

76 *French Light Infantry 1784-1815: From the Chasseurs of Louis XVI to Napoleon's Grande Armée* (Terry Crowdy)

77 *Riflemen: The History of the 5th Battalion 60th (Royal American) Regiment, 1797-1818* (Robert Griffith) (paperback edition)

78 *Hastenbeck 1757: The French Army and the Opening Campaign of the Seven Years War* (Olivier Lapray)

79 *Napoleonic French Military Uniforms: As Depicted by Horace and Carle Vernet and Eugène Lami* (Guy Dempsey (trans. and ed.))

80 *These Distinguished Corps: British Grenadier and Light Infantry Battalions in the American Revolution* (Don N. Hagist)

81 *Rebellion, Invasion, and Occupation: The British Army in Ireland, 1793 -1815* (Wayne Stack)

82 *You Have to Die in Piedmont! The Battle of Assietta, 19 July 1747. The War of the Austrian Succession in the Alps* (Giovanni Cerino Badone)

83 *A Very Fine Regiment: the 47th Foot in the American War of Independence, 1773–1783* (Paul Knight)

84 *By Fire and Bayonet: Grey's West Indies Campaign of 1794* (Steve Brown) (paperback edition)

85 *No Want of Courage: The British Army in Flanders, 1793-1795* (R.N.W. Thomas)

86 *Far Distant Ships: The Royal Navy and the Blockade of Brest 1793-1815* (Quintin Barry) (paperback edition)

87 *Armies and Enemies of Napoleon 1789-1815: Proceedings of the 2021 Helion and Company 'From Reason to Revolution' Conference* (Robert Griffith (ed.))

88 *The Battle of Rossbach 1757: New Perspectives on the Battle and Campaign* (Alexander Querengässer (ed.))

89 *Waterloo After the Glory: Hospital Sketches and Reports on the Wounded After the Battle* (Michael Crumplin and Gareth Glover) (paperback edition)

90 *From Ushant to Gibraltar: The Channel Fleet 1778-1783* (Quintin Barry)

91 *'The Soldiers are Dressed in Red': The Quiberon Expedition of 1795 and the Counter-Revolution in Brittany* (Alistair Nichols)

92 *The Army of the Kingdom of Italy 1805-1814: Uniforms, Organisation, Campaigns* (Stephen Ede-Borrett)

93	*The Ottoman Army of the Napoleonic Wars 1798-1815: A Struggle for Survival from Egypt to the Balkans* (Bruno Mugnai)	110	*The War of the Bavarian Succession, 1778-1779: Prussian Military Power in Decline?* (Alexander Querengässer)
94	*The Changing Face of Old Regime Warfare: Essays in Honour of Christopher Duffy* (Alexander S. Burns (ed.))	111	*Anson: Naval Commander and Statesman* (Anthony Bruce)
94	*The Changing Face of Old Regime Warfare: Essays in Honour of Christopher Duffy* (Alexander S. Burns (ed.)	112	*Atlas of the Battles and Campaigns of the American Revolution, 1775-1783* (David Bonk and George Anderson)
95	*The Danish Army of the Napoleonic Wars 1801-1814, Organisation, Uniforms & Equipment: Volume 3: Norwegian Troops and Militia* (David Wilson)	113	*A Fine Corps and will Serve Faithfully: The Swiss Regiment de Roll in the British Army 1794-1816* (Alistair Nichols)
96	*1805 – Tsar Alexander's First War with Napoleon* (Alexander Ivanovich Mikhailovsky-Danilevsky, trans. Peter G.A. Phillips)	114	*Next to Wellington: General Sir George Murray: The Story of a Scottish Soldier and Statesman, Wellington's Quartermaster General* (John Harding-Edgar) (paperback edition)
97	*'More Furies then Men': The Irish Brigade in the service of France 1690-1792* (Pierre-Louis Coudray)	115	*King George's Army: British Regiments and the Men who Led Them 1793-1815, Volume 1* (Steve Brown)
98	*'We Are Accustomed to do our Duty': German Auxiliaries with the British Army 1793-95* (Paul Demet) (paperback edition)	116	*Great Britain and the Defence of the Low Countries, 1744-1748: Armies, Politics and Diplomacy* (Alastair Massie)
99	*Ladies, Wives and Women: British Army Wives in the Revolutionary and Napoleonic Wars 1793-1815* (David Clammer)	117	*Kesselsdorf 1745: Decision in the Fight for Silesia* (Alexander Querengässer)
100	*The Garde Nationale 1789-1815: France's Forgotten Armed Forces* (Pierre-Baptiste Guillemot)	118	*The Key to Lisbon: The Third French Invasion of Portugal, 1810-11* (Kenton White) (paperback edition)
101	*Confronting Napoleon: Levin von Bennigsen's Memoir of the Campaign in Poland, 1806-1807, Volume I Pultusk to Eylau* (Alexander Mikaberidze and Paul Strietelmeier (trans. and ed.))	119	*Not So Easy, Lads: Wearing the Red Coat 1786–1797* (Vivien Roworth)
102	*Olmütz to Torgau: Horace St Paul and the Campaigns of the Austrian Army in the Seven Years War 1758-60* (Neil Cogswell) (paperback edition)	120	*Waging War in America: Operational Challenges of Five Armies* (Don N. Hagist (ed.)
103	*Fit to Command: British Regimental Leadership in the Revolutionary & Napoleonic Wars* (Steve Brown)	121	*Sailors, Ships and Sea Fights: Proceedings of the 2022 'From Reason to Revolution 1721–1815' Naval Warfare in the Age of Sail Conference* (Nicholas James Kaizer (ed.)
104	*Wellington's Unsung Heroes: The Fifth Division in the Peninsular War, 1810-1814* (Carole Divall)	122	*Light Troops in the Seven Years War: Irregular Warfare in Europe and North America, 1755-1763* (James R. McIntyre)
105	*1806-1807 – Tsar Alexander's Second War with Napoleon* (Alexander Ivanovich Mikhailovsky-Danilevsky, trans. Peter G.A. Phillips)	123	*Every Hazard and Fatigue: The Siege of Pensacola, 1781* (Joshua Provan)
106	*The Pattern: The 33rd Regiment in the American Revolution, 1770-1783* (Robbie MacNiven)	124	*Armies and Wars of the French East India Companies 1664-1770: European, Asian and African Soldiers in India, Africa, the Far East and Louisiana* (René Chartrand)
107	*To Conquer and to Keep: Suchet and the War for Eastern Spain, 1809-1814, Volume 1 1809-1811* (Yuhan Kim)	125	*Suffren Versus Hughes: War in the Indian Ocean 1781-1783* (Quintin Barry)
108	*To Conquer and to Keep: Suchet and the War for Eastern Spain, 1809-1814, Volume 2 1811-1814* (Yuhan Kim)	126	*The Russian Patriotic War of 1812: The Russian Official History* Vol.1 (Modest Ivanovich Bogdanovich, trans. Peter G.A. Phillips)
109	*The Tagus Campaign of 1809: An Alliance in Jeopardy* (John Marsden)	127	*The King and His Fortresses: Frederick the Great and Prussian Permanent Fortifications 1740-1786* (Grzegorz Podruczny)
		128	*A Swedish Soldier in the Napoleonic Wars: The Memoirs of Carl Magnus Hultin* (trans. Erik Faithfull)